The Global Phenomenon of Family-Owned or Managed Universities

Global Perspectives on Higher Education

Series Editors

Philip G. Altbach
(Center for International Higher Education, Boston College, USA)
Hans de Wit
(Center for International Higher Education, Boston College, USA)
Rebecca Schendel
(Center for International Higher Education, Boston College, USA)

This series is co-published with the Center for International Higher Education at Boston College.

VOLUME 44

The titles published in this series are listed at *brill.com/gphe*

The Global Phenomenon of Family-Owned or Managed Universities

Edited by

Philip G. Altbach, Edward Choi, Mathew R. Allen
and Hans de Wit

BRILL

SENSE

LEIDEN | BOSTON

All chapters in this book have undergone peer review.

The Library of Congress Cataloging-in-Publication Data is available online at http://catalog.loc.gov

Typeface for the Latin, Greek, and Cyrillic scripts: "Brill". See and download: brill.com/brill-typeface.

ISSN 2214-0859
ISBN 978-90-04-42341-1 (paperback)
ISBN 978-90-04-42342-8 (hardback)
ISBN 978-90-04-42343-5 (e-book)

Contents

PART 1
The Framework

PART 2
Countries and Institutions

PART 3
Conclusion

Preface

This pioneering volume, the first examining family-owned or managed higher education institutions (FOMHEI) is organized in three sections. The initial chapters provide an overview and analysis on the phenomenon and consider how the limited existing research is relevant. Most important however, are the institutional and national case studies that are the heart of this volume. The bulk of the book is dedicated to these specific institutional and national cases. The book concludes with a summary and final observations based on these cases.

Most of our authors are involved with the universities that they are writing about and in this respect this book differs from most research analyses. This has both advantages and drawbacks. Most of our authors are not academic researchers and they are rather deeply involved with their institutions. They bring a depth of commitment and understanding that is rare in more academic analyses. At the same time, they are clearly not objective observers.

Private higher education is the fastest growing segment of higher education globally and in 2019 a significant force in most of the world. In many countries, including most of Latin America and significant parts of Asia, private postsecondary institutions educate a majority of students. A surprisingly large part of global private postsecondary education consists of institutions owned or managed by families, often with family groups stretching back several generations. These family-owned or managed higher education institutions (FOMHEIS) are as diverse as private higher education itself. Despite the importance of FOMHEIS, this sector has received no attention from researchers or analysts and the institutions themselves have not conducted any analysis of their role in the broader postsecondary firmament. This book is the first effort to understand, describe, and analyze FOMHEIS. Even after the extensive research undertaken in the development of this volume, we still have no idea of the scope and size of this sector. We do know that it is much larger and more important than we anticipated.

The idea for this book came when Philip Altbach, founding director of the Center of International Higher Education (CIHE), noticed that several of his graduate students from Asia were sons or daughters of families who owned universities and who were being educated to go into the "family business." Altbach reflected on this phenomenon in his 2005 article "Universities: Family Style," perhaps the first article on this topic ever written (Altbach, 2005). Unable to find support for research, Altbach waited until 2017 to undertake this project in partnership with Hans de Wit, director of CIHE, and Edward Choi, a doctoral student and graduate assistant at CIHE at the time, and son of a family that owns a university in Korea. We undertook this project without any external funding, only with resources from the Center for International Higher Education at Boston College. Mathew Allen, faculty director for the Institute for Family Entrepreneurship at Babson College, joined the project. Allen was fascinated by this hitherto unresearched aspect of family businesses.

Given the extent and importance of FOMHEIS, it is somewhat surprising that there has been no research or analysis of this sector. Our research indicates that FOMHEIS number in the thousands globally and in a few countries (such as Brazil, Colombia, India, Korea, the Philippines) they constitute a large proportion of private higher education institutions. This pioneering book offers insights into this hitherto largely unknown dimension of global postsecondary education.

The organization of the book begins with consideration of private higher education with special reference to FOMHEIS. We were assisted in this effort by Daniel Levy, distinguished professor at the University at Albany, State University of New York, and a prominent scholar of private higher education. He provides an overview, placing FOMHEIS in the broader context of private higher education. Mathew Allen and Edward Choi provide an analysis of FOHMEIS from the perspective of family entrepreneurship. Finally, Edward Choi, Mathew Allen, Hans de Wit, and Philip Altbach reflect on the implications of our case study chapters.

The heart of the book is the case study chapters. We asked colleagues in twelve countries to write about their institutions as well as the broader situation of FOMHEIS in their country or region. These discussions yield important insights about FOMHEIS, including regional and institutional variations, varying patterns of ownership and governance, different family dynamics operating within the institutions and many others. Because of the paucity of research and researchers on this topic, we imposed no methodological strictures on our case study authors. This book is a first effort to describe and understand this important higher education phenomenon. What we might lack in traditional methodological rigor we more than gain in knowledge of an unexplored dimension of higher education.

Reference

Altbach, P. G. (2005). Universities: Family style. *International Higher Education, 39*, 10–11.

Acknowledgements

We wish to acknowledge the contribution of our case study authors. Most of our contributors prepared chapters on their intuitions while at the same time having ongoing institutional responsibilities as family administrators and faculty in their FOMHEIs. Others are scholars with interest and knowledge of this phenomenon in their country and provide a broader national perspective. We are indebted to them. They have provided important insights on their institutions concerning institutional management, the role of family groups in higher education and the context of private higher education in their country.

The Center for International Higher Education at Boston College, our institutional home, has provided critical support for this research. The Institute for Family Entrepreneurship at Babson College provided additional assistance. Mathew Allen brought insights from his study of entrepreneurship to the project. Liz Reisberg, a research fellow at the Center for International Higher Education, edited the manuscript. Edward Choi was central to this project. He contributed to several chapters in the book and handled the complicated project logistics. He is completing his doctoral thesis with a specific focus on researching how owner families in higher education negotiate decision-making in an organizational context where local regulatory conditions may place limitations on their authority.

Figures and Tables

Figures

Tables

Notes on Contributors

Mathew R. Allen
is associate professor at Babson College in the entrepreneurship division, faculty director for the Institute for Family Entrepreneurship, and academic director for the Global Successful Transgenerational Entrepreneurship Practices (STEP) Project. His expertise is in the effective management of human capital within entrepreneurial environments, especially family enterprises. He teaches entrepreneurship and family entrepreneurship courses at the undergraduate and graduate level. In addition, Professor Allen has been involved in executive education programs across the world with a special interest in Latin America. In addition to programs in the USA, he has worked with executive students from Argentina, Chile, Colombia, Germany, Korea, Mexico, Peru, and Uruguay. His research interests focus on the performance implications of leadership and effective management in entrepreneurial organizations. His research has appeared in publications such as *Personnel Psychology, Entrepreneurship Theory and Practice,* and *Strategic Organization.*

Philip G. Altbach
is research professor and founding director of the Center for International Higher Education in the Lynch School of Education at Boston College. From 1995 to 2013, he was the J. Donald Monan, SJ University Professor at Boston College. He was the 2004–2006 Distinguished Scholar Leader for the New Century Scholars initiative of the Fulbright program. He has been a senior associate of the Carnegie Foundation for the Advancement of Teaching and served as editor of the *Review of Higher Education, Comparative Education Review,* and *Educational Policy.* He is author of *Global Perspective on Higher Education* and many other books.

Gabriel Burgos Mantilla
has been a university professor in undergraduate and postgraduate programs, as well as dean of the faculty of law of the Universidad Autónoma de Bucaramanga (UNAB), and rector of the same university for 18 years. He has also been a member and president of the Asociación Colombiana de Universidades (ASCUN) and Red Universitaria Mutis (RUM). He was vice minister of higher education of Colombia from 2007 to 2010. He is an academic advisor to several Colombian universities and an active member of the Comité de Acreditación de la Red Latinoamericana de Cooperación Universitaria (RLCU).

Rodrigo Capelato

is the executive director of Sindicato das Entidades Mantenedoras de Estabelecimentos de Ensino Superior no Estado de São Paulo (Semesp). He is member
of the Consultative Council of the Brazilian Ministry of Education (CC-PARES/
MEC) and of the study group on indicators of higher education (GEIES-INEP/
MEC). He has bachelor's degree in economics and an MBA in IT from the University of São Paulo (USP) and is pursuing a PhD in contemporary studies from
the University of Coimbra. He is the author of books such as *New challenges in
higher education* and articles such as "Three Challenges to Education Management in the 21st Century" published by *Harvard Business Review.*

Edward Choi

is a PhD candidate in higher education at the Lynch School of Education and
Human Development, Boston College and Research Assistant at the Center
for International Higher Education, Boston College. Edward received a master's degree in international educational development from Teachers College,
Columbia University. His research interests include the organization and administration of higher education and family-owned institutions.

Hans de Wit

is Director of the Center for International Higher Education (CIHE) at Boston
College, USA. He is founding editor of the *Journal of Studies in International Education* (Sage), consulting editor of the journal *Policy Reviews in Higher Education,*
associate editor of *International Higher Education,* and co-editor of the book se-
ries *Global Perspectives in Higher Education* (Brill | Sense). He publishes a regular
blog in "University World News." He has (co)written books and articles on internationalization of higher education and is actively involved in assessment and
consultancy for organizations like the European Commission, UNESCO, World
Bank, IMHE/OECD, IAU, and European Parliament. He is founding member and
past president of the European Association for International Education (EAIE).

Mohammad Imranul Haque

is the program manager and quality assurance program evaluator with the Institutional Quality Assurance Cell of the American International University-
Bangladesh. He is engaged in various quality assurance activities as well as
coordinating workloads of the staff. He holds a master's in business administration (MBA) degree from the American International University-Bangladesh.
Mr. Haque was also a key person responsible for writing the manual of operation in connection with the university's ISO9001-2008 certification. Mr. Haque
is the university's representative to the Higher Education Management
Information System (HEMIS) organized by the University Grants Commission
(UGC), Bangladesh.

Chester D. Haskell

serves as interim vice-chancellor for academic affairs and university provost at Antioch University (USA). With four decades of academic leadership experience, he is an independent consultant working with universities in the USA and several other countries including Mexico, the Netherlands, Spain, Brazil, and the United Arab Emirates. His areas of expertise center on institutional governance and strategies, initiatives and requirements for effective international programs, consortia and governmental agencies. In addition, he has considerable knowledge about matters of academic quality, including accreditation. He also is a partner and director of Edu-Alliance Group (USA).

Farheen Hassan

is associate professor, director of the Bachelor in Business Administration Program, and deputy director of the Institutional Quality Assurance Cell (IQAC) at American International University Bangladesh (AIUB) and quality assurance practitioner as external peer reviewer. She has 20 years of working experience with non-government organizations, educational institutions and international organizations.

Carmen Z. Lamagna

was the first woman to be appointed vice-chancellor in Bangladesh. She earned a bachelor's of science in chemical engineering from Adamson University, a master's in arts from Rizal Technological University in the Philippines and a doctor of business administration from the California Coast University in the USA. Under her guidance from its inception in 1995, the American International University-Bangladesh, has earned distinction as a source of quality education. The university grew from 70 to more than 11,000 students distributed to faculties of science and technology, engineering, business administration, arts, and social sciences.

Daniel C. Levy

is a SUNY Distinguished Professor at the University of Albany. He is director of the internationally renowned PROPHE (Program for Research on Private Higher Education). His ten authored books, six edited books, and well over a hundred articles mostly focus on universities in the context of civil society and the state, either globally or in Latin America. He has lectured at most leading U.S. universities, lectured and worked in six continents, and been grantee and/or consultant with internationally leading foundations, development banks, and academic agencies. Levy has been awarded lifetime and long-term achievement awards from the leading academic associations in comparative and international education (CIES) and higher education (ASHE). His next book will be *The World of Private Higher Education*.

Kazuhito Obara

is a professor and associate dean of the college of education, Tamagawa University, Tokyo, Japan and head of the Center of Higher Education and Development, Tamagawa's research institute. He received his bachelor's (2001) and master's (2002) at Boston College, USA and a PhD (2005) from the University of California, Los Angeles. His research interests are comparative higher education, institutional research, enrollment management, university management, and real options under uncertainty.

Arevik Ohanyan

has served as the head of the Quality Assurance Centre at the Eurasia International University (EIU) since 2009, coordinating the implementation and enhancement of the internal quality assurance system as well as managing the external accreditation of the university. In 2019 she was tasked to improve the research environment and systems of the university and serve as head of newly established research incubator of EIU. She holds an MBA degree from the American University of Armenia. She has been a visiting scholar at the Center for International Higher Education (CIHE) of Boston College funded by the Bureau of Educational and Cultural Affairs (ECA) of the U.S. Department of State.

Fábio Reis

has a PhD in social history from the University of São Paulo (USP). He is director of academic innovation and cooperation networks at the Sindicato das Entidades Mantenedoras de Estabelecimentos de Ensino Superior no Estado de São Paulo (Semesp) and president of the STHEM Brazil Consortium. He was visiting scholar at Boston College in 2010, general director at the Salesian Center University (Unisal Lorena), coordinator of the laboratory of academic innovation at Unisal from 2016–2018, and coordinator and professor of the university management course at Unisal from 2007–2014. He was the editor of several books including *Cooperation Networks* (2018), *Creative Destruction* (2017), *Education Economics* (2016), *Sustainable Organizations in Higher Education* (2015), *Competitiveness and Changes in institutional DNA* (2014).

Alma Santiago-Espartinez

is the vice-president for academic affairs of Holy Angel University in Angeles City, Pampanga. She holds a bachelor's, master's and PhD in philosophy from the University of Santo Tomas, Manila. Alma was a Fulbright Scholar-in-Residence grantee in 2010–2011. She taught ethics and philosophy of the human person at the Dominican University of California for a year and delivered 23 lectures in 10 different states in the US during that period. She is also an author of several philosophy books.

Juan Carlos Silas Casillas

holds a PhD in educational policy and leadership from the University of Kansas, a master's degree in education and bachelor's in educational psychology from Universidad del Valle de Atemajac (UNIVA) in Guadalajara, Mexico. He is a full professor at ITESO, Universidad Jesuita de Guadalajara, and coordinator of the doctoral program in education. Silas Casillas is a member of the National System of Researchers (SNI) and the Mexican Council of Educational Research (COMIE). He is affiliated with the Program for Research on Private Higher Education (PROPHE) at the University of Albany and an active scholar in the field of private higher education in Mexico and Latin America

Wondwosen Tamrat

is associate professor and founding president of St Mary's University, Addis Ababa, Ethiopia. He is an affiliate scholar of the Program for Research on Private Higher Education (PROPHE) at the State University of New York at Albany, USA. He is also the coordinator of the private higher education sub-cluster set up for the realization of the African Union's Continental Education Strategy of Africa (CESA).

Leopoldo N. Valdes

has worked for international organizations, governments, and non-profits in three world regions. He has an MBA from Simon Fraser University, Canada and a master's in human resource management from the City University of Seattle, USA. After acquiring a British Columbia professional instructor diploma, he worked for several universities and career colleges in Canada. He returned to the Philippines in 2016 and joined Holy Angel University as senior internationalization officer.

Rene Joshua M. Verdote

is the corporate communications and social media officer of the University of the Cordilleras (UC) in Baguio City, Philippines. He is a part-time faculty member of the university's college of arts and sciences where he teaches courses in language and literature. He obtained his bachelor's degree in communication at the UC in 2014.

Charles C. Villanueva

holds a doctor of education (EdD). He is academic vice president, dean of the faculty of business administration, and director of quality assurance at the American International University-Bangladesh. He has participated in education and training in the Philippines and abroad including UNESCO/PROAP Bangkok and NIEPA India. He has taught in various colleges and universities in the Philippines, occupied managerial positions in the Philippine government, and been a consultant to UNESCO with assignments in Asian countries. He has published training manuals and modules in educational planning and management and in quality assurance. Villanueva has published in journals and presented papers at national and international conferences.

Vidya Yeravdekar

is the pro-chancellor of Symbiosis International University, a multi-disciplinary, multinational, multicultural international university, enrolling students from all states of India and 85 different countries. Dr. Vidya holds a postgraduate degree in medicine, a law degree and PhD in the internationalization of higher education in India. Her passion has been instrumental in the university's innovative approaches to promote internationalization. Her leadership has been key in creating strategic collaborations with universities across the globe for student and faculty mobility.

Kai Yu

is chief executive officer of the China Education Group Holdings Limited, a company listed on the Hong Kong Stock Exchange. Dr. Yu is a professor in education and has served as an educational consultant to the World Bank. He received his bachelor's of engineering degree in computer science (first class honors) from Queen's University of Belfast and master's of science and doctor of philosophy degrees in educational studies from the University of Oxford. Dr. Yu also received a master's of business administration degree in finance from the China Europe International Business School (CEIBS).

PART 1

The Framework

..

CHAPTER 1

Universities Family Style

Philip G. Altbach

A worldwide phenomenon in higher education that has been entirely left out of higher education scholarship is the study of private universities owned or managed by families. This phenomenon is especially relevant since private higher education has been the fastest growing segment of postsecondary education worldwide, enrolling at least one-third of students by 2019 or around 80 million. Latin America has the largest global proportion, around half of the student population studies in private postsecondary institutions.

There are no statistics concerning family-owned or managed higher education institutions (FOMHEIS). A few countries, such as Thailand, Ethiopia, Korea, and India, have significant numbers of FOMHEIS and they are also prominent in the private higher education sector in Latin America—indeed, up to half of the total private institutions. The number of FOMHEIS are in the thousands worldwide and exist in most countries. They are, without question, a key dimension of the private higher education environment.

A few FOMHEIS are respected high-status institutions that have existed for several generations and often include a research mission. A few even show up on regional and international rankings. The vast majority, however, were established more recently to serve the rapid expansion of higher education since around 1980, especially in developing and middle-income countries. They tend to be "demand absorbing," providing specializations and degrees in demand by the local marketplace and are prepared to quickly add fields that are deemed relevant to the job market. They are often able to quickly adapt to changing market needs and student interests. While these institutions seldom have the prestige more likely to be accorded to public universities in most countries, they serve a key role in diversified mass academic systems globally. FOMHEIS are often especially nimble in meeting market demands for specific kinds of higher education since their decision-making is generally concentrated within a small family group; decisions to shift staff and resources can often be reached quickly.

The overall quality of the private higher education sector and of FOMHEIS in particular is mixed. Many countries with numerous private institutions have weak quality assurance systems and thus it is difficult to accurately assess quality, but it is fair to say that the private sector has, on average, low prestige.

© KONINKLIJKE BRILL NV, LEIDEN, 2020 | DOI: 10.1163/9789004423435_001

The FOMHEI sector itself is increasingly diversified with a small number of institutions, especially older ones that have had several generations of family leadership, now well established in their countries. Degrees from such schools often are less valuable in the marketplace than those of more prestigious universities. Yet, as FOMHEIS are increasingly common and gaining stature in the higher education system, they are acquiring greater respect.

While FOMHEIS exist in most countries, they tend to be most common and influential in developing and middle-income countries that have recently undergone or are currently advancing towards the massification of enrollment. These are countries with an urgent need for skilled graduates that private institutions, including FOMHHEIS, can supply.

In addition to building higher education capacity, FOMHEIS have some market advantages. FOMHEIS sometimes permit new and innovative educational and management ideas to be developed and tested. Many were established by charismatic educational leaders with a zeal for reform, new ideas about education, or a desire to serve particular societal needs. These leaders are able to instill their ideas in their institutions and, insofar as they are able to concentrate resources, to build institutions with their imprint.

In some cases, FOMHEIS operate in private and secretive ways to make money or wield influence. Without the constraints of transparent management or faculty-led governance, many FOMHEIS operate with few internal constraints. There are, thus, both positive and negative aspects in FOMHEI organizational structures.

There is considerable diversity among FOMHEIS globally as well as within countries and thus it is difficult to generalize. Yet, common elements do exist and the importance of the phenomenon makes understanding this dimension of postsecondary education important to understand.

1   Definitions

Academic institutions controlled by family groups are often difficult to distinguish from other private universities. In fact, family institutions sometimes attempt to conceal that they are family-owned or at least avoid making this characteristic transparent. It may also be difficult to distinguish them legally and financially. Our definition is a simple one—a family-owned or managed university is an institution established by an individual or family group in which family members remain directly involved and generally dominant in the administration, governance, financial control, and/or direct ownership of the institution.

In some countries, family ownership may be unlawful or legally restricted, and as a result, patterns of ownership or control may be obscure. Institutional management may vary considerably due to legal requirements or historical circumstances or may be limited by governmental regulations. However, families often find sophisticated ways of maintaining control.

If family ownership is not respected in the local context, institutions may not advertise it. Where academic institutions are essentially business enterprises operated for profit, ownership, and financial structures are often kept opaque. In this respect some family universities do not differ markedly from other for-profit higher education institutions.

2   Motivations

Why do individuals and families establish and run universities? In many cases, there is a sense of philanthropy or social mission—a visionary thinker with ideas about education establishes a postsecondary institution that evolves into a family-controlled enterprise over time, especially when the founder must pass leadership on to others. Many of the best-known and most-respected universities that are family-owned, family-managed, or that stem from family roots are in this category. In some cases, families have a religious motivation and work with religious authorities to establishing an academic institution with links to a particular religion.

Universities confer prestige on those involved with them and may be established to bring honor or status to the founding individuals and families. In some countries, universities are established for political reasons—to help build a constituency for elected office among students and others, to maintain a political base or develop the local economy as a means of retaining political influence. Even if there is no direct monetary gain from a FOMHEI, other benefits may accrue.

Entrepreneurs frequently establish universities, especially in developing countries, with the idea of earning money. These institutions may be designed to remain under the control of families as a way of ensuring continuity and protecting income. Academic institutions can produce income. Of course, the most direct way is through tuition payments by students—finances can be structured so that tuition produces a profit. Some countries forbid for-profit higher education. In such cases, owners can still earn revenue by "renting" buildings, providing services such as maintenance, technology support, or through other ancillary means. Profit-oriented owners sometimes locate campuses within their own real-estate developments, thus increasing the value of other properties. Family-owned institutions can be a useful means for creating employment, not only for faculty and administrators, but also for support staff such as food service employees or cleaners.

In general, family ownership is seen as a way to ensure stability and control, keep financial aspects of the institutions as confidential as possible and maintain the original mission of the institution. Thus, there are many motivations for developing and maintaining FOMHEIS.

3   Characteristics

Family universities vary considerably and it is difficult to categorize them neatly. Institutional control is a key element since the family usually wishes to maintain its authority over the institution. Thus, family universities generally have structures that permit centralized control of the institution. Family members often occupy senior administrative and leadership positions, especially those relating to financial management. Powerful boards of trustees or directors dominated by family members that have responsibility for financial and academic decision-making are common. Although the structure of institutional control is subject to the norms and legal regulations of particular countries, family universities generally seek to ensure the maximum amount of direct and ongoing control over many aspects of the institution.

Family universities typically have very strong and centralized administrative control and hierarchy, even in countries where this is not the norm. Presidents, provosts, and other senior administrative officers have great authority over the institution, generally significantly more than would be the case in public universities. Concomitantly, faculty members may have little decision-making authority. Shared governance is much less common in private higher education in general and especially in FOMHEIS. Administrative offices are very often in the hands of family members with members of the owning family occupying the presidency and other key decision-making positions. Exceptions to this pattern include institutions established by individuals or families for philanthropic or idealistic reasons that lose their family links over time.

FOMHEIS are often subject to the initiatives—and sometimes to the whims—of the family leadership group, although in some countries, such as Japan and Korea, there are governmental restrictions on the number of family members who can serve on boards of trustees. Facing few checks and balances and little diffused academic authority, the leadership has considerable power over the direction of the institution. As already mentioned, this authority may permit innovative programs and new ideas about management to be implemented. The university may be in a position to respond to changes in the marketplace or to new pedagogical approaches. Or it can be subject to the whims of the controlling family, to academic fads of little value or to schemes to make quick money. Much depends on the motivations and judgment of the family owners.

Given the centralized control and a lack of a tradition with shared governance, FOMHEIS often limit the power of academic and other staff. There are often fewer guarantees of academic freedom, less scope for autonomy and the potential for more control over teaching styles. Family universities may be more efficiently managed because of tight central control or they may experience questionable policies implemented by the family group. These distinctive traits may also characterize other private universities—especially those at the lower end of the academic pecking order—but may be exacerbated in family-run institutions. Family ownership does not guarantee efficiency.

4   Challenges

Family-owned universities face some significant challenges—one of the most important is continuity. What happens when the charismatic founder-educator passes from the scene? Will other family members carry on the original mission or even continue to run the institution? Will family members possess the skills—or the desire—to provide leadership and manage a university? Will family-owned institutions established for academic, philanthropic or political reasons be able to sustain the founder's vision over time? Family institutions established for producing revenues may have fewer problems of continuity, but the complexity of academic institutions requires a level of sophistication that goes beyond a typical business enterprise.

In common with many family-owned businesses, FOMHEIS sometimes experience problems of leadership continuity over several generations. It is by no means guaranteed that succeeding generations of ownership families will be interested, or even qualified, to provide academic and managerial leadership. Such generational challenges may lead to non-family leaders being asked to take over, or in some cases the sale or even closure of the institution.

Building and maintaining academic quality demands a commitment from the academic community. Recent examples of newly established universities include some that are family owned, have quickly gained a reputation for high-quality academic programs, and that have developed impressive facilities. Some of the institutions that began with ample funds and academic enthusiasm have failed to achieve their potential, in part because of inconsistent leadership. Sustaining leadership and effective long-term management causes serious problems for family-owned universities as control inevitably passes from one generation to another.

5   Conclusion

It is hard to generalize about this special type of academic institution. Some are visionary institutions established by charismatic educational thinkers. Others are founded to solidify political power, while many others are founded to earn profit. In the rapidly changing and ever-expanding landscape of higher education, the phenomenon of family-owned or managed academic institutions is one that requires understanding—and scrutiny—as an emerging category of academic institutions. The case studies in this publication illustrate that variety of FOMHEIs as part of the private higher education sector. This first comparative global overview of FOMHEIs invites further study and understanding of this understudied and previously ignored yet substantive segment of private higher education.

CHAPTER 2

The Family Album inside the World's Private Higher Education Landscape

Daniel C. Levy

Family-owned or managed higher education institutions (FOMHEIS) are private. This chapter will thus place them into the wider landscape of private higher education (PHE). That wider landscape is in fact huge, now constituting a third of the world's total higher education enrollments. Although the FOMHEI share of the private sector is unknown, it is without doubt significant.

While most PHE is not FOMHEI, all FOMHEI is PHE and so this chapter should help readers see this volume's case-study chapters in their broader private context. Family-owned or managed higher education (FOMHE) often typifies major PHE characteristics. Of course, FOMHE is also part of the yet broader total higher education context, but on virtually all important matters—from growth to status and quality; finance; governance; function; institutional challenges and choices; and public policy issues—PHE provides a much more guiding and illuminating context (Levy, forthcoming) for understanding (even predicting) FOMHE reality than higher education overall does. It is therefore sensible that many of the volume's chapters (e.g., on Armenia, Brazil, China, Ethiopia, and Mexico) highlight general developments in their country's PHE.

At the same time, much of what is documented throughout this book is not particular to the family form. Characterizations of FOMHEIS as distinctive can be misleading when, though they are in fact largely different from the public sector (usually the majority sector), they are typical of the private sector. Tuition dependence, institutional size, hierarchical internal governance, and struggles with legitimacy are just a few examples common not only to FOMHEIS but to all PHEIS.

Yet beyond painting the general landscape of PHE, we will highlight those parts of PHE into which FOMHEIS most often fit best. The largest point in this regard is that FOMHEI overwhelmingly fits into the "non-elite" private subsector as opposed to what we will depict as the "elite" and "identity" subsectors. As our PHE portrait gets more detailed, including *types* within subsectors, and other *forms* of private institutions, we will be able to identify where typical FOMHEIS concentrate as well as where significant, exceptional FOMHEIS make their way.

© KONINKLIJKE BRILL NV, LEIDEN, 2020 | DOI: 10.1163/9789004423435_002

While our main purpose is to paint the PHE landscape in order to contextualize and illuminate the FOMHEI terrain, we perforce achieve a complementary purpose. The chapter, like the volume overall, contributes importantly to our understanding of PHE. Until now, the fast-growing literature on PHE has lacked much descriptive work on the family reality. The extant PHE literature refers only in passing to FOMHEIs. That those references turn out to be generally accurate owes to both luck and the PHE literature's generally accurate depiction of the non-elite subsector. From here forward, however, the PHE literature can be more detailed and surer handed about how it incorporates FOMHE.

This chapter proceeds from this introduction to focus consecutively on the following staple PHE topics and fitting FOMHE into each: definition; growth; size; the non-elite subsector, including for-profit PHE; the elite subsector; the identity subsector; conclusion. However, these sections are not rigid boundaries so that the subject matter itself leads us to refer recurrently, for example, to non-elite PHE.

1   Definition

Definition is a frequent issue in PHE discussions. We expect this in popular and policy discussions as participants change cast, promote different connotations based on beliefs and self-interest and do not often pause to read PHE literature. Definition is also a frequent issue in scholarship. There the reasons more often concern the complexity of the subject matter, nuances of meaning, ambiguity between empirical and normative formulations (just as in "what is a university?"), and a confusing mingling of "private" with "privateness." Related to the last point is the great overlap with the massive subject of "privatization," a term that itself has many varied meanings in higher education and beyond. While FOMHE is integral to the growth of PHE, it lies apart from the privatization most analyzed in higher education—the advance of "privateness" in finance and governance within public higher education (Hoang, 2018). Public universities do not become family owned or managed.

Notwithstanding the myriad complexities in defining private, the PHE literature, especially the leading empirical literature, has had comparatively little difficulty developing a reasonable definition that facilitates analysis of the real world. It takes as private whatever is so defined legally within a sovereign jurisdiction, usually a country. Admittedly, this brings certain limitations to cross-country comparison, as different countries can use somewhat different defining criteria. In practice, however, the definitions of PHE are rather standard internationally even as the PHE reality varies greatly. The legal definition commonly depends on ownership of the institution and, despite newsworthy exceptions, ownership is typically rather clear-cut.

Yet such simple definitions are formalistic, themselves telling us little about complex reality. The same is true, however, of this volume's definition of FOMHEIs. Like it, the definition of private is only a starting point for analysis. Such definitions have operational value and allow us (like governments and international agencies) to identify and count. Once we have identified which are the PHE institutions or the FOMHEIS we can empirically identify and explore their major characteristics. We can see, for example, how often they receive public funds, operate under government regulations, and perform public functions. As we identify patterns of variation, we can create and define PHE sub-categories. This is how the PHE literature has developed the subsectors, types, and forms that allow us to convey a meaningful overview of PHE here and see how FOMHEI fits within it.

This book's introduction similarly lays out a definition of FOMHEIs that sets the starting point for its national and institutional case studies. The definitional component of ownership harks back toward the legal core of our PHE definition, while the ongoing management component moves beyond it. Mostly, however, like the PHE definition, the FOMHEI definition leaves open for investigation what are the main characteristics of FOMHEIs. By definition the family remains involved in finance, governance, *or* ownership but the extent and shape of the family's role and those of other actors must then be studied. Some institutions will prove to have more "family-ness" than others. In particular cases, reasonable observers may even differ on whether there is enough family involvement to classify the institution as a family one. For example, the formal owners of Mexican FOMHEIS are civil associations. Certainly, the goals, resources, practices, and outputs of FOMHEIS will vary. As more is learned about the empirical reality of FOMHEIS we should be able to create meaningful categories within the overall FOMHEI form, or perhaps even to tweak the overall FOMHEI definition. For now we can note that key similarities exist in the definitional approach to PHEIS and FOMHEIS; it is more often difficult to identify which are FOMHEIS than which are PHEIS; but such greater difficulty is common when we move from the general category of PHEI to specific categories within it, family being just another example alongside elite, religious, non-profit, etc.

2   Growth

The growth of PHE has been astounding. This is the main reason that growth has been the most studied reality of PHE, a more prosaic reason being the availability of private-public data in many countries. But only now do we have a sectorial comprehensive *global* enrollment dataset. Built at PROPHE (Program for Research on Private Higher Education), this dataset allows us to discover much about PHE's present size. Unfortunately, neither this nor any global dataset reaches back prior to 2000. Further reach has been achieved for only one region, Latin America, indeed back to 1955 (Levy, 1986), and for scattered individual countries that have been individually studied in the rest of the world. Nonetheless, the comprehensive data compiled since 2000 (through 2015, though we cite more reliable 2010 data except where otherwise noted), national case studies and general historical knowledge about higher education allow us to say much with assurance about growth and size (Levy, 2018).

Whatever private precursors existed the advent of the nation state generally meant that higher education would be public. The "continental model" (Clark, 1983) that guided European development and, through colonialism the pre-national and early national periods in much of Latin America, Asia, and Africa, was state dominated. Countries considered higher education a public good that required the state to have both the right and responsibility to fund it and direct it (though in cooperation with senior professors). The model left no room for private interests, business, religion—or PHE. Of course, inevitably, a model does not correspond to more varied historical reality, just as the quite contrasting "US model" does not correspond fully to US historical reality and both models are increasingly far from capturing contemporary reality. But until the middle of the last century most of the world had no, or only marginal, PHE. Many countries still had no or little PHE until late in the century or even into the present century.

PHE's growth to its present one-third share of total enrollment is yet more remarkable considering also the notable general growth of government in social and economic fields in much of the last century with a notable spike (very much including higher education) in the post-war era. Even as an era of broad economic and social privatization arose in the last quarter of the 20th century, the strong normative preference has continued globally for public over private higher education. Moreover, public universities often continue to use their political might to oppose private growth, although they sometimes partner with it, and public enrollment has grown globally in absolute terms as never before. Yet by 2000, PHE had risen to 28 percent of total global enrollment. And while the private share has risen only modestly further in the new century, its raw enrollment has continued to soar, more than doubling from 27 to 57 million in the first decade, then rising to some 70 million by 2015, and probably well over 80 million by 2019. The number of countries without any PHE continues to dwindle, probably to fewer than 10. PHE today exists in nations of all development levels, cultures and political regimes, including even communist countries.

The reasons for PHE growth vary by sectoral component. Religious, women's, and ethnically oriented institutions grow to protect or promote group interests and opportunities, sometimes when the public sector denies access or quality. Semi-elite (elite within their country but not world-class) PHEIs often grow to serve business and class interests, often as a reaction to public university turmoil or other perceived loss of status and quality. Non-elite PHEIs mostly result from soaring demand for HE outstripping public capacity.

We correctly understand FOMHE as part of the world's exploding higher education enrollment. Yet it is more acutely understood as part of the world's exploding PHE enrollment, especially its non-elite PHE enrollment. Whatever profit focus, status, community, educational, or philanthropic purpose individual founders and managers may have for their FOMHEIs, soaring demand is a big facilitating factor, sometimes a necessary one albeit insufficient without family initiative. As with much of non-elite PHE overall, FOMHEIs are not infrequently institutions of access more than institutions of choice. This may be vivid where FOMHEIs emerge in regions not amply covered by the public sector, as with the rural location of many Japanese FOMHEIs. It is likely that just as entering students often do not know whether a HEI is owned by a private, public, for-profit, non-profit, or religious entity or how religious or profit-driven an entity is, so they often do not know whether or how much their institution is family-owned or managed. Of course, the dynamic is different for exceptional higher status FOMHEIs with well-known, often famous owners.

The non-elite nature of most FOMHEIs makes them especially vulnerable to the vagaries of the marketplace, including demographically induced stagnation or even declines in demand (Levy, 2013). The volume's case studies of Japan and South Korea show this in stark contrast to the boom in FOMHEIs where non-elite PHE skyrockets as in India and Brazil. Non-elite FOMHEIs are likewise particularly vulnerable to decline, merger, and even death when "delayed regulation" emerges after an almost laissez-faire space for easy growth. Weak institutions generate dissatisfaction among clientele, public opinion, and government culminating in crackdowns. Much depends on political regimes, as seen in the 1960s-70s in South Korean where heavy regulation was sandwiched between and periods of more market-friendly regimes. The point is that regulatory costs and standards or stagnant demographics that hardly faze the strongest PHEIs imperil weak non-elite ones including many FOMHEIs. There is thus no guaranteed future for them in all countries. Regardless, for several decades the dominant global tendencies have been favorable to major non-elite and FOMHE growth.

3   Size

Decades of growth have led to the remarkable present size of the private sector. The 57 million students just mentioned represented 32.9 percent of total enrollment in 2010 and, as noted, a still increasing number, albeit with a steadier rather than rapidly rising private share.

Whereas the PROPHE dataset shows the figures for each individual country, we highlight here the salient features of the global PHE's country configuration. Countries with both private and public sectors hold 98 percent of the world's HE enrollment. On the other hand, we discover an also remarkable concentration of PHE in countries with the largest HE systems (Table 2.1).

Of course, some correlation between PHE and total enrollment is unremarkable and the 10 largest systems account for 58 percent of global total enrollment. Yet they account for 69 percent of global PHE, close to the 71 percent if we selected the 10 countries with the largest private enrollment, in descending order—India, US, Brazil, China, Japan, Indonesia, South Korea,

TABLE 2.1   Ten largest systems' individual and aggregated private shares

Country	% private	Private enrollment	Total enrollment	Rank by total enrollment	Rank by private enrollment
China	19.6	4,664,531	23,856,345	1	4
India	58.3	12,443,748	21,350,427	2	1
United States	27.5	5,617,069	20,427,709	3	2
Russia	14.7	1,323,348	8,984,977	4	3
Brazil	72.7	4,764,498	6,552,707	5	3
Indonesia	58.2	2,908,383	5,001,048	6	6
Japan	78.6	3,016,964	3,836,314	7	5
Iran	44.9	1,702,572	3,790,859	8	8
Turkey	5.2	181,829	3,529,334	9	35
Rep. of Korea	80.7	2,636,972	3,269,509	10	7
Total-top ten	39.0	39,259,914	100,599,229		
Total-global	32.9	56,722,374	172,545,175		
Top ten global share		69.2%	58.3%		

SOURCE: HTTP://PROPHE.ORG/EN/GLOBAL-DATA

Iran, Philippines and Russia. For a list of the 10 largest systems overall, nine would remain the same, while Turkey would replace the Philippines.

What then can we say about FOMHE within this global and country land-scape of PHE size and shape? Unfortunately, there is no shortcut around the need to gather reliable FOMHE data at a country level. There is no global FOMHE dataset as we now have for PHE. However, much it helps that this book's editors provide a guiding definition for their authors, other country case studies may not attempt to follow this path. Nor is it always easy to match defi-nitional features to real-world phenomena. This contrasts to the comparative ease of labeling private versus public and the existence of a global PHE dataset.

Fortunately, however, we can now get much better bearings on FOMHE size and shape. First, we know the size of the whole private pie. Second, we know that most of it is non-elite. Third, we know that FOMHE is a significant part of the non-elite enrollment in many countries. All three of these observations hold firmly for the global aggregate. All three observations also guide coun-try estimations but with more complete applicability as well as empirical base regarding the first two than the third.

Taking informed speculation further, the 10 countries with towering private enrollment probably hold a significant share of the world's FOMHE, though we are not in a position to venture an estimate. We are on strongest ground where we couple the PROPHE database with country FOMHEI case studies. We can contingently estimate that FOMHE has around 851,852 students, 18 percent of all private enrollment. Where the Colombian case study shows that FOMHE has 29 percent of total enrollment and we separately know that PHE holds 45 percent of total enrollment; we discover that whereas Brazilian FOMHE enrollment is higher than Colombian FOMHE enrollment, Colombia far outdistances Brazil in the FOMHE share of both private and total country enrollment. At the same time, our general knowledge of non-elite PHE warns us to recognize the limitations of national figures showing FOMHE's share of institutions given that non-elite PHEIs tend to be smaller in enrollment than PHEIs average and especially smaller than public institutions' average size. We need further research on where, why, and how much mid-size FOMHEIS exist, as in Mexico and Thailand, albeit alongside small FOMHEIS, and we must remember that "mid-size" within PHE is often rather small within the totality of higher education (PROPHE, 2018).

On geographical concentration within countries, the PHE literature has found and explained PHE roots in urban centers with its spreading out only recently getting scholarly attention (Navarro Meza, 2016). Whereas the vol-ume's Colombian and Ethiopian chapters place roughly half the FOMHEIS in the capital cities, the Brazilian, Japanese and Korean chapters refer to a significant rural or other non-urban presence. What is the configuration in other countries? And what about "chains" of institutions? This volume includes several references to grouping of institutions under common family ownership. One working hypothesis might be that while many PHE chains, prominently including international chains, are business-owned and often involve conglomerates dealing with non-education enterprises as well as sometimes both higher and other education levels, a major form of family chain focuses on a pathway from lower through higher education, with preferential passage for those already in the chain, as in Thailand (PROPHE, 2018). To be sure, there is plenty of overlap between the business and family form and only case studies can give a better sense of FOMHE chain characteristics.

When it comes to the regional configuration of FOMHE, we cannot escape the need to accumulate more country case studies and scholars might perhaps work with regional agencies to design regional surveys about FOMHE. But again too, our PHE dataset now provides some good guidance for informed estimates and understanding.

The duality of dispersion and concentration that characterized the world's country PHE configuration also characterizes the regional configuration as Table 2.2 shows. Counting the US as its own region, 7 of 7 regions have at least a tenth of their enrollment in PHE. No region remains outside the PHE growth phenomenon. Clearly, the PHE dispersion is global. Yet we should highlight the regional PHE concentration in two regions. Asia has by far the largest private enrollment, some 32 of the world's 57 million, while Latin America has the largest private share, 49 percent. And while Asia is highest in raw private enrollment and Latin America is highest in private share, Latin America is second highest in raw enrollment and Asia is second highest in private share. Integrating with country data, most of the top 10 largest private sectors are Asian, most of the next 10 Latin American. The concentration in two regions obviously means lower shares elsewhere. Still, the US holds a prominent 3rd place in both raw private enrollment and private share (while the importance of US PHE is obviously much greater in research, faculty, graduate education, finance, quality, status, and impact than it is in enrollment size). Meanwhile, although Africa, the Arab region and the developed British Commonwealth (Australia, Canada, and New Zealand) have come to PHE only in recent decades, all have seen great private growth that shows little sign of abating. Eastern Europe had a private boom only after the fall of communism, though private growth there has recently become problematic. Western European PHE, however proportionally small compared to average global reality, shows vibrancy, most dramatically with the UK opening to true PHE only after 2010.

TABLE 2.2   Regional concentration of private enrollment

	Regional percent global private	Regional percent global total	Private share (percent)	Regional private enrollment	Regional total enrollment
Global	100.0	100.0	32.9	56,722,374	172,546,175
Africa (Sub-Saharan)	1.6	3.0	17.8	930,016	5,218,120
Arab States	2.5	4.8	17.4	1,423,630	8,201,861
Asia	56.9	44.4	42.1	32,267,911	76,568,246
Developed British Commonwealth (Canada, Australia, New Zealand)	0.6	1.8	10.1	318,033	3,162,889
Europe	9.7	21.5	14.9	5,526,851	37,177,470
Latin America and the Caribbean	18.8	12.6	48.8	10,638,863	21,789,880
United States	9.9	11.8	27.5	5,617,069	20,427,709

SOURCE: HTTP://PROPHE.ORG/EN/GLOBAL-DATA

Concentration in Asia and Latin America carries with it another salient discovery about PHE's geographic configuration. It is mostly a developing world phenomenon. Including Japan and South Korea, with their large majority private sectors, the developed world holds 30 percent of global PHE, the developing world 70 percent (PROPHE, 2010). Moreover, as both 2000–2010 data and post-2010 data show, growth is faster in the developing world with its share of PHE rising. Although we cannot put firm figures to the crucial point, undoubtedly non-elite PHE concentrates even more in the developing world than it does worldwide.

Definitively knowing the overall regional configuration of PHE with strong reason to believe it is accentuated for non-elite PHE, we can greet the volume's ensuing information on FOMHE in that context. FOMHE is surely dispersed to most of the world and just as surely concentrates in the developing world. It is by no means unrepresentative that this volume's cases come predominantly from the developing world. Nor that its only two clearly developed world cases

(Japan and South Korea) feature stagnation and threat while the great majority of country chapters feature growth. Though not included in the volume, US FOMHE, historically prominent within the US's PHE landscape, is presently on the defensive in recent years facing the regulatory burdens and enrollment declines of fellow institutions concentrated in the for-profit arena (PROPHE, 2018). Surely too, the twin giant PHE regions of Asia and Latin America again give us a "base rate" for thinking about the regional concentration of FOMHE (as again the volume's chapter representation reflects). However, we also sense provocative indications of greater prevalence in Asia than in Latin America, especially if much of the latter's family educational presence concentrates at the lower levels (PROPHE, 2018).

4   The Non-Elite Subsector

As geography is one common and useful way to portray the PHE landscape, highlighting the chief subsectors of the private sector is another and it too proves useful for sketching the FOMHE portrait. Originally, the main PHE three-part typology featured religious, elite, and demand-absorbing subsectors (Levy, 1986). Based on accumulating case studies, we have on the one hand, broadened the subsectors to be respectively identity, elite, and non-elite. On the other hand, we have made considerable progress in identifying types within each subsector.

Admittedly, the definition of non-elite PHE often comes by exclusion—that PHE that is neither identity nor elite. Thus, non-elite PHE is non-identity PHE that is unselective and low in status and quality. Salient characteristics of non-elite PHE include the limited abilities of the student body and faculty. Meager institutional resources mean scant budgets, heavy reliance on part-time teaching, and the near absence of both research and subject matter expensive to teach. All this is clear. Less clear is the socioeconomic student profile in non-elite PHE. Critics often indiscriminately refer to the private sector's privilege, but non-elite PHE does not easily fit that stereotype. While families do have to pay tuition and loan programs remain scarce or often ineffective, tuition is often comparatively low, many students both study and work part-time, and of course, the lower rungs of higher education overall are generally where children of less well-to-do and less well-educated parents disproportionately land. Compared to the rest of PHE and indeed the rest of total higher education, non-elite PHE is likewise disproportionately concentrated in non-universities (vocational colleges, short-cycle, college affiliates of public universities, international branch campuses, and others). The non-elite subsector is typically the numerically largest private subsector, often constituting a majority of private enrollment and in some countries even the majority of total enrollment.

The largest type within the non-elite subsector is demand-absorbing. This type derives fundamentally from the surge in demand for higher education that the current supply does not accommodate. Demand-absorption is thus central to PHE's concentration in the rapidly growing developing world. Much demand-absorbing PHE is mediocre and rather non-descript, frequently seeking ease and legitimacy by copying public-sector practice, often facilitated by employing public university "full-time" professors, part-time. Simultaneously, much demand-absorbing PHE is worse than mediocre, rife with abysmal quality and fraud. Accordingly, this is where institutional death is most common. Government closes demand-absorbers for minimal quality. Or government's rising regulations (including accreditation requirements) set levels or impose burdens demand-absorbers cannot manage. Or market demand slows from demographic stagnation (presently most lethal in Eastern Europe).

Partly offsetting this bleak forest on the non-elite private landscape are not only the run-of-the-mill mediocre institutions but also "product-oriented" PHEIs. The product in question is nearly always a job. These seriously managed institutions orient themselves to the labor market, hire able part-time instructors from local businesses, arrange student internships and counseling, and tailor their curriculum to practical subject matter attractive to students. Such institutions often claim to be the most student and job friendly institutions.

While FOMHEIs are mostly non-elite, we need more research to know whether they are overwhelmingly non-elite. Juxtaposing the budding FOMHE literature to the PHE literature, we can venture the hypothesis that while a significant share of non-elite PHE is family-owned or managed, a yet higher share of FOMHE is non-elite. Whatever the respective shares, a related research agenda challenge will be sorting out how much non-elite FOMHE is demanding-absorbing, abysmal, demand-absorbing mediocre, product-oriented, and the like.

Leaving aside ownership itself, it is thus far unclear if any common characteristics of non-elite PHE manifest themselves prominently at FOMHEIs. This is powerful testimony to the strong overlap between FOMHEI and non-elite PHE. From the above summary of non-elite PHE, we can point to characteristics of much FOMHE—meager institutional resources, narrow and inexpensive offerings, reliance on part-time staff, demand-absorption, tuition dependence and claims of student and job-centeredness. Most, if not all of South Korea's junior colleges, are family institutions. Unfortunately, negative realities and stereotypes about poor, non-elite PHE abound when it comes to FOMHE as well as fraud, notably through the transfer of funds and unwarranted provision of jobs to family members and associates. Against this background, many FOMHEIS are among the weak, non-elite PHEIs that struggle to gain trust and legitimacy.

At the same time, much of what is best in non-elite PHE can also be found in FOMHE. Several of the volume's chapters suggest that some of their country's better, though not semi-elite FOMHEIS, have a true educational mission, seek to serve the community, teach seriously, care about student development into responsible citizens and endeavor to professionalize management, even if through ownership families. Many FOMHEIS are job oriented. Yet a very tentative impression might be that FOMHEIS also offer a kind of general higher education, even with quasi-liberal arts formation, more often than do typical non-elite PHEIS. Many FOMHEIS are established by well-known figures, including ex-professors or administrative leaders from public universities.

It is within our extended discussion of non-elite PHE that we should include an analysis of the for-profit presence. Even in PHE generally, almost all for-profit institutions are non-elite, a key question then being the relative balance between demand-absorbing and product-oriented types. Within the FOMHE slice of the for-profit presence, the non-elite predominance is even greater than for for-profit in general, the key question of balance between the demand-absorbing and product-oriented types remaining. The comparatively small part of for-profit PHE that achieves the semi-elite level concentrates in business-heavy institutions rather than family institutions, though the two ownership forms can overlap. One supposes further that while many business-heavy for-profits are publicly traded on the stock exchange (as in Brazil, Indonesia, and Malaysia), for-profit FOMHEIS would generally be private companies.

Even among non-elite for-profit HEIs serious education exists. Nor is it simply that some of these HEIs put education above profit. There is also the proposition, admittedly heatedly contested, that good education and profits are achievable together. How unusual that is, what the obstacles are and so forth are open questions where much more research could help. What appears true from scattered observation including national studies is that for-profit activity includes a disproportionate amount of the worst of PHE as well as egregious corruption. It is crucial to highlight, however, that such behavior is not limited to legally for-profit institutions. Many countries do not legally allow for-profit PHE. In those cases the incentives are often particularly high for profit-seekers to establish and run non-profit PHEIs that are really "for-profits in disguise" (Weisbrod, 1988).

Acknowledgement of this disguised reality provided much of the stimulus for Brazil and Peru in the 1990s making the for-profit form legal and, uniquely in Vietnam in 2006, making PHE exclusively for-profit (Chau, forthcoming;

Salto, 2018). Whether as legal for-profits or for-profits in disguise, FOMHEIS come in for their share of criticism leveled against for-profit PHE in general. Further, nepotism is obviously particularly associated with the family form, a chronic issue when hiring and rewards stem primarily from nepotism or family member competence, commitment, and loyalty.

Several of the volume's chapters underscore how pivotal for-profit variables are for their country's FOMHE reality. In countries that allow for-profit legally, FOMHEIS often take this form. All Armenian FOMHE is for-profit with at least a high overlap in Brazil. As Tamrat finds not just for Ethiopia but also for much of Africa (Benin, Botswana, Ghana, Mozambique, South Africa, Sudan, and Uganda), the tremendous growth of FOMHE is intertwined with the tremendous growth of for-profit PHE. Further research might explore the relative weight of for-profit FOMHEIS that are primarily for-profit institutions with family ownership or primarily family institutions in for-profit form.

Meanwhile chapters on Mexico and South Korea have shown what separate Thai and other studies have shown—that where the law proscribes for-profit PHE and thus all FOMHE is legally non-profit, FOMHE sometimes raises the specter of for-profits in disguise. Clearly, just like other non-elite PHE, FOMHEIS take three basic forms regarding profit—legally for-profit, legally and for the most part behaviorally non-profit, and for-profit in disguise. The more researched US case shows also that FOMHE can change its for-profit versus non-profit shape over time, as it can change other aspects of its shape over time. Historically, most US for-profit HEIS had been small, family operations but in the 1980s corporate for-profits burst onto the scene and many FOMHEI for-profits had to merge or close, though family-owned remains a notable subform of for-profits (PROPHE, 2018).

5   The Elite Subsector

While non-elite is easily the largest PHE subsector, whether by number of students or number of institutions, the two other subsectors are now also large and their importance, especially for the elite subsector, transcends these numbers. But in a chapter emphasizing FOMHE's place within the PHE landscape, neither of these two other subsectors merits as much space as the non-elite subsector. Even so, these two subsectors still merit some attention. One reason is that, as in PHE generally, the importance of semi-elite FOMHEIS transcends their numbers. Another reason is that appreciating the PHE characteristics that FOMHE generally does not have, helps us recognize more clearly those it does have abundantly.

We have found it fruitful to divide the world's elite PHE into two principal types—world-class and semi-elite. A sharp reader might immediately note that this chapter has referred several times to semi-elite and only once in passing to world-class. The explanation is simple—semi-elite is the almost exclusive type of elite PHE outside the US. World-class PHE is almost non-existent outside the US with the chief exceptions being South Korea and a handful of European universities that are officially private even though understandably often seen as public. Japan has a few private universities on the cusp of world-class. Virtually all mainstream definitions of world-class give special weight to research and scholarly publication along with reputation, selectivity of students and financial resources. Translated into global rankings, the top 200 universities include just a handful of private universities outside of the US (Levy, 2018). Yet even in the US there is no world-class FOMHEI. Stanford was family-run during its early decades and institutions like Carnegie-Mellon bear the names of family founders or endowers but not ongoing owners and managers.

How then can we understand semi-elite? Not world-class, but private institutions towering above the bulk of the private sector and commanding respect for their quality, status and selectivity in the upper echelons of a country's higher education. Moving from definition to empirical reality, semi-elite PHE usually flourishes below the public system peak, often sharing status in some important respects, often matching and competing with widely respected public universities below the peak.

Semi-elite universities typically make their mark in teaching and training in commercially related fields, orientation to upper rungs of the job market, especially in business, internationalism that markedly emulates western forms (with particular attraction to things American) and contact with the west and less often in basic research and the hard sciences. Semi-elite universities are also often pointedly pro-market and display deep and broad hostility towards the state in general and public universities in particular. In fact, first in Latin America and later in Africa, South Asia, and elsewhere, semi-elite universities have often arisen partly in rebuke of perceived political disorder or bureaucratic stagnation in the public sector.

In many ways, semi-elite PHE remains within the general characteristics of the private sector, as opposed to the public sector, but not to the extreme seen in non-elite PHE. For example, income is mostly private and from tuition, but it has a more diverse income profile than non-elite PHE does. Likewise, these institutions concentrate in commercial fields and fields inexpensive to offer but less overwhelmingly or narrowly than non-elite PHE does.

If readers focused only on the institutional case studies of the volume, they might suppose that much of FOMHE is semi-elite. This is because most of the institutional case studies portray successful institutions with more than marginal semi-elite characteristics, but to whatever extent the portrayals are accurate, what they portray remains far from typical for FOMHEIs. Accordingly, by reading the national case studies as well as the volume's introduction and conclusion, readers will see the totality of FOMHE more clearly. The key to this divergence is that while the bulk of FOMHE is non-elite, often institutions known only locally and rarely internationally, semi-elite FOMHEIs enjoy much higher profiles and, frankly, importance. It is not unlike the tendency of foreigners to think of US PHE and picture the Ivy League.

One could reasonably highlight several institutional examples from the volume. For example, the Symbiosis International University in India appears as innovative and with the academic quality and breadth to move from being one of the country's numerous private-affiliated colleges to become a "deemed university" in 2002. We limited ourselves, however, to examples from Bangladesh and Armenia.

The American International University of Bangladesh (AIUB) appears to be semi-elite according to its detailed description in this volume. Established in the mid-1990s, it sits alongside Bangladesh's best-known semi-elite universities such as BRAC and the North-South University. Strikingly, AIUB is almost surely better known for being high quality than for being family-owned. "American" and "International" are both attractive semi-elite names to convey orientation and status though the worldwide reality for both is quite mixed—some institutions are truly semi-elite, Americanized and internationalized in practice; others far from meriting any such characterization. AIUB courses are in English and partnerships abound with international universities and associations. The founder is a nationally known medical doctor. A driving mission is to have high quality higher education that helps blunt the nation's notorious brain drain. While the flagship fields are computer and business studies, two of AUIB's other principal units are engineering and science & technology. Serious efforts are made to encourage research. The university claims to have a 90 percent full-time faculty, extraordinary probably even for semi-elite universities. Other characteristics include an ample campus, extra-curricular activities and student counselling. Surely this is not the portrait of Bangladesh's typical FOMHEI. Yet neither is it nationally unique in all important respects; chapter author Lamagna reports, for example, that at least six Bangladeshi FOMHEIs claim to have nearly a similar share of full-time faculty.

A second likely example of a semi-elite FOMHEI, though depicted in less firmly established terms than the AUIB, is Armenia's Eurasia International University, established in 1997. Again, "International" appears in the name, self-portrait, and myriad characteristics. Founding ideas came largely from

Europe with reforms invoking the Bologna Process. Reforms have included lessening the original family dominance that can pose a serious challenge to semi-elite status. Eurasia has been keen to emphasize accreditation and its strong orientation to the job market. It receives no public funding, draws its income mostly from tuition, but seeks to diversify its income streams. This last desire becomes a need as, like many post-communist countries, Armenia faces a demographic threat to higher education, especially PHE. With diminished student demand, Eurasia admits students less selectively than it had in the past. To offset this threat, Eurasia is more actively recruiting students internationally and opening programs taught in English. Crucially recognizing that much of Armenia's educated citizenry realizes that Armenian PHE is largely non-elite, often shoddy, Eurasia labors hard to distinguish itself from the PHE crowd.

6   The Identity Subsector

The final subsector to consider is the identity subsector. In a sense, the first shall come last in that the identity sector is noteworthy for often being a country's first private subsector whereas we treat it last here. Typically, the identity is religious. And religious remains by far the largest and most widespread globally of the identity types, the others being gender and ethnic. Identity institutions then are group-oriented institutions. A prominent mission is to promote or preserve group identity. As with FOMHEIS, a definition must specify whether founding orientation is sufficient, or some noteworthy contemporary presence is required. For us, identity PHEIS do definitionally require some mission continuity, though not ongoing management by the founding group. An identity institution is one that prominently features group orientation in its official written mission statement.

More than other private subsectors, identity faces the challenge of mission dilution (or drift) over time. We see internal manifestations where the further removed we get from the founding generation and spirit, the harder it is to maintain a faculty and student body, or eventually even leadership, committed to the original mission. Much of the problem has external roots, from a changing society with a diminishing share of its population practicing a religion or placing high priority on distinctive ethnicity over inter-generational assimilation. Such evolution may occur alongside the opening of public institutions to groups previously excluded, undoing the prior necessity for separate private havens such as women's colleges or historically black colleges and universities in the US. A downward spiral of diminishing demand for identity institutions and diminishing mission at the institutions makes identity institutions vulnerable to perishing.

In our judgment FOMHEIS are not identity institutions. Not founded to promote or preserve a group identity, FOMHEIS do not make such ends prominent in their mission statements. Their mission does not highlight teaching about the family. Yet if FOMHEIS are not identity institutions, then why not simply note the identity subsector as a significant part of the overall PHE landscape and leave it at that with no further reference to FOMHE? Two reasons follow.

One reason is that the line between identity and family institutions is not always clear-cut. Families are groups of a sort, pivotally so in some societies. A family may promote its ethnic or religious affinities and FOMHEIS' missions certainly often include promotion of family interests and even perhaps a little preservation, if only in the institution carrying the family name. Such considerations are not enough for us to see an identity institution, yet we need not recoil if another observer prefers to think of some or even all family institutions as identity institutions of a kind.

The second reason to juxtapose family and identity institutions is that several parallels illuminate each category. Again, we benefit from viewing FOMHE within the broader PHE landscape. First is great commitment by the founders, linked with both initial ownership and mission statements as seen, for example, in the (Indian) Symbiosis University case. Second, however, is the shared vulnerability to mission dilution over time. Third, and closely related, is the commonality of wrenching policy choices between mission commitment and pragmatic survival. Hold the line because that is where true cause lies or let out the line more and more to salvage what is possible without the whole ship sinking (Levy, forthcoming).

Alongside such notable similarity, we nonetheless illuminate also by noting differences. One is that FOMHEIS are often strikingly more vulnerable than identity institutions during the first generational transition. More generally, FOMHEIS are particularly vulnerable to "internal" erosion. The volume's Ethiopian case vividly portrays how the founding voluntary zeal of public-spirited family members (businesspeople, physicians, or professors) yields to salaried employee or investor priorities on profits. This story unfolds in Vietnam, China, and probably many other countries. While it sometimes turns on the shift from family-member management to professional managers outside the family, it also involves generational shifts within the family. In contrast, FOMHEIS are less vulnerable than identity institutions to changes in the wider society insofar as they are less dependent from the outset on a particular segment of the wider society. Beyond the matter of mission dilution, when it comes to actual declining enrollment and even death, the FOMHEI may be inherently more vulnerable than the typical identity institution because of both the FOMHEI's narrower base and overwhelmingly non-elite nature. "Death" can involve closure or mergers or selling to profit-seekers or other PHEIS as the case of two Chilean FOMHEIS recently sold to religious congregations (D. C. Levy, personal communication, 2018).

One final difference between identity PHEIS and FOMHEIS is of a different nature from those involving decline and death. Identity institutions of all types have public cousins. Islamic public universities are common in Muslim-majority Asian countries and there are even a few public Catholic universities; public ethnic HEIS appear in China for disadvantaged minorities and in Latin America for indigenous populations. Historically common in the US, public women's colleges now flourish elsewhere; historically black public HEIS are also part of the US higher education landscape but there is no public family university. Even in the Saudi autocracy, the country's first university (1957) was established as a public institution bearing the name King Saud University, but it is no public cousin of private identity institutions.

7   Conclusion

Were there space for a separate section devoted to how FOMHE fits into general patterns of PHE distinctiveness from the public sector, we would find again the salient reality discovered in our analysis of definition, growth, size, and each of the private subsectors. This is that FOMHE is an integral part of PHE, understandable mostly by its similarities to other PHE. At the same time, we would again find that the similarities and even overlap are most prevalent regarding non-elite PHE. Furthermore, where the FOMHEIS are for-profit, the similarities and overlap with for-profit non-elite come to the fore; where the FOMHEIS are non-profit, the similarities and overlap with non-profit non-elite PHE come to the fore.

Consider the following examples that all contrast both FOMHE and non-elite PHE to the public sector norm. In finance, while public higher education globally continues to depend largely, although decreasingly, on public funds, FOMHE, especially non-elite and particularly for-profit non-elite PHE, depends overwhelmingly on tuition, though some leading FOMHEIS benefit from family philanthropy and family business. In function, the typical concentration is on teaching over research, and on fields of study that are inexpensive to offer. In governance, institutional rule is narrow and hierarchical, usually with owner and board dominance over faculty while students have influence as consumers, choosing or leaving the institution, much more than as voice within the institution. The institutions usually enjoy autonomy that allows diverse routes, and also often allows low quality and shoddy practice, though over time this frequently provokes "delayed regulation" from government. Like most non-elite PHEIS, most FOMHEIS are at once part of a diverse system and narrow in internal governance.

The bulk of FOMHE is non-elite and shares many of its salient characteristics. Venturing further, apart from the family role itself, it is difficult to find any significant activity or tendency within FOMHE as detailed in chapter after chapter that follows that is unique or lacks a significant non-family counterpart. Something at least similar is true in reverse—what we typically find in non-family, non-elite PHE generally has a family counterpart. In contrast, other major PHE terrain finds comparatively little family counterpart, as with semi-elite PHE, while yet other major PHE terrain finds no true family counterpart, as with identity PHE, or even no remotely proximate family counterpart, as with world-class PHE.

Aided by this volume's case material, this chapter has been able to contribute to our knowledge about PHE by beginning to fill a major hole with information about FOMHE, a prevalent PHE form. Yet more central to this chapter's purpose has been to contextualize a portrait of FOMHE inside the much larger global landscape of higher education's private sector.

References

Chau, Q. (forthcoming). *The U-turn from nonprofit to for-profit private higher education in Vietnam* (Doctoral dissertation). SUNY Albany, Albany, NY.

Clark, B. R. (1983). *The higher education system: Academic organization in cross-national perspective*. Berkeley, CA: University of California Press.

Hoang, L. (2018, March). Twin privatization in Vietnam higher education: The emergence of private higher education and partial privatization of public universities. *Higher Education Policy, 32*, 359–380. https://doi.org/10.1057/s41307-018-0086-8

Levy, D. C. (1986). *Higher education and the state in Latin America: Private challenges to public dominance*. Chicago, IL: University of Chicago Press.

Levy, D. C. (2013). The decline of private higher education. *Higher Education Policy, 26*(1), 25–42.

Levy, D. C. (2018). Global private higher education: An empirical profile of its size and geographical shape. *Higher Education, 76*(4), 701–715.

Levy, D. C. (forthcoming). *A world of private higher education*.

Navarro Meza, E. E. (2016). *Las políticas de educación superior en México y la oferta privada en zonas no metropolitanas* (Master's thesis). Mexico City: FLACSO.

PROPHE. (2010). *Developed vs. developing regions.* Retrieved from
    https://www.prophe.org/en/global-data/regional-tables/developed-vs-
    developing-regions/

Salto, D. J. (2018). To profit or not to profit: The private higher education sector in Brazil.
    Higher Education, 75(5), 809–825.

Weisbrod, B. (1988). *The nonprofit economy.* Cambridge, MA: Harvard University Press.

CHAPTER 3

Family Involvement in University Management

Mathew R. Allen and Edward Choi

Research on family-owned enterprises has a long and rich history (Chrisman, Kellermanns, Chan, & Liano, 2010) but has focused predominantly on issues related to family-owned businesses (Chrisman, Steier, & Chua, 2008) addressing governance (Eddleston, Chrisman, Steier, & Chua, 2010), communication (von Schlippe & Frank, 2013), succession (Jaskiewicz, Lutz, & Godwin, 2016), strategies (Chrisman, Chua, & Sharma, 2005; Chrisman et al., 2008) and entrepreneurship (Brockhaus, 1994). While much is known about the performance drivers of both family businesses and business families, research has not, to date, delved deeply into family business behavior within specific industries.

One area in particular that lacks in-depth study is family-owned or managed universities (FOMHEIS). Anecdotally, it seems that families are present in a very significant way in the ownership and management of universities across the globe regardless of cultural context or national level of development (Altbach, 2005; Martin & Samels, 2010; Poole & Chen, 2009). In some countries, especially in Asia and Latin America, FOMHEIS may be found in large numbers and occupy a significant presence within the higher education system. However, surprisingly little is known about these particular family-owned enterprises (Altbach, 2005) with the exception of some case studies (Tsamenyi, Noormansyah, & Uddin, 2008) or indirect references (Grubb, Sweet, Gallagher, & Tuomi, 2009; Poole & Chen, 2009). These cases, however, do very little to contribute to an understanding of family-owned or managed universities and many questions remain unanswered. What exactly is a family-owned or managed university? Why do families become involved in higher education? What is their role and what are the motivations that explain their continued involvement?

1   What Is a Family-Owned or Managed University?

Altbach (2005) suggests that a family university is "an institution established by an individual or family group in which family members remain directly involved and generally dominant in the administration, governance, financial control and/or direct ownership of the institution" (p. 11). A key point is the preservation of the family's involvement and influence in management over successive generations—control over the firm stays within the family unit.

This definition is consistent with what is referred to as the "components-of-involvement" in the family firm literature. According to Kraiczy (2013), a family firm is defined by satisfying at least one of the following conditions—a family is the owner; a family manages the firm; or a family controls the firm. The components of involvement approach are concerned with the extent, modalities, and family member(s) involvement in the management, ownership, and governance of a firm (Astrachan, Klein, & Smyrnios, 2002; Klein, Astrachan, & Smyrnios, 2005; Sharma & Salvato, 2013).

However, Altbach's (2005) definition, as well as the components-of-involvement approach, does not capture one defining characteristic of the family-owned or managed enterprise. According to several scholars (Litz, 1995; Sharma & Salvato, 2013; Shanker & Astrachan, 1996), a family firm embodies the vision, purpose(s), and intent of the family unit as well as the distinctive behaviors of the family unit that lead to the pursuit of firm outcomes desirable to the family. These characteristics may be found in the "essence model" defined by four key criteria—a family's influence over the strategy of the firm; a family's vision and intention to maintain control over the firm throughout successive generations; family firm behavior; and distinctive "familiness" as explained below (Chrisman, Chua, & Litz, 2003; Kraiczy, 2013). The essence definition builds on the characteristics of the components-of-involvement approach and more intentionally incorporates the dimensions of the family's intent, vision, and behaviors associated with their managerial involvement.

The essence approach also captures what Habbershon and Williams (1999) refer to as "familiness," understood as the bundle of non-financial resources or behaviors that dominant family coalitions (DFCs) or the families involved in ownership and management generate in their firms. A firm's "familiness" includes a participatory culture that promotes care and loyalty among familial and non-familial employees; family language that manifests as a style of communication that allows for more privacy and efficiency among family members; a stewardship orientation to employees where owners treat and nurture employee relationships as a valuable resource of the firm; the unification of beliefs and vision; flexibility allowing both family and non-family personnel to adapt to multiple roles while maintaining strong social bonds; and a culture that promotes creativity and innovation. Chua, Chrisman, and Sharma (1999) propose a family firm definition that accounts for all the components just discussed.

The family business is a business governed and/or managed with the intention to shape and/or pursue the vision of the business held by a dominant coalition controlled by members of the same family or a small number of families in a manner that is potentially sustainable across generations of the family or families. (p. 25)

Indeed, for the purpose of this study we draw on Chua, Chrisman, and Sharma (1999) and Altbach (2005) to suggest the following expanded definition.

A family university is an institution established by an individual or family group in which family members remain directly involved and generally dominant in the administration, governance, financial control, and/or direct ownership of the institution with the intent to shape a distinctive vision through distinctive behaviors.

It may helpful to elaborate what is meant by intent in the above definition. There seems to be some intent or vision driving a founder (or family unit) to establish and maintain control over an institution. It is useful to imagine a founder's intent as a continuum with philanthropy on one end and economic gain on the other. Of course, no higher education enterprise, family-based or other, falls at either extreme of this continuum, but different combinations of profit and social mission place some institutions closer to one end than the other. For example, it is not unreasonable to say that for-profit ventures give greater priority to making a profit than maximizing social impact. However, this is not to say that for-profit institutions do not value the academic mission. It is only that the objective of economic gain is emphasized as part of the operating model.

In addition to adding clarity to the characteristics that describe a family firm, the revised definition also suggests a reason for involvement that falls on this spectrum between a philanthropical and financially motivated vision held by the founder and family members.

However, a definition alone does not provide a comprehensive framework to fully understand the family-owned enterprise. Thus, it is useful to consider a theoretical model that has been widely accepted by family firm scholars as defining and explaining family firms. This theory is socioemotional wealth theory or SEW (Berrone, Cruz, Gomez-Mejia, & Larraza-Kintana, 2010). It may provide more robust theoretical structure to examine the number of families involved in these types of ventures. SEW theory provides a framework within which the role and intent of the family unit become clearer.

2   Socioemotional Wealth

The socioemotional wealth model argues that in addition to a focus on the
creation and preservation of financial wealth, business families are also motivated by the creation and preservation of socioemotional wealth (SEW). Like
Habbershon and Williams' (1999) "familiness" SEW may also be understood as
a firm's resources linked to familial managerial involvement and influence. The
model contends that this non-financial wealth creation can be more important than economic gain. In one study (Berrone, Cruz, & Gomez-Mejia, 2012),
these non-financial benefits are organized into five dimensions captured by
the acronym FIBER—family influence, identification of family members with
the firm, binding social ties, emotional attachment of family members and
renewal of family bonds through dynastic succession. These non-financial
benefits of ownership are briefly described below. As mentioned earlier, these
elements overlap with the conditional requirements of the essence approach.

2.1   *Family Influence*
In family-owned businesses, the dominant family coalition's ability to exercise
influence rests on a strong ownership position derived from an ascribed status (Berrone, Cruz, & Gomez-Mejia, 2012; Schulze, Lubatkin, & Dino, 2003)—a
social status given at birth or assigned later in life. Typically, family members
will control most, if not all, of the key top management positions within a firm
(Tagiuri & Davis, 1996) that include seats on the board and executive roles
such as chief executive officer (CEO), vice president, and chief financial officer
(CFO). It is often the case that a single family member occupies multiple top
management positions on the board and at the executive level.
      Therefore, family influence is cemented into governance that gives family
members a positional advantage in the decision-making hierarchy (Ashwin,
Krishnan, & George, 2015; Davis, 1983; Habbershon & Williams, 1999; Jones,
Makri, & Gomez-Mejia, 2008; Tagiuri & Davis, 1996). In addition, family influence is strengthened through the preferential treatment of DFC members in
hiring and promotion activities (Bertrand & Schoar, 2006; Cambreleng, 1969;
Lansberg, 1983; Deephouse & Jaskiewicz, 2013; Gomez-Mejia, Nuñez-Nickel &
Gutierrez, 2001; Schulze et al., 2003; Tagiuri & Davis, 1996). According to
Bertrand and Schoar (2006) business founders tend to hire and promote from
within family networks rather than potentially more competent and professional non-family candidates. Trust seems to play a large role in these decisions (Fukuyama, 1995) as well as, in some cases, pressures stemming from
family members who feel entitled to company profits and positions (Lansberg,
1983).

2.2   *Identification with Firm*

This sew dimension refers to the psychological attachment that forms between the DFC and the firm and the identity that reflects back on both the firm and family unit. To members of the DFC the firm is perceived as an extension of the family's reputation (Berrone et al., 2012; Craig & Dibrell, 2006; Dyer & Whetten, 2006; Klein et al., 2005; Vardaman & Gondo, 2014). This perception compels the DFC to "be more emotionally invested in the firm than non-family members should be at family or non-family firms" (Deephouse & Jaskiewicz, 2013, p. 342), and thus family members demonstrate more loyalty to the firm. Further, the integrated family and firm identity is reported to have a positive (as well as perhaps negative) impact on firm activities, the social relationships that are external and internal to the firm and the services and products offered by the firm (Berrone et al., 2012).

2.3   *Binding Social Ties*

This dimension captures the stock of relational capital at the family firm, internal and external to the firm such as relationships between personnel and those between the firm and the community. Socioemotional wealth theory has a positive view of these relationships and likens the family firm culture to what Coleman (1990) refers to as closed networks where relationships are part of a collective culture of social capital and relational trust. Family and non-family members (internal and external) are integrated into this culture and share in the affective outcomes of trust, loyalty and interpersonal solidarity (Cennamo, Berrone, Cruz, & Gomez-Mejia, 2012). Scholars suggest that DFCs pursue the welfare of constituents located within the firm, but also those in the surrounding community with special attention paid to addressing issues of "poverty, environmental degradation, and social justice" (Cennamo et al., 2012, p. 22). Often, corporate investments are made to help the surrounding community even in the absence of economic gains (Brickson, 2005; Berrone et al., 2010; Lyman, 1991). Further, these relational investments are part of what Cennamo et al. (2012) describe as a family firm's "generational investment strategy," a concept referring to the need of DFCs to cultivate a positive reputation through philanthropic giving (Stavrou, Kassinis, & Filotheou, 2007), performing acts of goodwill in the community and providing greater job security to employees (Block, 2010; Stavrou, Kassinis, & Filotheou, 2007) as a means to legitimize their continued involvement in firm activities.

2.4   *Emotional Attachment*

Emotional attachment refers to the emotional positions that family members develop toward one other within the firm (Berrone et al., 2012). They manifest as either positive projections such as pride or love or in negative forms such as disappointment or anger. Emotions often run high at family firms and may blur the boundaries between family and corporation. In other words, intra-family emotions tend to spill over into the interactions, practices and dealings of the business and vice versa. To many scholars (Benedict, 1968; Berrone & Gomez-Mejia, 2012; Breton-Miller, Miller, & Steier, 2004; Davis, 1983; Lansberg, 1983; Tagiuri & Davis, 1996) the intersection of the family and business systems is a distinctive family firm trait that creates either conflict or harmony among DFC members with implications for the business and non-family personnel. In words, the emotional dissonance or harmony among family members may disrupt or have a positive effect on business practices.

2.5   *Renewal through Dynastic Succession*

Renewal through dynastic succession corresponds to the final dimension of FIBER. It refers to the mechanism by which familial influence and the other dimensions of SEW capital are passed on to successive generations. It is also the most discussed SEW dimension (Ayres, 1990; Beckhard & Dyer, 1983; Benedict, 1968; Birley, 1986; Breton-Miller, Miller, & Steier, 2004; Gómez-Mejía et al., 2007; Tagiuri & Davis, 1996; Zellweger et al., 2012), not to mention the most import-ant dimension of a DFC's vision alluded to in the discussion of definitions.

Based on the behavioral agency model (Wiseman & Gomez-Mejia, 1998), the socioemotional wealth model is founded on the idea that firms commit to decisions based on the "dominant principles" (Berrone et al., 2012) espoused by the organization. These principles drive owners or managers to make deci-sions that aim to preserve what is most important to them and the business. In the case of family businesses, dominant family coalitions are understood to frame decisions in reference to the preservation of the non-financial benefits described above. In other words, a greater premium is placed on decisions that preserve or augment socioemotional wealth as opposed to those that concern the preservation and/or gain of financial resources (Gomez-Mejia et al., 2001).

In sum, socioemotional wealth preservation has been shown to drive various behaviors in family businesses including their approach to succession (Jaskiewicz et al., 2016), orientation to the community (Cruz, Larraza-Kintana, Garcés-Galdeano, & Berrone, 2014), and other factors (Berrone et al., 2010; Firfiray, Cruz, Neacsu, & Gomez-Mejia, 2018; Gomez-Mejia, Patel, & Zellweger, 2018).

3   Socioemotional Wealth and Family-Owned Universities

While the literature does not provide direct evidence of a connection between socioemotional wealth preservation and family decisions to become involved in owning and operating universities, there are some potential connections. One is the potential link between non-financial social benefits and the prestige and respect often afforded institutions of higher learning. For example, because of the educational nature and prominent role that universities play in their local community, the potential for a family to gain significant reputational wealth as a result of owning and operating a university is perhaps higher than it might be in owning another kind of a business.

Another is the potential fit between a family's long-term approach, effort to avoid significant risks, and the slow rate of change often found in higher education (Altbach, 2016; Austin & Jones, 2015; Birnbaum, 2004; Hazelkorn, 2015; Kezar, 2004). Research has shown that in an effort to preserve socioemotional wealth, business-owning families will avoid risk and seek out less risky decisions and situations (Gómez-Mejía et al., 2007). Business-owning families have been shown to invest less in research and development (R&D) due to the risk associated with investing in new technologies (Gomez-Mejia, Campbell, Martin, Hoskisson, Makri, & Sirmon, 2014). They have also been shown to avoid firm diversification due to the possibility of having to share family authority with outside members (Gomez-Mejia, Makri, & Larraza Kintana, 2010). While owning and operating a university is most certainly not a risk-free endeavor, the longer-term nature of institutions of higher education and the comparably slow rate of change within the industry might be appealing to families based on a preference for a longer term, lower risk business approach. In support of this viewpoint, family businesses have been shown to seek out industries that are aligned with their management and leadership styles over industries such as high tech where those approaches would be less feasible (Naldi, Cennamo, Corbetta, & Gomez-Mejia, 2013).

Thus, while not explicitly addressed in current family business research, the prevalence of family involvement in universities across the globe can be understood through socioemotional wealth and the desire for families to build and maintain the non-financial benefits of business ownership.

4   Family Values and Family Involvement

While the socioemotional wealth model is perhaps the most prominent theoretical tie linking family business research to family-owned or managed universities, there are other links. One potentially interesting connection is the influence of the family and family values on the decision-making within the family business (Hubler, 2009) and the potential benefits arising from familial influence.

As mentioned earlier, "familiness" (Habbershon, Williams, & MacMillan, 2003) refers to the unique resources, attributes, or behaviors that families bring to or generate in the business as a result of their influence. These attributes lend competitive advantages in the marketplace (Carnes & Ireland, 2013). For example, advantageous behaviors include a long-term business approach (Kachaner et al., 2012) with a focus on future generations (Miller, 2014) and a participatory family culture. Another beneficial outcome of family involvement is the influence that family values and ideals have on business decision-making. In particular, DFCs tend to prioritize stakeholder concerns and interests in decision-making (Bingham, Dyer Jr., Smith, & Adams, 2011). As mentioned earlier under binding social ties, prioritizing stakeholder concerns creates positive outcomes for employees and the community.

5   Conclusion

The research cited does not focus directly on family-owned or managed universities. It does, however, provide some insight into why families might be interested in owning and operating a university. Indeed, a social mission represents a pronounced, consecrated, and fundamental function of academe (Birnbaum, 1988; Eckel & Kezar, 2011). Thus, founders and their families who feel strongly about effecting positive social change may regard higher education as a natural fit with their family's values. In this way, the concept of "familiness" (Pearson, Carr, & Shaw, 2008), the influence of family values and behaviors and the caring exhibited by families for stakeholders, provides a theoretical framework for understanding for the prevalence of family-owned or managed universities across the globe.

In conclusion, despite of the prevalence of family-owned universities across the globe, very little research has looked specifically at families who own and operate universities. Most family business research has focused on performance issues in family businesses and has not been industry specific or addressed the decision to become involved in a particular type of family business. That said, current literature does provide some insights into why families might be interested in universities as a type of business. Specifically, the socio-emotional wealth model, the concept of "familiness," and the importance of higher education to both families and family businesses all provide theoretical evidence for why business-owning families might be interested in owning and operating a university.

While prior research provides a theoretical basis for the existence of family-owned universities, very little is known about these entities. The purpose of this research is to delve into some of the more salient questions that have not been addressed in family business research such as how decision-making, succession planning, family involvement, and myriad other activities actually take place in these organizations.

References

Altbach, P. G. (2005). Universities: Family style. *International Higher Education, Spring*(39), 10–12.

Altbach, P. G. (2016). *Global perspectives on higher education.* Baltimore, MD: Johns Hopkins University Press.

Ashwin, A. S., Krishnan, R. T., & George, R. (2015). Family firms in India: Family involvement, innovation and agency and stewardship behaviors. *Asia Pacific Journal of Management, 32*(4), 869–900.

Astrachan, J. H., Klein, S. B., & Smyrnios, K. X. (2002). The F-PEC scale of family influence: A proposal for solving the family business definition problem. *Family Business Review, 15*(1), 45–55.

Austin, I., & Jones, G. A. (2015). *Governance of higher education: Global perspectives, theories, and practices.* Abingdon: Routledge.

Ayres, G. R. (1990). Rough family justice: Equity in family business succession planning. *Family Business Review, 3*(1), 3–22.

Beckhard, R., & Dyer, W. G. (1983). Managing change in the family firm: Issues and strategies. *Sloan Management Review, 24*(3), 59.

Benedict, B. (1968). Family firms and economic development. *Southwestern Journal of Anthropology, 24*(1), 1–19.

Berrone, P., Cruz, C., & Gomez-Mejia, L. R. (2012). Socioemotional wealth in family firms: Theoretical dimensions, assessment approaches, and agenda for future research. *Family Business Review, 25*(3), 258–279.

Berrone, P., Cruz, C., Gomez-Mejia, L. R., & Larraza-Kintana, M. (2010). Socioemotional wealth and corporate responses to institutional pressures: Do family-controlled firms pollute less? *Administrative Science Quarterly, 55*(1), 82–113.

Bertrand, M., & Schoar, A. (2006). The role of family in family firms. *The Journal of Economic Perspectives, 20*(2), 73–96.

Bingham, J. B., Dyer Jr., W. G., Smith, I., & Adams, G. L. (2011). A stakeholder identity orientation approach to corporate social performance in family firms. *Journal of Business Ethics, 99*(4), 565–585.

Birley, S. (1986). Succession in the family firm: The inheritor's view. *Journal of Small Business Management, 24*, 36–43.

Birnbaum, R. (1988). *How colleges work: The cybernetics of academic organization and leadership.* San Francisco, CA: Jossey-Bass.

Birnbaum, R. (2004). The end of shared governance: Looking ahead or looking back. *New Directions for Higher Education, 127,* 5–22.

Block J. (2010). Family management, family ownership, and downsizing: Evidence from S&P 500 firms. *Family Business Review, 23,* 109–130.

Breton-Miller, I. L., Miller, D., & Steier, L. P. (2004). Toward an integrative model of effective FOB succession. *Entrepreneurship Theory and Practice, 28*(4), 305–328.

Brickson, S. L. (2005). Organizational identity orientation: Forging a link between organizational identity and organizations' relations with stakeholders. *Administrative Science Quarterly, 50,* 576–609.

Brockhaus, S. R. H. (1994). Entrepreneurship and family business research: Comparisons, critique, and lessons. *Entrepreneurship Theory and Practice, 19*(1), 25–38.

Cambreleng, R. W. (1969). The case of the nettlesome nepot. *Harvard Business Review, 47*(2), 14.

Carnes, C. M., & Ireland, R. D. (2013). Familiness and innovation: Resource bundling as the missing link. *Entrepreneurship Theory and Practice, 37*(6), 1399–1419.

Cennamo, C., Berrone, P., Cruz, C., & Gomez-Mejia, L. R. (2012). Socioemotional wealth and proactive stakeholder engagement: Why family-controlled firms care more about their stakeholders. *Entrepreneurship Theory and Practice, 36*(6), 1153–1173.

Chrisman, J. J., Chua, J. H., & Litz, R. (2003). A unified systems perspective of family firm performance: An extension and integration. *Journal of Business Venturing, 18*(4), 467–472. Chrisman, J. J., Chua, J. H., & Sharma, P. (2005). Trends and directions in the development of a strategic management theory of the family firm. *Entrepreneurship Theory and Practice, 29*(5), 555–575.

Chrisman, J. J., Kellermanns, F. W., Chan, K. C., & Liano, K. (2010). Intellectual foundations of current research in family business: An identification and review of 25 influential articles. *Family Business Review, 23*(1), 9–26.

Chrisman, J. J., Steier, L. P., & Chua, J. H. (2008). Toward a theoretical basis for understanding the dynamics of strategic performance in family firms. *Entrepreneurship Theory and Practice, 32*(6), 935–947.

Chua, J. H., Chrisman, J. J., & Sharma, P. (1999). Defining the family business by behavior. *Entrepreneurship Theory and Practice, 23*(4), 19–39.

Coleman, J. (1990). *Foundations of social theory.* Cambridge, MA: Belknap.

Craig, J., & Dibrell, C. (2006). The natural environment, innovation, and firm performance: A comparative study. *Family Business Review, 19*(4), 275–288.

Cruz, C., Larraza-Kintana, M., Garcés-Galdeano, L., & Berrone, P. (2014). Are family firms really more socially responsible? *Entrepreneurship Theory and Practice, 38*(6), 1295–1316.

Davis, P. (1983). Realizing the potential of the family business. *Organizational Dynamics, 12,* 47–56.

Deephouse, D. L., & Jaskiewicz, P. (2013). Do family firms have better reputations than non-family firms? An integration of socioemotional wealth and social identity theories. *Journal of management Studies, 50*(3), 337–360.

Dyer, W. G., & Whetten, D. A. (2006). Family firms and social responsibility: Preliminary evidence from the S&P 500. *Entrepreneurship Theory and Practice, 30*(6), 785–802.

Eckel, P. D., & Kezar, A. (2011). The intersecting authority of boards, presidents and faculty: Toward shared leadership. In P. G. Altbach, P. J. Gumport, & M. N. Bastedo (Eds.), *American higher education in the twenty-first century: Social, political, and economic challenges* (pp. 238–280). Baltimore, MD: Johns Hopkins Press.

Eddleston, K. A., Chrisman, J. J., Steier, L. P., & Chua, J. H. (2010). Governance and trust in family firms: An introduction. *Entrepreneurship Theory and Practice, 34*(6), 1043–1056.

Firfiray, S., Cruz, C., Neacsu, I., & Gomez-Mejia, L. R. (2018). Is nepotism so bad for family firms? A socioemotional wealth approach. *Human Resource Management Review, 28*(1), 83–97.

Fukuyama, F. (1995). *Trust: The social virtues and the creation of prosperity.* New York, NY: Free Press Paperbacks.

Gomez-Mejia, L. R., Campbell, J. T., Martin, G., Hoskisson, R. E., Makri, M., & Sirmon, D. G. (2014). Socioemotional wealth as a mixed gamble: Revisiting family firm R&D investments with the behavioral agency model. *Entrepreneurship Theory and Practice, 38*(6), 1351–1374.

Gómez-Mejía, L. R., Haynes, K. T., Núñez-Nickel, M., Jacobson, K. J. L., & Moyano-Fuentes, J. (2007). Socioemotional wealth and business risks in family-controlled firms: Evidence from Spanish olive oil mills. *Administrative Science Quarterly, 52*(1), 106–137.

Gomez-Mejia, L. R., Makri, M., & Kintana, M. L. (2010). Diversification decisions in family-controlled firms. *Journal of Management Studies, 47*(2), 223–252.

Gomez-Mejia, L. R., Nuñez-Nickel, M., & Gutierrez, I. (2001). The role of family ties in agency contracts. *Academy of Management Journal, 44*(1), 81–95.

Gomez-Mejia, L. R., Patel, P. C., & Zellweger, T. M. (2018). In the horns of the dilemma: Socioemotional wealth, financial wealth, and acquisitions in family firms. *Journal of Management, 44*(4), 1369–1397.

Grubb, W. N., Sweet, R., Gallagher, M., & Tuomi, O. (2009). *Korea: OECD review of tertiary education.* Retrieved from http://www.oecd.org/education/skills-beyond-school/38092630.pdf

Habbershon, T. G., & Williams, M. L. (1999). A resource-based framework for assessing the strategic advantages of family firms. *Family Business Review, 12*(1), 1–25.

Habbershon, T. G., Williams, M. L., & MacMillan, I. C. (2003). A unified systems perspective of family firm performance. *Journal of Business Venturing, 18*(4), 451–465.

Hazelkorn, E. (2015). *Rankings and the reshaping of higher education: The battle for world-class excellence.* Basingstoke: Palgrave Macmillan.

Hubler, T. M. (2009). The soul of family business. *Family Business Review, 22*(3), 254–258.

Jaskiewicz, P., Lutz, E., & Godwin, M. (2016). For money or love? Financial and socio-emotional considerations in family firm succession. *Entrepreneurship Theory and Practice, 40*(5), 1179–1190.

Jones, C., Makri, M., & Gomez-Mejia, L. R. (2008). Affiliate directors and perceived risk bearing in publicly traded, family-controlled firms: The case of diversification. *Entrepreneurship Theory and Practice, 32*(5), 1007–1026.

Kachaner, N., Stalk, G., & Bloch, A. (2012). What you can learn from family business. *Harvard Business Review, 90*(11), 102–106.

Kezar, A. (2004). What is more important to effective governance: Relationships, trust, and leadership, or structures and formal processes? *New Directions for Higher Education, 127*, 35–46.

Klein, S. B., Astrachan, J. H., & Smyrnios, K. X. (2005). The F-PEC scale of family influence: Construction, validation, and further implication for theory. *Entrepreneurship Theory and Practice, 29*(3), 321–339.

Kraiczy, N. (2013). *Innovations in small and medium-sized family firms: An analysis of innovation related top management team behaviors and family firm-specific characteristics.* Wiesbaden: Gabler Verlag.

Lansberg, I. S. (1983). Managing human resources in family firms: The problem of institutional overlap. *Organizational Dynamics, 12*(1), 39–46.

Litz, R. A. (1995). The family business: Toward definitional clarity. *Family Business Review, 8*, 71–81.

Lyman, A. (1991). Customer service: Does family ownership make a difference? *Family Business Review, 4*, 303–324.

Martin, J., & Samels, J. E. (2010). All in the family: America's family-owned and operated career universities. *University Business.* Retrieved from https://www.universitybusiness.com/node/2531/manage/page/0/media

Miller, S. P. (2014). Next-generation leadership development in family businesses: The critical roles of shared vision and family climate. *Frontiers in Psychology, 5*, 1–14.

Naldi, L., Cennamo, C., Corbetta, G., & Gomez-Mejia, L. (2013). Preserving socioemotional wealth in family firms: Asset or liability? The moderating role of business context. *Entrepreneurship Theory and Practice, 37*(6), 1341–1360.

Pearson, A. W., Carr, J. C., & Shaw, J. C. (2008). Toward a theory of familiness: A social capital perspective. *Entrepreneurship Theory and Practice, 32*(6), 949–969.

Poole, G. S., & Chen, Y. (2009). *Higher education in East Asia.* Rotterdam, The Netherlands: Sense Publishers.

Schulze, W. S., Lubatkin, M. H., & Dino, R. N. (2003). Toward a theory of agency and altruism in family firms. *Journal of Business Venturing, 18*(4), 473–490.

Shanker, M. C., & Astrachan, J. H. (1996). Myths and realities: Family businesses' contribution to the US economy – A framework for assessing family business statistics. *Family Business Review, 9*(2), 107–123.

Sharma, P., & Salvato, C. (2013). A balancing act between continuity and change. In P. F. Pérez & A. Colli (Eds.), *The endurance of family businesses: A global overview* (pp. 34–56). Cambridge: Cambridge University Press.

Stavrou, E., Kassinis, G., & Filotheou, A. (2007). Downsizing and stakeholder orientation among the Fortune 500: Does family ownership matter? *Journal of Business Ethics, 72,* 149–162.

Tagiuri, R., & Davis, J. (1996). Bivalent attributes of the family firm. *Family Business Review, 9*(2), 199–208.

Tsamenyi, M., Noormansyah, I., & Uddin, S. (2008). Management controls in Family-Owned Businesses (FOBs): A case study of an Indonesian family-owned university. *Accounting Forum, 32*(1), 62–74.

Vardaman, J. M., & Gondo, M. B. (2014). Socioemotional wealth conflict in family firms. *Entrepreneurship Theory and Practice, 38*(6), 1317–1322.

von Schlippe, A., & Frank, H. 2013. The theory of social systems as a framework for understanding family businesses. *Family Relations, 62*(3), 384–398.

Wiseman, R. M., & Gomez-Mejia, L. R. (1998). A behavioral agency model of managerial risk taking. *Academy of Management Review, 23*(1), 133–153.

Zellweger, T. M., Kellermanns, F. W., Chrisman, J. J., & Chua, J. H. (2012). Family control and family firm valuation by family CEOs: The importance of intentions for transgenerational control. *Organization Science, 23*(3), 851–868.

PART 2

Countries and Institutions

∴

CHAPTER 4

Armenia: Challenges and Prospects—The Case of Eurasia International University

Arevik Ohanyan

The practice of individuals and families establishing schools in Armenian communities worldwide has deep historic roots. Schools have traditionally been key centers of community organization during Armenia's mostly stateless history with a crucial role for maintaining culture and national identity. With the collapse of the Soviet Union and contemporary Armenia's rise as a new state, democratic state-building rather than community survival has been the overarching task of the educational sector in the country. The role of individuals and families in spearheading this process has had deep resonance with Armenia's pre-Soviet past.

Subsequent to the collapse of the Soviet Union and Armenia's transition to a market economy in the 1990s, private entrepreneurship emerged as a key force in reshaping the landscape of higher education. A number of educational establishments were founded by individuals, families, and organizations across all levels including pre-K, K-12, vocational, undergraduate, and graduate study. However, success in carving a space within the largely state-dominated public education sector varied. The early and emerging private pre-K and K-12 institutions were characterized as elite establishments with very high tuition fees that locked out most of the population. The major advantages of these institutions included low student-teacher ratios; alternative and innovative educational programs; highly trained teachers and staff; and a focus on student-centered learning. These private initiatives addressed market demand but struggled to offer access to broader segments of society.

In contrast to the pre-K and K-12 sectors, private initiatives in the higher education realm met with greater resistance from the state and were limited to serving economically marginalized segments of the society that were locked out of higher education during the Soviet era. The family-owned or managed institutions (FOMHEIS) continue serving this segment in an increasingly competitive environment populated by public entities, international, and inter-governmental higher education institutions. Inter-governmental universities are established on the basis of agreements between multiple agencies in Armenia and a foreign country. For example, the French university in Armenia

© KONINKLIJKE BRILL NV, LEIDEN, 2020 | DOI: 10.1163/9789004423435_004

was founded by the Ministry of Education and Science, the Ministry of Foreign Affairs, the French Ministry of Foreign Affairs and International Development and the French Embassy in Armenia.

This chapter examines the challenges and factors constraining the development of private higher education institutions and FOMHEIS in present-day Armenia. It explores whether the recent political changes underway as a result of the "Velvet Revolution" pose new challenges and whether Armenia's democratic progress can create a competitive environment for FOMHEIS while addressing issues of access and economic inequalities. In the first section of the chapter the current landscape of FOMHEIS in Armenia is summarized followed by an institutional case study of one of the earliest FOMHEIS, Eurasia International University, with a focus on its organizational development and future strategic possibilities.

1   The National Higher Education Context

The collapse of the Soviet Union in 1991 and subsequent transition to a market economy and democracy in Armenia created unique opportunities for the development of private higher education. This transition liberalized the higher education system with new private actors emerging and necessitated a reevaluation of the higher education system overall.

Among the 25 private higher education institutions in Armenia, 19 are registered as limited liability companies (LLCs), five as cooperatives, and one as an educational foundation. Twenty-three of the existing private higher education institutions were established during the period 1989–1996. Eight universities were established during the final years of Soviet collapse, between 1989–1990; these were established mostly as "production cooperatives" as legislation giving entrepreneurial endeavors legal status was not yet approved.

All FOMHEIS and private institutions in Armenia are for-profit private LLCs and cooperatives and they are all treated like commercial organizations. These institutions are not granted any specific benefits as educational institutions; they have no public or external funding and are completely tuition-supported. One private institution is registered as an educational foundation but still does not receive any public funding.

1.1   *Overregulation and Under-Regulation: Learning to Live with the Private Sector*

The politicization of public universities was a significant issue in Armenia's higher education system and one that severely challenged the democratic prospects of Armenian statehood. This was effected through governmental control that reached into the university's administrative apparatus. From student unions supporting the governing party and its platforms to members of the government serving on the governing boards of state universities, the state maintained a firm grip over the public sector. University administrators and leadership were sheltered by the state from competition as universities provided a political base for acquiring votes during elections. Even drastic cuts to state funding failed to diminish the political control of the state over public universities.

Centralized regulation also applies to newly established FOMHEIS. The Law of Enterprises and Enterprise Activity passed in 1992 allowed private institutions freedom and autonomy to engage in entrepreneurial activities with limited state oversight or regulation. However, strict licensing and accreditation requirements enforced by the Law on Higher and Postgraduate Professional Education passed in 2004 restrained the autonomy of FOMHEIS and other private educational establishments. For example, while Article 6 of the Law on Higher and Postgraduate Education highlights the autonomy and academic freedom of higher education institutions, Article 8 limits the autonomy with a requirement to adhere to a pre-defined and specific set of state educational standards. The educational standards prescribe the number of required general courses (e.g., Armenian history, Armenian language and literature, philosophy, sociology, law, political science, Russian, another foreign language, physical education) as well as specialized courses for all degrees at the undergraduate level at all private and public institutions (Republic of Armenia, 2011a). This leaves very limited room for adapting the curriculum to the evolving needs of the labor market. It also curtails the potential for innovation.

In 2012, changes to the law on higher and postgraduate professional education introduced requirements for the admission process at both state and private tertiary institutions. Still, the law failed to ensure a level competitive environment between state and private entities giving important advantages to public institutions. For example, public educational institutions in Armenia receive block grants annually from the government based on enrollment and additional funding for research. Until 2017, some male applicants to state and inter-governmental universities were exempt from compulsory military. These factors helped state universities in recruitment, particularly in light of Armenia's protracted border conflicts. In contrast, private higher education institutions and their students were ineligible for any state funding or exemptions from military service.

For non-state institutions that were categorized as inter-governmental or international universities, state intervention was comparably less visible and limited which skewed the competitive landscape further. These universities managed to bypass the state educational standards and had enough flexibility and external funding to adapt and modernize their educational content and curriculum. The American University of Armenia (AUA), for instance, was generously supported by the United States government through a Congressional allocation of US$9.58 million towards endowment. Another funding source for AUA was the Armenian General Benevolent Union (AGBU) that underwrote a major share of the operational budget needed to launch the AUA and later established an endowment fund to sustain the university.

As there was no legislative restriction, these institutions also managed to sidestep the requirement of the centralized admission exams and maintained the freedom to organize and administer their own admission processes. Such complete autonomy has provided the freedom to innovate and modernize academic programs, flexibility generally denied to both state and private institutions.

1.2   *The Velvet Revolution: Impact and Projected Consequences*

The demand for high quality education was a key concern voiced by young people in Armenia's Velvet Revolution in April 2018. The prevalence of politicized student unions and university administrations linked to the ruling political party and the government and the lack of fair competition within the system were among the protesters' grievances. The newly appointed Deputy Minister of Education and Science, Hovhannes Hovhannisyan, stated that the new government was interested in the development of private higher education in the hope that it would stimulate quality improvements at state universities and improve the overall efficiency of the system (Interview with Hovhannisyan, 23 August, 2018).

The new government has continued a policy of encouraging mergers of private establishments to consolidate the education sphere, indicating that only larger private institutions will be able to compete with state universities. Despite consistent pressure from successive governments for private university mergers very few have actually happened. Rather, many private institutions have ceased operation. The reason may be personal. According to the deputy minister, "Many of the leaders of private institutions tend to be familiar with one another and personal ambition may prevail when considering decisions related to mergers." Another reason may be concern for properties and buildings and other ownership issues that might arise from a merger.

Government authorities are interested in developing a fair, competitive environment that will be shaped by future legislation to regulate management, accountability, and funding schemes and ensure the autonomy and academic independence of all types of higher education institutions.

2   The Nature of FOMHEIS in Armenia

Within ten years of the Soviet collapse, non-state institutions of higher education in many countries of the former Soviet sphere experienced rapid growth.
In Armenia, Georgia, Kazakhstan, Latvia and Moldova the number of private institutions exceeded the number of publics (Smolentseva, Huisman, &
Froumin, 2018). In Armenia, 98 public and private universities were operating
during the 1999–2000 academic year with a total student enrollment of 61,274
and nearly 21,500 (35 percent) studying in private institutions (Armenian Statistical Agency, 2000). The number of private universities during this period
grew to 82 (Armenian Statistical Agency, 2000). By 2018, the Ministry of Education and Science of Armenia listed only 25 private institutions with a total
enrollment of 9,371 students (Armenian Statistical Agency, 2018).

Based on government data, 20 of 25 (80 percent) operating universities
are individually or family-owned or managed (FOMHEI). These universities
are defined as, "established by an individual or a family group and the family
members remain directly involved and generally dominant in the administration, governance, financial control, and/or direct ownership of the institution"
(Altbach, 2005).

Most of the FOMHEIS were initially established to absorb excess demand for
higher education in Armenia that was not met by the state universities. With
the emergence of the international and inter-governmental universities and
demographic decline, the state universities lowered admissions requirements
to address a growing shortage of applicants. These moves within state sector
universities challenged student recruitment at private institutions.

By 2018 the total student enrollment in the higher education system was
78,747 for both master's and bachelor's programs where 9,371 students (12 percent) were enrolled in private universities (Armenian Statistical Agency, 2018).
The larger private higher education institutions, those enrolling more than
500 students, are FOMHEIS and account for most of the cohort. The remaining
institutions serve fewer than 100 students each.

As evident above, the number of private higher education providers has
decreased from 82 to 25 since 1999 and the share of students enrolled in the
private sector decreased by nearly half. Many of the private tertiary institutions that were closed were established by an individual or family. The reasons
for this dramatic decline are varied. Some of the institutions were closed by
decision of their founders and family members, often due to inadequate financial or succession planning. Others ceased operation after the introduction of
tightened state requirements and control resulting from the Bologna reforms.
In these cases, institutions lacked the required minimum human and financial
resources and infrastructure to ensure sufficient quality. Many of the FOMHEIS

that closed were operating out of private properties with inadequate facilities signifying that their initial license had lacked a thorough state audit.

In 2018, 15 FOMHEIS owned their own properties and buildings outright. These institutions have generally directed most of their profits and expenses toward continuously improving infrastructure and ensuring compliance with minimum state licensing requirements. As a result, financial resources were rarely directed to research activities or to faculty training and professional development. The remaining five FOMHEIS continue to lease their facilities and in some cases operate within a state university facility by renting classroom space, library space, etc.

The state licensing requirements focus on infrastructure and resources as well as the adherence of educational programs to state standards newer accreditation requirements (Republic of Armenia, 2011b) are directed towards establishing quality systems and promoting greater accountability and transparency within the institution. Research and development are central to these requirements and a major challenge for FOMHEIS that have limited resources to devote to these activities. Consequently, accreditation will serve as another quality filter and with all likelihood leave only a few FOMHEIS in the market. In a meeting with rectors of non-state universities following the Velvet Revolution, Arayik Harutyunyan, Minister of the Education and Science, disclosed that the future landscape will be composed only of those institutions that have the capacity to comply with quality assurance requirements and that have sufficient financial resources to apply for accreditation.

External institutional accreditation is mandatory. Although new standards were introduced in 2000, most private institutions continue operating with accreditation awarded under the old system. Under the previous system accreditation did not expire, leaving institutions without any obligation or incentive to renew accreditation under the new system. These institutions argue that the new law is not retroactive and cannot be enforced on institutions with prior accreditation. This controversy will likely be resolved in the courts or through negotiation and compromise.

As of 2018, the National Registrar of the Institutional Accreditation of the National Centre of Professional Education Quality Assurance Foundation (ANQA) listed only three accredited private institutions; all three institutions are FOMHEIS. One of the accredited FOMHEIS is the Eurasia International University and a case study of this institution follows.

2.1   *Exit, Merge, or Regroup*

As discussed above, more than 50 FOMHEIS closed during a 20-year period. These were often controversial institutions enrolling a very small number of students and frequently accused of improper activities and corruption. These types of institutions were somewhat predatory, focused on profit and often described as diploma mills based on their low admission standards, lack of an academically rigorous curriculum, lack of facilities, absence of research initiatives, and poor job placement rates. These institutions harmed the status of FOMHEIS in society, creating an environment of public mistrust towards the sector as a whole. In the ensuing context, it was challenging for legitimate and better quality FOMHEIS to thrive.

The new government formed in 2018 after the Velvet Revolution continues to audit and ensure compliance from FOMHEIS and other non-state institutions with state licensing and accreditation requirements while advocating for mergers and consolidation. The push for mergers of non-state universities has met some resistance, especially from leadership at the larger FOMHEIS. As already indicated, most of the non-state institutions currently operating in Armenia are FOMHEIS that own properties and buildings and the risks associated with these investments complicate mergers. In addition to these challenges, there are non-monetary difficulties. Cultural differences between the organizations, norms and values of the founding families and the fear of losing influence and institutional identity are also factors. There is a keen desire of founding families to maintain ownership after a merger to ensure that institutions built over years survive and can be transferred to future generations.

A number of FOMHEIS have attempted to merge while maintaining some level of independence and autonomy under the umbrella of the merged entity. This experience has proven to be problematic as most of the FOMHEIS had overlapping specializations such as economics, law, pedagogy, and languages that didn't integrate easily. In theory, merging two different institutions should create a larger, more diversified institution and it should be easier to find win-win solutions, but this has not proved to be the case.

While the current post-revolutionary government promotes the idea of mergers, it is also expecting private HEIS and FOMHEIS to rethink strategies such as implementing innovative alternatives to state universities, differentiating themselves in the market, designing specializations targeted to labor market needs, and supporting the government in defining and meeting quality standards. The current government, in contrast to previous ones, announced that it considers private higher education as a mechanism to enhance the national competitiveness of all institutions in the country.

2.2   *Family Succession or Professional Management?*
The family name and family reputation become the best collateral for building FOMHEIS. Families are socially invested in seeing their institutions succeed.

A failure of the institution reflects on the family name, which in many traditional societies like Armenia, is of high value. At the same time, limiting the institution's leadership and management to the family carries its own risks such as excluding diverse perspectives and professional knowledge that the family may not possess. In considering trajectories moving forward, FOMHEIS will be weighing costs and opportunities for family-based versus professional models of administration with the latter opening the door to experts outside of the family.

December 2018 was the deadline for the institutional accreditation of all higher education institutions in Armenia based on new standards and guidelines. Three of the 20 operating FOMHEIS received accreditation; two have been reaccredited; the rest remain in a process of self-assessment, either having been rejected or not having applied at all. The accreditation process is costly and requires professional management to ensure compatibility with new state and European Union requirements.

In most FOMHEIS, with only a few exceptions, there are consistent patterns of governance and decision-making. Power and authority are often centralized with institutional leadership and the rector (often a founding family member is involved in handling even minor, non-strategic issues). Most financial decisions are made by the rector alone or in consultation with family members. Most of the FOMHEIS are headed by family members who lived and studied in the Soviet system. By 2018, 12 out of 20 FOMHEIS were still headed by their founders. The average number of years of service as a rector in these cases is 24 years. In all cases, the rector is also on the board of founders. Following an average of 18 years under the initial leadership, eight universities transitioned to the second generation with new rectors. In these cases, the successors were immediate family members and continued the family tradition of centralized, somewhat authoritarian, management reflected in centralized decision-making, lack of consultation with the board and other stakeholders of the university, and lack of strategic planning.

With one exception, the second generation owns and controls its own private facilities and properties. This might explain the decision to maintain direct ownership control and active involvement in management. In all cases the successions were automatic and not based on a succession plan.

Will families be able to meet the tightened state requirements, survive competition and meet market demands? Will the Bologna requirements for stakeholder involvement in decision-making shape future management practices? Will the FOMHEIS choose to merge based on the demands of the Ministry of Education and Science? The coming years will be transformative for FOMHEIS and for the higher education system in general.

3   The Case Study of the Eurasia International University

Eurasia International University (EIU) was founded by the Ohanyan family in 1997 in Yerevan, Armenia. The rector of the university, Suren Ohanyan,
received his Candidate of Sciences Degree in Geography from Moscow's
Lomonosov State University in 1974 and Doctor of Sciences Degree in Economic Geography from Saint Petersburg University in 1991. For more than 20
years prior to founding EIU, Ohanyan taught and conducted research in state
universities, having led the department of economic geography of the Armenian State University of Economics. In the mid-1990s Ohanyan moved to the
private sector, establishing a multi-level educational complex comprised of
K-12 and a university. The development of the educational complex occurred
over time. Eurasia International University was established first, followed by
the K-12 school. The motivation for adding the K-12 grades was in part the poor
preparedness of applicants to the college level from a state educational sector
that was under severe stress in the aftermath of the Soviet collapse. This holis-
tic educational approach enhanced EIU's efforts in student recruitment. The
educational complex serves more than 1,000 students across all levels—600
are bachelor's, master's, or doctoral students; 400 study at the K-12 school; and
130 are children in the kindergarten. The educational complex employs more
than 150 teaching, administrative, and support staff.

EIU and its related schools began in leased facilities in line with the state
licensing requirements of the time. In 2005, the family decided to sell their
residence in central Yerevan in order to finance a down payment on a permanent building in a suburb of the city. Subsequent loans and grants allowed the
family to purchase, expand, and renovate the facility and move the university
to this permanent location.

The EIU, provides education on the three levels of the National Qualification Framework—bachelor's (VI level); master's (VII level); researcher, scientific degree candidate of science (VIII level). The major degree programs are
management, jurisprudence, foreign languages, and pharmacy. Since 2013
the university has offered candidate of sciences degree programs in the fields
of economics and management, Germanic languages, and public law (constitutional, administrative, financial, municipal, environmental, European
and governmental). The specializations at the master's level include, but are
not limited to, constitutional law, civil law and procedure, criminal law and
procedure, international and European law, management, project management, electronic business management, hospitality management, English
language and literature (TEFL), and pharmacy. The university is establishing an information technologies (IT) department with an emphasis on the

development of management and information systems in collaboration with ICT companies.

The university has been implementing reforms directed toward the implementation of the Bologna Declaration and was among the first institutions in Armenia to implement the European Credit Transfer System (ECTS) in 2005 and adopt a two-cycle system of education. EIU has been actively involved in mobility programs and ensures mobility for students, administrative and academic staff at the university through agreements with various institutions and the programs financed by the European Union.

The university has been accredited twice—in 2015 for two years and in 2018 for four years—based on the "Standards and Guidelines for Quality Assurance in the European Higher Education Area" (ESG) by the National Center for Professional Education Quality Assurance Foundation (ANQA). It is one of only three private universities to receive a four-year accreditation.

3.1   *Mission and the Strategic Prospects*

The administration and leadership have articulated a vision to position EIU in Armenia and the region as an institution with "dynamic management directed towards educating professionals with practical skills and abilities as well as theoretical knowledge in line with evolving labor market demands" (Eurasia International University, 2014a). This vision is backed up by the EIU mission statement which is outlined in three levels—teaching, research, and public service. The current mission statement strongly emphasizes the role of the university as a teaching institution despite the lack of legislative distinction between research and teaching institutions in Armenia. Based on the mission statement, the role of EIU is to provide higher-level professional and postgraduate education in the fields of social, humanities, and information technology consistent with the demands and needs of the labor market.

Internationalization is a central priority and is reflected in management board meeting minutes, scientific board and department meetings, strategic plans, and institutional and operational action plans. Taken together, they reveal that EIU institutional managers and leaders connect the strategic opportunities for the university with internationalization evident in the number of dual and joint degrees, programs taught in a foreign-language, exchange programs, number of ongoing joint research programs, and number of exchange and international students (Eurasia International University, 2018). Among the major incentives to promote course development and teaching in foreign languages is a 30 percent salary bonus for professors teaching in English or another foreign. The knowledge of foreign languages is also among the major promotion criteria for administrative and academic staff by the Human Resources

Development Centre (EIU, 2012, 2016). External international and domestic experts involved in EIU's two accreditation reviews ranked EIU positively on external relations and internationalization.

> [T]aking into account the separate planning on internationalization in the EIU Strategic Master Plan, an existence of an internationalization Strategy and the separate responsible division, the active involvement in international programmes and projects, as well as willingness of faculty to teach in foreign languages, the expert group believes that the institution meets the requirements of the Criterion 9, International Relations and Internationalization. (National Center for Professional Education Quality Assurance Foundation, 2018)

The expert panel involved with the accreditation process commended EIU for the sharp increase in the number of international students. There has been significant growth in international student numbers, increasing from 19 in 2016–2017 academic year to 79 in 2017–2018 (National Center for Professional Education Quality Assurance Foundation, 2018). That number is expected to double during the academic year, 2019–2020. The efforts of the university toward internationalization—internationalization of curriculum, academic and administrative staff and international marketing—appear to be reflected in the numbers and these developments are among the major outcomes of 2014–2018 strategic plan implementation. The financial inflow from international students is also contributing to the financial stability of the university, particularly significant considering the domestic demographic decline and fierce competition in the domestic market.

3.2   *Governance and Administration*

A self-study conducted in 2009 concluded that EIU's operations were highly dependent on subjective decisions made either by a founding family member or by key personnel working at the university for more than 10 years. Although certain operational regulations did exist on paper, they were not observed in practice. Key processes such as fiscal control and budgeting; purchasing; human resource recruitment; evaluation; promotion and development; strategy development and monitoring; program; and course development and monitoring were poorly regulated. The final decision in these domains was often made by the rector, also the founder, or by the board of founders consisting of the founding spouse and four adult children. Other internal and external stakeholders had a limited voice in operational and strategic decisions. It was concluded that this practice led to subjective and arbitrary choices. For example, the core decisions on educational program development and revision were made by the rector or board of founders. In most cases those decisions were based upon the educational background of some of them, but also reflected personal preferences and perspectives. The lack of staff or other non-family stakeholders in management bodies distanced educational content from labor market requirements to the detriment of student learning and placement outcomes.

Realizing the need for more professional management and the importance of stakeholder involvement in decision-making processes, EIU completely restructured its organizational chart in 2011. The changes were key to developing an internal quality management system. Within the revised EIU charter, the scope of strategic decision-making authority by the rector and the board of founders was reduced. A management board comprised of the university's academic and administrative staff, employees, students, and alumni was empowered to review and approve university structure, strategy, annual and long-term budgets, define tuition fees and determine scholarship criteria among other functions. The rector's annual plan and report and their correspondence to the strategic action plan are now regulated by the management board. The activities of the board of founders have been limited to the election of the rector and decisions on university real estate.

The vision of the current EIU leadership is that the reduced role of the board of founders and the rector and the strengthened role of management committees and bodies will create participatory decision-making at EIU and a solid basis for the smooth transition and succession of management to new leadership without personal or familial connections to the founding family.

3.3 *Financial Management and Control*

The university currently receives no state funding and is predominantly tuition-supported. Family-member shareholders have always reinvested any profits into programs and toward the continuous improvement of educational services, infrastructure, and human resource development. Additional funding has been allocated towards research activities.

Prior to 2014, there was no formal process for the allocation of financial resources. Long-term financial decisions were made by the board of founders, while the rector made daily decisions. Financial revenue and expenditures were not planned or forecasted creating short and long-term risks. The implementation of the internal quality management system, the development of an EIU quality manual, and regulations on financial management have completely revised the decision-making process.

The financial planning process at EIU begins with defining priorities at the beginning of the academic year in accordance with the strategic plan. The budget is discussed, revised and the initial version is approved by the rector. The final version is submitted for discussion and review to the management board. The rector can make revisions to the extent that they are not more than 20 percent of the budget approved by the management board. The financial management department presents monthly, quarterly, and annual statements to the rector who later reports to the management board. These statements include the overall financial position that includes profit or loss, income, cash flow, and changes to equity.

While short-term financial management has become better regulated, the university continues to struggle with longer-term financial projections. This shortcoming was noted by the two external accreditation panels. Both groups noted that the link between the EIU strategic plan and financial planning is weak and that the university is lacking sound mid and long-term financial forecasts. (National Center for Professional Education Quality Assurance Foundation, 2015, 2018). The EIU financial management department is working on the design of realistic mid and long-term financial projections, something that is particularly challenging in light of the institution's tuition dependence.

3.4 *Future Challenges and Prospects for Eurasia International University*

As already indicated, most FOMHEIs in Armenia have struggled to qualify for institutional accreditation. Only a few FOMHEIS have received external accreditation and for the rest this process remains challenging. While EIU has successfully received accreditation twice and was positively acknowledged for the implementation of its internal quality assurance system, another challenge remains—a new process for the external accreditation of individual academic programs that will impose new requirements on both state and non-state institutions in Armenia. This process will be especially challenging for smaller institutions as the accreditation of each program is expected to be costly.

This program-specific process is challenging in terms of the criteria for educational programs. During the first institutional accreditation, the academic programs criterion was criticized by the external experts. They noted the lack of clear mechanisms for program development, continuous improvement, and monitoring. The experts recommended a revision to existing educational programs and the adoption of an outcomes-based approach. Based on the recommendations, EIU revised program practices completely and each academic program was redesigned in accordance with new, outcome-based methodologies. The review of these changes was positive during the second accreditation process.

The diversification of income sources is another challenge for the university. This is an issue for the FOMHEIS, all other non-state institutions in Armenia, as well as state institutions. Because of the demographic decline, limited national budgets, and increased competition from inter-governmental and international universities, the acceptance rate has been very high in both state and private institutions with the exception of a few specializations. Based on statistics published by the Appraisal and Testing Center of the Republic of Armenia, the overall acceptance rate for the 2018–2019 academic year in public universities was close to 85 percent of the applicants who passed the examination on the first or second attempt. Students who do not pass the state examination for full-time studies usually have the option to enter a state higher education institution as a part-time student. This option translates into a 100 percent acceptance rate. Public opinion still leans towards a preference for state universities due to lingering mistrust of private institutions. As a result, most applicants prefer to enroll at either a state or inter-governmental university.

Against this backdrop EIU has managed to decrease its dependence on national students by enrolling more international students through various international recruitment initiatives and plans to build upon this success. With dramatic and continued instability in international higher education (de Wit & Altbach, 2018), this strategy might prove risky, but the "new world order" of higher education internationalization (Marginson, 2011) may open opportunities for developing countries as alternative study destinations. Vertical and horizontal mobility among developing countries could be an opportunity for EIU. Students from post-conflict zones including Iraq and Syria have been one source of applicants who see Armenia as a safe country with affordable higher education. Another target population is the Armenian diaspora and Armenians with international passports. It has been estimated that while the population in Armenia is around 3 million, some 6 million ethnic Armenians live outside its borders. The largest Armenian diaspora (more than one million) community is in Russia which has been the major source of international students for Armenian institutions and is a target for EIU as well.

The university has a number of additional initiatives towards the diversification of resources including the development of courses for working professionals and specific lifelong learning programs. Developing research projects with third-party funding via cooperative mechanisms with industry or other partners is another strategy discussed by the faculty and administrators.

The university is also developing marketing efforts to address stereotypes that affect public trust of non-state universities like EIU. In doing so, EIU is aiming to position itself as a quality-oriented and student-centered university led by dynamic and responsive management. Changing the image of the private sector will be problematic as long as the market allows diploma mills to operate. The bad actors make it difficult for responsible private universities to grow and consolidate. The government has taken steps toward addressing the problem. "The quality-oriented universities are overshadowed by the ones with inferior quality selling diplomas internationally and the Ministry of Education and Science will address the issue by tightening the monitoring mechanisms" (Interview with Hovhannisyan, August 23, 2018).

The challenges may be offset by the emerging opportunities afforded by the law on higher education under development. The draft law appears quite promising for quality oriented FOMHEIs and non-state universities in that the law will ensure a more level competitive environment for all types of tertiary institutions. There would be fewer distinctions between public and private and the categorization will change to accredited versus non-accredited. Institutions without accreditation will not be authorized to issue diplomas, only a completion certificate. This would help to diminish the operation of the low-quality institutions that have undermined the legitimacy of the private higher education sector in general.

EIU sees a number of opportunities for differentiation in degree specializations developed in close cooperation with relevant industries. The pharmacy degree has recently been implemented in cooperation with a local pharmaceutical company. This is a unique university-industry collaboration, providing an innovative model for Armenia. The theoretical component of the education is delivered by EIU at its premises and most of the practical, laboratory-based education is carried out within the company where pharmaceuticals are developed and produced. Another university-industry cluster is in the development stage and will be offered in the field of management information systems and information systems development. These degrees are developed primarily in English, targeting international students and diaspora Armenians.

4   Conclusion

Most of the non-state institutions in Armenia, including EIU, founded and sustained since the mid 1990s have been owned and managed by families. Family enthusiasm, values, and reputation served as collateral of sorts and flexible, intuitive management was their hallmark during the early development of the sector. Management and administration of FOMHEIs in Armenia have generally suffered due to a lack of short, mid, and long-term planning mechanisms or a clear strategy for generational transitions. The existing FOMHEIS, including those founded by families and transitioning to second-generation family leadership, tend to be more authoritarian in their approach to governance. The new accreditation scheme in Armenia emphasizes the importance of democratic, participatory management, and stakeholder involvement in decision-making processes.

Considering the structural challenges to the higher educational sector, social resources and family ties that have enabled the rise of private universities will likely be insufficient for their consolidation. Institutional leadership with sound governance will be necessary for these institutions to move forward. The FOMHEIS must rethink the practice of automatic familial succession in favor of succession planning that is open to professional management, particularly in cases when technical expertise is lacking within the founding family.

The FOMHEIS also need better patterns of investment. While most of the existing FOMHEIS directed financial recourses to infrastructure development, facilities, and real estate in the past, the future will require considerable resources directed to areas such as the design and monitoring of educational programs, scientific research, human resources development, and promotion. This is not only a requirement for sustaining a tertiary-level institution but also a requirement for institutional and educational program accreditation that will pose a challenge to most FOMHEIS.

In line with global trends, the higher education system in Armenia is continuously evolving and institutions with more dynamic and nimble management are more likely to gain a competitive advantage. While previously some players were sheltered by the state, the post-revolutionary political landscape of higher education in Armenia appears to be constructive and portends a truly competitive environment for the sector. This is an opportune moment for FOMHEIS to re-think their strategies for growth and consolidation in an increasingly global educational context.

References

Altbach, P. G. (2005). Universities: Family style. In P. G. Altbach & D. C. Levy (Eds.), *Private higher education: A global revolution*. Rotterdam, The Netherlands: Sense Publishers.

Armenian Statistical Agency. (2000, January). *Socio-demographic indicators*. Retrieved from https://www.armstat.am/file/article/sv_12a_99_57.pdf

Armenian Statistical Agency. (2018). *Socio-demographic indicators*. Retrieved from https://www.armstat.am/file/article/sv_03_18a_5190.pdf

de Wit, H., & Altbach, P. G. (2018, August 11). Dramatic instability in international higher education. *Inside Higher Education*. Retrieved from https://www.insidehighered.com/blogs/world-view/dramatic-instability-international-higher-education

EIU. (2012, March 11). *Regulation on academic staff asessment and incentive compensation, 29–01*. Retrieved from http://eiu.am/oeVS4

EIU. (2014, October 20). *The strategic plan of Eurasia International University for 2014–2018*. Retrieved from http://eiu.am/HnQA8

EIU. (2016, March 18). *Regulation on administrative and management staff evaluation, incentive compensation and promotion, 32-01*. Retrieved from 2018, from http://eiu.am/EU8nR

EIU. (2018, May 5). *Internationalization: The DNA of Eurasia*. Retrieved from http://eiu.am/bbDyc

Marginson, S. (2011). The new world order in higher education. *Higher Education Research in the 21st Century Series, 3*, 3–20.

National Center for Professional Education Quality Assurance Foundation. (2015). *Expert report on the institutional accreditation of Eurasia International University*. Yerevan.

National Center for Professional Education Quality Assurance Foundation. (2018). *Expert report on institutional accreditation of Eurasia International University*. Yerevan.

Republic of Armenia. (2004, December 14). *Law on higher and postgraduate professional education, HO-62-N*. Retrieved from https://bit.ly/2WbXjxR

Republic of Armenia. (2011a, April 1). *State educational criteria for bachelor qualification of the Republic of Armenia, N 271*. Retrieved from https://bit.ly/2G3JHhL

Republic of Armenia. (2011b, July 30). *Statute on state accreditation of institutions and their academic programs in the Republic of Armenia, N 978*. Retrieved from https://bit.ly/2AYAkNI

Smolentseva, A., Huisman, J., & Froumin, I. (2018). Transformation of higher education institutional landscape in post-Soviet countries: From Soviet model to where? In A. Smolentseva, J. Huisman, & I. Froumin (Eds.), *25 Years of transformations of higher education systems in post-Soviet countries*. London: Palgrave Macmillan.

CHAPTER 5

Bangladesh: Family Members—The Key to University Success

Carmen Z. Lamagna, Charles C. Villanueva, Farheen Hassan and Mohammad Imranul Haque

For this chapter, 14 family-owned universities were reviewed where ownership is primarily based on certain conditions such as being established and funded by a single family or clan or by a member of a family with family members appointed to the board.

1 The Context of the Bangladeshi Higher Education

Bangladesh has a population of approximately 166 million people. Educating this huge population is a significant challenge for the country and the higher education system. The particular challenge for Bangladesh is how to make higher education more accessible to university-aspiring students. The introduction of private universities in the 1990s increased opportunities for students to pursue a university education.

All private universities in Bangladesh are non-profit institutions as mandated by the Private University Acts of 1992 and 2010. Private institutions can offer education up to the master's level while public universities offer education through the PhD level. The challenge remains how to guarantee quality education, especially with the rapid growth of universities in Bangladesh, a phenomenon welcomed due to pent-up demand. The quality of services offered to students is a concern to all stakeholders. A well-designed quality assurance strategy is needed to ensure a strong academic foundation for the country. The task of maintaining standards for quality education is the responsibility of the University Grants Commission Bangladesh or UGC.

Bangladesh is a developing country and its economy is in transition from agriculture to industry, manufacturing, and service sectors. Bangladesh intends to leverage the opportunities offered by globalization to build a knowledge-based economy. Improving the quality of tertiary education is vital to spur the country to middle-income status. Tertiary education in Bangladesh is currently beset with many deeply rooted and intertwined challenges. These

© KONINKLIJKE BRILL NV, LEIDEN, 2020 | DOI: 10.1163/9789004423435_005

include an inadequate environment for improving the quality of education and research; weak governance and accountability; poor planning and monitoring capacities; and insufficient funding.

The Bangladesh government (GoB) recognizes that the country is at risk of being marginalized in the highly competitive global economy because its tertiary education system is not prepared to capitalize on the creation and application of knowledge. The government also realizes that the state has a responsibility to put an enabling framework in place to encourage tertiary institutions to be more innovative and responsive to the need for rapid economic growth and to empower graduates with the right skills to successfully compete in the global knowledge economy.

2   The Academic Ecosystem

In Bangladesh, most private universities are stand-alone universities, meaning they only offer tertiary degree programs. The minimum requirement for admission is the higher secondary certificate (HSC). Students with an HSC may enroll in bachelor's degree courses. After successful completion of a bachelor's degree program, one can enroll in a master's degree program. For those aspiring to a PhD program, an additional 3–4 years of study is required. Higher education is being offered in universities, colleges, and institutes of diversified studies in professional, technical, technological, and other special types of education.

According to 2017 data from the UGC, approximately 3.2 million students were enrolled in tertiary level education compared to only 31,000 in 1972. Total tertiary enrollment during the decade 2016–2026 is projected to reach 4.6 million (Mannan, 2017) with 65 percent of students enrolled in private universities (Neazy, 2018).

There are 150 universities in Bangladesh—47 universities in the public sector and 103 in the private sector. There are three international universities operating in Bangladesh as well. The Bangladesh Open University (BOU) conducts distance education programs, especially programs in the field of teacher education that lead to a bachelor's of education (BEd) and master's of education (MEd). The total number of family-owned universities is not known as no data on that issue are available, but there appear to be at least 14 of them.

Bangladesh National University functions as an affiliating university with different colleges and institutions in various fields of study that offer undergraduate and postgraduate-level education. After successful completion of a course, BNU conducts a final examination and awards a degree, diploma, or certificate to successful candidates. Degrees awarded are BA, BSS, BSc, BCom (Pass & Honours) BFA(Pass), MA, MSc, MSS, MCom, MFA, LLB, and other degrees. Bangladesh National University offers part-time training to university teachers.

3   The Present Scenario

In Bangladesh, the literacy rate among the population aged 15 years and older is 72.76 percent—75.62 percent for males and 69.9 percent for females (UNESCO, 2016). The educational system in Bangladesh is three-tiered and highly subsidized. There was a time when higher education was considered a luxury in a society of mass illiteracy. However, towards the turn of the last century, the need for highly skilled manpower started to be acutely felt in every sphere of the society for development and poverty alleviation. Highly trained manpower contributes towards human resource development by supplying teachers, instructors, researchers and scholars to institutions such as schools, colleges, technical institutes, and universities. These institutions are instrumental in bringing about a technological revolution in agriculture, industry, business and commerce, medicine, engineering, transport, and communication (UGC, 2005).

The University Grants Commission (UGC) of Bangladesh acts as the intermediary between the government and all universities, regulating most institutional affairs. Private universities are no exception despite not receiving any government funding. Currently, there is no recognized quality assurance (QA) mechanism for public or private universities in Bangladesh. This deficiency was recognized in the UGC's "Strategic Plan for Higher Education 2006–2026," and in GoB's "National Education Policy (NEP)" in 2010. The strategic plan recommended the establishment of an independent accreditation council for both public and private universities in Bangladesh.

There are five types of postsecondary education available in the country—general education; science; technology and engineering education; medical education; and agricultural education. The higher education sector also provides vocational and Islamic *madrasha* education. About 900,000 students completed higher secondary education in 2017 and were eligible to enter universities in Bangladesh (Hassan, 2017).

4   Private Higher Education

The establishment of private universities in Bangladesh over the last two decades was somewhat of a revolution. Gone are the days of extremely limited university seats. The large number of private universities today can provide sufficient places to meet demand.

The increase in higher education supply is a result of the Private University Act, 1992. Among its provisions, the act states: "Whereas, it is necessary to establish private universities in order to meet the increasing demand of, and to extend pervasively, higher education in the country, to facilitate the access of the general public to higher education and to create in this way a class of skilled persons; and whereas, several individuals, associations, charitable funds, and institutions in the country are eager to establish and manage private universities." The law requires the establishment of a syndicate or board of trustees to manage the university. This board represents the highest authority of the university to make final decision on all academic and administrative matters.

The following year, the parliament approved a revision to this act, the Private University Act, 2010. The bill was introduced to ensure that certain problems with private universities were not allowed to fester. The Minister of Education stated that

> aside from the trustee board and government representatives, an acclaimed academician nominated by UGC would be a member of the syndicate. The administrative and academic control is in the hands of the vice-chancellor. The syndicate would ensure transparency in university activities and block secrecy, corruption, and misrule.

The bill was introduced to stop private universities from becoming business-oriented organizations.

5   The Landscape of Family-Owned or Managed Universities

A group of universities emerged that were founded by a member or members of families where family members were named to the board of trustees and other strategic roles within the administrative, managerial, and academic framework to control the activities of the university. The founders defined roles and responsibilities so that they have the final say and a controlling stake in all matters pertaining to university operation.

> Family universities enable new and innovative educational and management ideas to be developed and tested. They give rein to charismatic educational leaders with a zeal for reform. They may also permit private higher education institutions to operate in the most private and secretive ways to make money or wield influence. (Altbach, 2007)

TABLE 5.1   Family-owned universities in Bangladesh

	University	Location
1	American International University Bangladesh (AIUB)	Dhaka
2	University of Liberal Arts Bangladesh (ULAB)	Dhaka
3	Daffodil International University	Dhaka
4	Royal University of Dhaka	Dhaka
5	International Business Administration and Information System University (IBAIS)	Dhaka
6	International University of Business, Agriculture and Technology (IUBAT)	Dhaka
7	Leading University of Sylhet	Sylhet
8	Metropolitan University	Sylhet
9	Premiere University	Chittagong
10	North Bengal International University	Rajshahi
11	Dhaka International University,	Dhaka
12	University of Information Technology and Sciences,	Dhaka
13	Varendra University	Rajshahi
14	Uttara University	Dhaka

A small group of family-owned or managed universities exist in Bangladesh. The universities listed in Table 5.1 may not be complete.

These private, family-run universities represent around 15 percent of private higher education institutions. The majority are located in Dhaka with only a few located outside the capital. A brief introduction to each institution follows.

American International University Bangladesh's (AIUB) computer science and IT programs are considered the flagship programs of the university. AIUB has produced thousands of graduate and postgraduate degree holders who serve the length and breadth of the national economy. AIUB has become one of the premier universities in the country due to its reputation in computer science, IT, engineering, business, arts, and social sciences programs. It is a pioneer in the quality assurance and accreditation of its academic programs.

The University of Liberal Arts (ULAB) presented itself as the country's first university specialized in the arts.

Daffodil International University was founding in the early 2000s as a small institution providing diplomas and IT training to professionals at a time when this was a beyond the skill of most people in Bangladesh. Over the years, Daffodil has grown to encompass business, engineering, and other faculties.

Royal University targets students from less-privileged backgrounds. The Royal University is run by a Bangladeshi banking family and is expanding to a second, larger campus in a suburb outside of Dhaka.

The International Business Administration and Information System University (IBAIS), although established as a university focuses on professional courses and diplomas for professionals. The university works with NGOs and government ministries to extend formal language and management courses to thousands of government and NGO employees. IBAIS has a much-respected English language training program for public hospital nurses designed to enhance the professional level of nursing in Bangladesh.

The International University of Business, Agriculture, and Technology (IUBAT) is a family-run university aspiring to international standards. The institution is one of a few private universities offering a dedicated nursing college, a tourism and hospitality management college, and agricultural sciences college in addition to the more traditional programs in engineering and business. IUBAT is oriented towards a contribution to socio-agroeconomic development through human resource development and scientific collaboration.

Leading University is a traditional university that focuses on academic rigor and the personal development of students. Under dynamic leadership, the programs engage students in education complemented by sports and other extra-curricular activities. The university offers engineering, science, business, law, and social sciences. Leading University of Sylhet along with Metropolitan University are pioneering research initiatives in Bangladesh, an activity not typically pursued by private institutions. Subsequently, these private universities are making significant contributions to the human resource development needed by the country.

Metropolitan University was established in 2003 offering business administration, computer science, and engineering. Over time, new departments were opened creating additional academic programs. The university prides itself on its research-oriented academic programs and faculty.

Premiere University is geared towards developing effective and competent human resources. The university has traditional departments including law, business, and engineering.

The North Bengal International University and Varendra University are located in the commercial and industrial hub of Rajshahi City. The universities are small educational institutions, relatively new, founded around 2013. The universities are backed up by a robust group of professors and academicians. What these universities lack in longevity and maturity, they make up for with highly professional faculty and senior scholars. These universities have a well-rounded list of academic programs including business, engineering, social science, and law.

The Dhaka International University is a multi-campus educational institution. The relatively new university has a significant number of students across 4 campuses. The university fulfills a low-tuition fee niche in particular communities in the capital.

The University of Information Technology and Sciences, located in the capital city, was established in 2003 and is an older institution in this category. Despite still being relatively young, the university is one of the most professional institutions in the country. The institution boasts IT, engineering, science, business, law, language, and social welfare departments. The university focuses on research in IT and science.

Uttara University remains a small community-oriented university located at the capital city's outer limits. Like Royal, it targets students from low-income backgrounds.

Practically, all the above mentioned privately, family-owned universities have affiliations with international universities and organizations. They host foreign students, especially in computer science and in master's programs in public health. Some Bangladeshi faculty who have emigrated are contracted to teach while home on vacation; others are contracted after returning from abroad for other reasons.

6   Traits of Family-Run Universities

Family members at family-owned or managed universities in Bangladesh generally maintain majority voting and decision-making authority on the board of trustees due to their majority on the board. This arrangement presents both benefits and challenges for the university in terms of management. There is no opposition from non-family board members as they are usually designated by the family resulting in an absence of infighting. Despite variations in governance, family-run boards tend not to suffer from insurmountable differences. As a result, decisions are deliberated and resolved in a short amount of time.

This kind of arrangement facilitates long-term planning and implementation without challenges or changes to board policy or strategy. Family-run universities in Bangladesh have the benefit of being able to formulate a long-term vision efficiently and pursue a set of strategies to achieve that vision. From an operational perspective, the day to day decision-making process runs smoothly as there is little debate among multiple stakeholders on the board before an action is taken.

Some family-owned universities are subsidiaries of established businesses like banks, garment manufacturers or others, but the rest, like AIUB, were established from the passion and vision of an individual. By virtue of the

Private University Act, all private universities, including family-owned institutions are non-profit institutions.

Human resource management tends to be more efficient as well. It is easier to "indoctrinate" employees in the institution's culture and workplace ethics. Expectations at the workplace are made clear by the board and since only one culture operates, management style and operation are consistent.

At family-run institutions relationships between the employees and employers tend to be friendly which results in lower employee turnover. Employees and their contributions are well known to members on the board. The presence of the family members in management positions helps to share vital information about university operations widely.

7   Challenges of Family-Run Universities

Family-run institutions in Bangladesh face challenges as well. These stem from a singular management approach that, while conducive to operational efficiency, poses risks. These universities usually lack diversity of opinion. Management is usually influenced by the family-run board of trustees. The absence of diverging opinions on the board limits debate before major or minor decisions are taken and implemented. With more diversity there would be challenges and discussion that would contribute to greater possibilities for success.

The board often includes some members outside the family who are professors or former government officials. According to UGC rule, there must be representation from the UGC and government in the syndicate at all private universities. These individuals usually present their opinions at board meetings before critical decisions are made. However, their minority status on the board means that they have little influence on the decision-making process beyond making their concerns heard.

The board is not always competent in matters of education despite their passion and good intentions. The management decisions coming from the board may not be as professional or sound as those that might be expected from a board with more academically oriented members. The family-run board, and the university in turn, may simply function as a means to increase the family's influence in the socioeconomic sphere nationally. The individuals on the board may not be trained, experienced or enlightened in the art and science of university management. This may result in the poor academic and administrative performance of the university.

The family running the board are often businesspersons with well-established business ventures. The university might simply be a non-profit venture designed to enhance the reputation of the business group and increase the socioeconomic footprint of a business conglomerate. Hence, the university may be seen as an initiative for business diversification, despite its non-profit status. A key challenge is that these business owners are often too busy managing other businesses and may lack time and expertise to dedicate to the operation of the university. At the same time, family owners are often unwilling to delegate decision-making authority to others. The university may suffer the consequences.

A disadvantage of the family-run structure is the absence of relevant policies and strategies for student success. This might occur due to poor priority development. The family-run universities might give priority to the institution's reputation and student admissions over educational priorities consistent with the mission and vision of the institution. For example, the family-owned university might not prioritize research or innovation and, as a result, not disburse adequate funds for either. Other areas such as curriculum development, increasing staff capacity, strategic industry affiliations or industry research collaborations might not be adequately addressed. This is not unique to family-run institutions and may happen at other private universities.

Family conflict might jeopardize smooth management in some cases. The interlacing of family and university matters also becomes a challenge. This sometimes results in mismanagement or mishandling of university funds. Family-run institutions also suffer from sexism due to dominant societal values and cultural beliefs; men in the family might tend to accumulate power leaving women relatives without influence, a situation common in the cultural context of Bangladesh.

While family-owned or managed universities in Bangladesh have made a positive impact on the higher education sector, these universities require better management and mechanisms for internal change. The greatest challenge for the family-run university will be to keep family matters distinct from and outside of board discussions and separate from the various offices held by family members. In other words, there should be a clear separation between personal and professional functions and roles.

Family-run universities often have the distinct advantage of stable management, succession, and vision in Bangladesh. There are seldom any rapid changes on the board and hence, very limited uncertainty.

8   The Case Study

The American International University-Bangladesh (AIUB), a government approved, private university was founded in 1994 by philanthropist Anwarul

TABLE 5.2   AIUB statistics a glance

Faculty	Total students		Total faculty		Graduates after 18 years
	Undergraduate	Graduate	Full-time	Part-time	
Faculty of Arts & Social Sciences	276	78	41	13	866
Faculty of Business Administration	1973	907	70	24	14160
Faculty of Engineering	2704	84	101	0	6609
Faculty of Science & Information Technology	3671	69	112	2	3172

SOURCE: OFFICE OF RECORDS, VIRTUAL UNIVERSITY EXPERT SYSTEM (VUES) OFFICE

Abedin, a renowned physician. It envisioned creating and promoting a learning environment through state-of-the-art facilities and an expanded frontier of research-based knowledge.

AIUB offers several degree programs at the graduate and undergraduate level in four faculties—arts and social science; business administration; engineering; science and information technology. By its 18th convocation the university had graduated over 24,807 students. In 2017, the university enrolled more than 10,000 students and employed more than 363 faculty members of which 324 (89 percent) were full-time and 39 (11 percent) were part-time (Table 5.2).

8.1   History of the American International University-Bangladesh (AIUB)

During his final year of study in AMA Computer College (AMACC) in the Philippines, Ishtiaque Abedin, the second son of Dr. Anwarul Abedin, dreamt of establishing a private university in Bangladesh. With support from family members, he presented his vision to Carmen Z. Lamagna, director of student affairs at AMACC in 1994. This led to a formal meeting with the vice-president of student affairs, a visit to Bangladesh by the chairman and president of AMACC and an official meeting with the former education minister. Dr. Anwarul Abedin offered financial support to advance the AIUB project.

The sons of Dr. Abedin who were living abroad returned to help set up the university. The eldest son, Hasanul Abedin Hasan, completed a Doctor of Business Administration in the US and played an active role in the success of this project. AMA International University-Bangladesh (AIUB) launched on November 6, 1994 under the leadership of Carmen Z. Lamagna. In September 1995, AIUB started its first year of operation and the prime minister of People's Republic of Bangladesh signed the establishment document in November 1995.

The partnership between the AMACC and AIUB failed after one semester. According to the vice-chancellor, "The separation was done as they want me to implement lots of Philippine policies which were not suitable for a university in Bangladesh as policies need to be revised and modified according to the culture and environment" (Habib, Pathik, & Chowdhury, 2013, p. 9). Official separation took place in March 1996 and the institution was renamed the American International University-Bangladesh (AIUB). "American" was selected to retain the acronym and there was no restriction in the use of the term "American." In fact, there is no relationship or affiliation to US higher education or any other university outside of the US using "American" in their name.

At AIUB the curricula and instruction are written and delivered in English. This was intended to minimize the outflow of Bangladeshi students to foreign universities. From 1980 to 1990 a good number of talented Bangladeshi students who were financially able, left the country for higher studies elsewhere which alarmed the educational sector of Bangladesh. Additionally, a large number of students passed the HSC (Higher Secondary Certificate) every year in Bangladesh but could not continue their studies due to the limited number of places at public tertiary institutions. For this reason, it was important to allow the creation of new universities in the private sector to increase access and at the same time motivate the improvement of university quality. Due to the success of the business sector in the early 90s, demand for highly educated and capable graduates increased. This further justified the development of AIUB (Habib, Pathik, & Chowdhury, 2013).

8.2 *Vision, Mission, Goals and Quality Policy*

The vision, mission, goals, and quality reflect the AIUB's strong commitment to individual student welfare and development but also addresses national and global challenges. The university follows developments of the new millennium with a commitment to the development of the country. This is reflected in the various policies and programs developed and implemented by the university. Awareness of the vision and mission is reinforced in university documents such as the admission application, handbooks, website, and banners placed in strategic places of the campus.

8.3   *The Founders*

The AIUB was founded by Dr. Anwarul Abedin and his wife, Hasna Abedin, along with their three children—Hasanul A. Hasan, Ishtiaque Abedin and Nadia Anwar. As stated in the university statutes, "The founders and their legal successors shall be and remain forever hereafter, a body politic and foundation, in fact and in name by the founders. By that name shall and may have continued succession forever hereafter, and in law to sue and be sued, implead and be impleaded, answer and be answered unto, defend and be defended, in all courts and places whatsoever, and may have a common seal, and may change and alter the same at their pleasure" (AIUB Statute, 2017). This statement was adopted by the board of trustees to ensure succession to the next generation of family members.

8.4   *Chronology of Development*

With two rooms, ten computers, three faculty members and 70 students, AIUB launched in the Hosaf Tower, Mohakhali, Dhaka in 1994. The campus grew to include rented spaces on four campuses and eventually eight.

Government policy specified in the Private University Act 2010 requires all private institutions to have a permanent campus. This prompted management to purchase more than 8 acres of land and build infrastructure to house all academic programs on one campus. AIUB shifted to its permanent campus with state-of-the-art academic and instructional facilities in 2017. From 1994 to the present, the AIUB built more than 100 classrooms and acquired about 1,600 computer units.

8.5   *Degrees and Accreditation*

AIUB currently operates four faculties—science and technology; engineering, business administration; and arts and social sciences. A total of 20 academic programs are offered—13 are undergraduate and seven are graduate. In addition to the academic degree programs, the university also offers short-term professional international and local courses and training through the Continuing Education Center (CEC).

The BBA, MBA/EMBA, CS, CSE, CSSE, SE, CIS and EEE programs are accredited by the Philippine Accrediting Association of Schools, Colleges and Universities (PAASCU), a member of Asia Pacific Quality Network (APQN), International Network for Quality Assurance Agencies in Higher Education (INQAAHE), National Committee on Foreign Medical Education and Accreditation (NNCFMEA), Council for Higher Education Accreditation (CHEA) International Quality Group. This is the first university among public and private universities in Bangladesh to have achieved this level of recognition for quality and excellence. Accreditation from PAASCU was pursued because there is no existing accreditation body in Bangladesh.

The university also involves local professional bodies to ensure quality standards for the engineering and architecture programs. The graduates of a program accredited by the professional bodies have better opportunities in the job market. The Institute of Engineers (IEB) is the most prestigious professional organization in the country. AIUB's EEE and COE programs are accredited by the IEB. The Institute of Architects Bangladesh (IAB) is a professional institution safeguarding, promoting and developing the profession of architecture in Bangladesh and accredits architecture programs. The architecture program of the university is accredited by IAB.

In addition to pursuing the accreditation of academic programs, the university embarked on ISO 9001:2008 Certification with the Société Générale de Surveillance (SGS) and United Kingdom Accreditation Service (UKAS) that covers management operations. AIUB is an ISO 9001:2008 certified university.

The university has established the Institutional Quality Assurance Office to implement and monitor quality assurance and accreditation activities. Since 2008, this body has been strengthened and was subsequently aided by a project on quality assurance funded by the World Bank in 2015. The Quality Assurance Office undertakes continuous evaluation of the university to identify areas for improvement and validation through the processes of accreditation and certification.

The Office of Planning and Development is involved with long-term development and strategic planning of the university.

8.6   Research and Development

A major thrust of the university is towards research. Together with instruction and community engagement, research capacity needs to be improved through cultivation of the faculty's ability to conduct research. Resources are provided in the budget of the university. However, the allocation is not sufficient to cover all research activities within the university. The university has to pursue additional sources of funding through commissioned research projects. Institutional incentives include the provision of research grants to faculty to present research papers at international conferences. Research productivity is a major criterion for faculty promotion and permanence.

Research is published in the *AIUB Journal of Science and Engineering* (ISSN#1608-3679) and *AIUB Journal of Business and Economics* (ISSN#1683-8742). Since the first publications in 2002, two issues per year have been published and the journals have been recognized by academics in Bangladesh and abroad.

Collaborative research opportunities with partner universities are added to the pipeline for identifying potential areas of focus including industry, cross-cultural environments, and integrative analytical frameworks. To boost the university's research culture, the AIUB Center for Research Planning and Development was established. The Center envisages strengthening and expanding the research horizon of the university and promoting excellence in academic programs through collaborative and internationally funded research projects.

8.7   Scholarships

The scholarship program of the university is based on demands to increase access to university education and mandates from the government to offer scholarship to children of freedom fighters. Merit-based scholarships are awarded to students in recognition of their academic performance. The Private University Act 2010 mandates that private higher education institutions should allocate grants to six percent of the total enrollment. This is a challenge, but for AIUB this is addressed through different programs. Different types of scholarships and financial waivers are offered based on academic merit, need, or special talent in sports and art. A range of additional scholarships fall under the category of social responsibility and target specific groups.

8.8   Facilities and Services

The best feature of the university might be the state-of-art facilities that include modern computer labs, an Apple Macintosh lab, an animation lab, electrical and electronic engineering labs, an architecture design studio, physics and chemistry labs. IT offers 24-hour, high-speed Internet access, in-house software development facilities, an in-house developed Virtual University Expert System (VUES) and a modern university management system. The campuses are fully secured with the latest monitoring devices.

The library has a collection of about 65,000 volumes including books; printed and online references; journals; periodicals; and audiovisuals covering more than 80 academic areas.

The university provides extra-curricular services such as academic counseling and support to students with serious academic deficiencies through the Office of Probation. The Office of Placement and Alumni is an initiative to assist students to find employment and internships required for graduation. The Office of Student Affairs coordinates off-campus and on-campus student activities. (Villanueva & Haque, 2013).

AIUB has a wide network of clubs and associations offering different co-curricular activities. These clubs plan activities and programs throughout the year. The clubs and student organizations are under the supervision of selected faculty members and university officers. Student organizations are active in undertaking projects and planning study tours, exhibits, stage plays, cultural events and sports competitions. Students are encouraged to participate in activities that contribute to the development of their talents. Programs and activities are evaluated to determine their effectiveness for student development. There are several national and international outreach programs conducted on regular basis to monitor student engagement and development.

8.9   *Management Structure*

The university is managed by men and women preserved in the dictum, "Praesidium, Disciplina and Civitatis," as well as in the motto of the university, "Where leaders are created."

Efficiency and effectiveness emanate from top executives, but management is participatory in practice. The management has to respond to concerns and challenges and encourage efforts towards continued excellence. Survival in the competitive academic world requires determination, ingenuity, creativity, technology, and thoughtful planning. The spirit of teamwork and coordination among key officials is essential to reach objectives and desired results.

The organizational and management structure of the university offer guideposts that delineate all operations of the university. AIUB has bodies and committees as prescribed by the Private University Act. These committees have been organized to provide coordinated support to the overall operation of the university. All committees are active and meet regularly. The university has formulated a long-term strategic plan (2010–2020) that defines the priorities of the university for the next ten years.

8.10   *Strategic Alliances*

In a constant effort to internationalize its education and improve its global competitiveness, AIUB has been increasing affiliations with universities in North America, Europe, Australia, and South East Asia. The university has entered into a memorandum of understanding (MOU) with a number of international institutions such as Monash University of Australia, University of Gavle, Sweden, St. Mary University of Canada, and others to promote academic cooperation that includes collaborative research, student exchange, faculty exchange, and other development activities.

AIUB also partners with local, multinational and foreign organizations such as the International Association of Universities (IAU), Asia Pacific Quality

Network (APQN), British Council, Microsoft, World Bank-IFC, European Union (EU) and many other organizations. The cooperation includes opportunities for research, student internships, student placement, projects and other development activities. The partnerships provide opportunities for wider horizons and enrichment to the curriculum and contribute to internal capacity building.

Industry is consulted in program development through surveys, seminars, workshops, talk shows, internship programs, job fairs, roundtables, convocations, and through the involvement of CEOs who are regular partners in student placement. The partnerships encourage the exchange of valuable ideas and suggestions that are considered for the development and improvement of the university.

9   Conclusion

The case of American International University-Bangladesh demonstrates how success can be achieved under the leadership of a family. From the start, the Abedin family has been a key element in the establishment and operation of the university. As described in this chapter, family-owned universities in Bangladesh reflect direct family influence over the operation of their universities. While there are positive effects of familial involvement, some negative aspects and risks were noted—the lack of unity among family members, personal interest over institutional welfare, lack of a long-term vision for the university, lack of knowledge and skill to manage a university, and owner attitudes that inhibit cooperation from the non-family members in the academic community.

At AIUB, these challenges are not apparent. Although there may be some disagreements, differences are settled taking into account the overall welfare of the university. Strong and consistent leadership defines the governance of AIUB, influenced by concern for the benefit of all. Hence, after 25 years the university has become a leading institution and landmark in higher education in Bangladesh. It is expected that the success will be sustained while at the same time allowing for any changes needed to respond to the growth, development, and the continued excellence of its academic programs and services. Stability is protected by the unequivocal support of both the academic and non-academic staff and the leadership of the vice-chancellor and the board of trustees. The AIUB will continue to build the institution and the capacities of all of the young men and women involved with the organization.

References

Habib, M., Pathik, B. B., & Chowdhury, T. M. (2013). *An Academic Odyssey: Chrono-logical Advancement of American International University-Bangladesh (1994–2011)*. Germany: LAP Lambert Academic Publishing.

Lamagna, C., Villanueva, C. C., & Hassan, F. (2017). *The effects of internal quality assur-ance on quality and employability: American International University-Bangladesh*. Paris, France: International Institute for Educational Planning, UNESCO.

UNESCO. (2018). *Bangladesh*. Retrieved from http://uis.unesco.org/country/BD

University Grants Commission of Bangladesh. (2018). *Public universities*. Retrieved from http://www.ugc-universities.gov.bd/home/university/public/120

University Grants Commission of Bangladesh. (2018). *Private universities*. Retrieved from http://www.ugc-universities.gov.bd/home/university/private/75

Villanueva, C. C., & Haque, M. I. (2013). AIUB's quest for quality and excellence: Strengthening academic reputation. *The FBA Journal, AIUB, 1*(1), 19–44.

World Population Review. (2018). *Bangladesh population 2018*. Retrieved from http://worldpopulationreview.com/countries/bangladesh-population/

CHAPTER 6

Brazil: Family-Founded Higher Education Institutions

Fábio Reis and Rodrigo Capelato

The Brazilian private higher education system expanded dramatically after the University Reform of 1968 and the National Education Guidelines and Framework Law (LDB) of 1996. At the time of the LDB, Brazil had 922 higher education institutions (HEIS) of which 211 were public and 711 were private. At the conclusion of 2018 there were 2,448 institutions—2,152 private and 296 public. The election of Jair Bolsonaro as president in 2018 portends more change. It is difficult to predict how the number of institutions in each category might change in the future.

The 1990s were conducive to sector expansion as there was growing demand for access from people who had not had the opportunity to enroll at this level previously. In many cases, it was during this decade that children from families with limited financial resources were entering higher education for the first time.

The public sector was not able to meet widening enrollment demand due to limitations on government spending, the high cost of maintaining public universities and the concentration of public institutions in capital cities and large metropolitan areas limiting their reach. Private higher education represented 75.3 percent of the enrollment in Brazil by 2017 and had become essential to the expansion of access.

The patterns of expansion have changed over recent years, especially in the area of traditional, face-to-face teaching. Competition, limited public resources to expand traditional infrastructure, and the growth of distance education have forced the development of new higher education business models. It has become difficult for small, traditional private institutions to remain sustainable within Brazil's higher education system and this has led to many mergers.

The for-profit private higher education sector is controversial in Brazil. All of the family-owned institutions operate within this sector, but the expansion of FOMHEIS was not always accompanied by the capacity within families to manage a university properly. Critics insist that families prioritize financial gain over quality, but others see FOMHEIS as responsible for expanding access

© KONINKLIJKE BRILL NV, LEIDEN, 2020 | DOI: 10.1163/9789004423435_006

to higher education and paving the way for more young people to enter the labor market at a higher skill level.

1   Enrollment Expansion

Brazil currently enrolls 8.3 million undergraduate students in traditional face-to-face and distance education. Despite the seemingly high number, this still does not place Brazil near the participation rate of most developed countries. In 2017, only 17.8 percent of 18–24 age group was enrolled in higher education. The National Education Plan approved by the national Congress in 2014 established a 33 percent net enrollment target by 2024 as one of its goals, but the economic crisis of 2015 and the lack of long-term policies are decreasing the likelihood that Brazil will reach this goal.

Enrollment growth can be seen in two distinct periods during the 44 years between 1974 and 2017. From 1974 to 1995 enrollment grew by an average of 1.62 percent per year. From 1995 to 2017 enrollment grew by an average of 7.3 percent per year. Growth by decade and distribution by sector is shown in Table 6.1.

The LDB opened the door to private participation in higher education that included for-profit companies and stimulated the creation of many FOMHEIs. Prior to the LDB, family participation within higher education was limited to non-profit institutions. Subsequent to the LDB, several other public policies were established that created additional opportunities for higher education that are elaborated later in this text. Figure 6.1 presents enrollment growth in relation to national policy initiatives.

TABLE 6.1   Higher education enrollment from 1960 to 2010 in Brazil

Year	Enrollment (Public HEIs)	Percentage	Enrollment (Private HEIs)	Percentage	Total enrollment
1960	59,624	58.6	47,067	41.4	101,691
1970	210,613	49.5	214,865	50.5	425,478
1980	492,232	35.7	885,054	64.3	1,377,286
1990	578,625	37.6	961,455	62.4	1,540,080
2000	887,026	26.9	1,807,219	67.1	1,694,245
2010	1,643,675	25.7	4,764,061	74.3	6,407,733

SOURCE: SINDATA/SEMESP

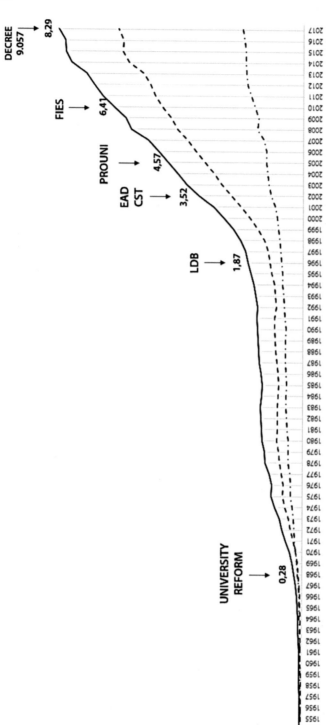

FIGURE 6.1   Higher education enrollment in Brazil (in millions). (Source: SINDATA/SEMESP)

During 2002 and 2003, the first undergraduate courses to be offered through distance education appeared along with strong incentives to expand technical and technological courses (shorter courses with strong ties to the labor market). Both initiatives spurred a new wave of growth attuned to labor market demands.

In 2005, two social inclusion programs for low-income youth were created. ProUni (University for All) facilitated tuition-free placement in private HEIs for underprivileged students by providing tax waivers to the host institution. Reuni (Restructuring and Expansion Plans of Federal Universities) expanded available places in public universities. In 2010, the federal government reformulated the Student Financing Fund (FIES) reducing interest rates while increasing the grace and amortization periods. This allowed more than 50 percent of the Brazilian population considered to be lower middle class to enter higher education.

In 2017, the Ministry of Education (MEC) published Decree 9,057 stimulating an expansion of distance education courses. The number of distance learning providers grew by almost 250 percent in just one year.

In this context, entrepreneurial families who founded institutions of various types and in all regions of the country, from large cities to small towns in remote places, were a main driver of the expansion of higher education in Brazil.

By 2018, the higher education system in Brazil consisted of 2,448 institutions, of which 2,152 were private and 296 public. The private sector encompassed 1,157 for-profit institutions (including 647 family-owned) and 991 non-profit. FOMHEIs represent 56 percent of the for-profit institutions and 26 percent of all HEIs in Brazil.

The contribution of FOMHEIs to national enrollment is almost equivalent to that of the entire federal system. In 2017, the number of students enrolled in federal public universities reached 1.3 million with 1.05 million in FOMHEIs. Family-owned institutions are also responsible for 13 percent of the country's first-degree graduates or 156,000 of the 1.2 million university graduates in 2017. Federal public institutions graduated 151,000 first-degree students that year.

Private, for-profit institutions reported a total of approximately US$12 billion in revenue in 2017; 25 percent or nearly 3 billion in revenue was reported by FOMHEIs.

2   Consolidation

After 2005, higher education began a period of consolidation with many mergers and acquisitions, mainly by institutions managed by families. Foreign funds and backing from publicly-owned companies helped finance new education groups, many acquiring smaller, FOMHEIs to grow into enormous enterprises. Brazil hosts the largest higher education company in the world. Kroton Educacional enrolls approximately one million students. Ten of the largest education groups account for 49 percent of private enrollment. Among these four are public companies listed on the São Paulo Stock Exchange; two are owned by American groups; and one is a limited public company with private equity fund participation.

The consolidation of the higher education market happened mainly through the acquisition of HEIs. Laureate Education, Inc. acquired Anhembi Morumbi University in 2005. The IPOs of Anhanguera Educacional, Kroton Educacional, Estácio Participações, and Grupo SEB on the São Paulo stock exchange in 2007 provided revenue for further market consolidation through additional acquisitions.

Other international educational groups such as Adtalem Global Education (formerly DeVry) and Ilumno (former Whitney University System)—both American—entered the Brazilian market by acquiring family-owned institutions. Simultaneously, private equity funds invested in educational groups boosting their purchasing power. In 2013 two more companies, SER Educacional and Anima Educacional, launched IPOs in the stock exchange.

Another important market shift resulted from the merger of two of the largest companies, Kroton and Anhanguera. Announced in 2013 and approved in 2014, the merger resulted in the largest education company in the world. At the same time, Estácio acquired SEB Group's higher education holdings. These mergers presented a new phase of massive consolidation in the Brazilian private higher education sector. The attempted merger of Kroton and Estácio in 2016 would have created a single group with more than 1.5 million students. However, the Ministry of Justice denied permission, concerned about the potential to close off market competition. The decision, coupled with the country's economic crisis, cooled the pace of consolidation.

Acquisitions continue to take place in Brazilian higher education, but at a slower pace. According to the "Fusion & Acquisitions" report produced by KPMG Corporate Finance (2018), the education sector in Brazil registered more than 260 mergers and acquisitions from 1999 to 2017. Brazil still has more than 1,600 private companies, both for-profit and non-profit, that own more than 2,100 private HEIs. The average number of students is 2,000 per institution.

3   Impact of Private and For-Profit Institutions

The expansion of private higher education in the country was facilitated by the 1968 university reform, the 1996 LDB, and the approval of the 1998 Constitution.

In 1968, the intention was for private education to play a complementary role to public education; however, what occurred was that private enrollment eventually surpassed public enrollment (Corbucci, Kubota, & Meira, 2016).

Community and religiously-affiliated HEIS (Catholic, Presbyterian and Evangelical among other religions) play a critical role in Brazil. They represent almost five percent of total Brazilian HEIS and enroll eight percent of Brazilian students. These are non-profit institutions that prioritize a humanistic approach to higher education and have strong links to their local community. The Pontifical Catholic universities are benchmark institutions with regard to quality in Brazil and have solid results in international rankings.

According to critics of the 1968 University Reform, the law allowed for the emergence of a type of education driven by business models and market forces, changing the features of Brazilian higher education, formerly limited to public or private confessional institutions, to a scenario with the for-profit sector as a third actor (Corbucci, Kubota, & Meira, 2016).

University of Brasilia professor, Carlos Benedito Martins, criticizes the for-profit sector because of the influence of profit and demands of the educational market (Martins, 2009). For Martins, for-profit HEIS remain profitable by offering teaching, and professional training taught by teachers with poor academic qualifications contracted on an hourly basis, while not investing in research or graduate programs. Martins sees the private sector as shaped by the "free market game."

4   Family-Owned HEIS

The history of family-owned institutions is marked by the pioneering initiatives of families contributing to improved access to higher education in Brazil, particularly in the more remote parts of the country.

The founding families of the 647 FOMHEIS sustain their activities through the profits obtained from elementary, middle, and high schools as well as HEIS. There are cases where the entire family lives off income generated by a school. Many proprietary families began their business in education with elementary schools slowly expanding activities that culminated with the creation of higher education institutions. Currently the reverse is happening with educational groups launching their business within higher education and subsequently venturing into elementary, middle, and high schools. Kroton Educacional, for example, worked solely with higher education historically. However, in early 2018 Kroton bought Somos Educacional for US$1.2 billion and launched into the primary and secondary education market.

A very common critique of family-owned institutions is that they provide poor quality. However, based on the General Course Index (IGC), a quality indicator published annually by MEC, it is possible to document that institutions vary in quality regardless of their financial structure or sector. The IGC runs on a scale from 1 to 5, with 3 being the minimum satisfactory score. The results across sectors are surprising similar. The following list shows the percent of institutions with an IGC of 3 or better by sector:
- Public: 87.1 percent
- Private, non-profit: 84.3 percent
- Private, for-profit: 85.3 percent
- Family-owned: 83.3 percent

Therefore, conclusions about quality cannot be generalized to a sector, but would appear to result from other institutional characteristics.

Even though the system as a whole may have quality problems, this is not limited to the private, for-profit sector. Moreover, allowing FOMHEIS to earn profits does not necessarily mean that quality is affected.

5   Legal Framework

Article 7 of Law 9,131, passed in December 1995, allowed "entities that maintain private higher education institutions to be constituted under any of the legal categories provided for in the civil code" (Covac & Coimbra, 2013). The LDB classified institutions as public or private. Private HEIS were defined within the following categories:
- Private institutions. HEIS established by one or more individuals or legal entities governed by private law and can be for-profit or non-profit.
- Community institutions. HEIS created by individuals, legal entities or non-profit educational cooperatives and have members of civil society on their board.
- Religiously affiliated institutions. HEIS created by individuals or legal entities that are confessional in orientation and ideology (Covac & Coimbra, 2013).

These institutions can be colleges, university centers, or universities. Colleges focus on undergraduate degrees but can offer some graduate courses; university centers have the autonomy to open new undergraduate courses without additional permission from the Ministry of Education; universities focus on research and offer at least four master's and two PhD programs as well as undergraduate programs. Many family-owned higher education institutions opt for the private, for-profit category in order to distribute earnings to

family members. For-profit HEIs are eligible to participate in the government's
PROUNI program and receive tax benefits that can be as high as 10 percent of
total revenue.

The Brazilian higher education system is probably unique due to the strong
presence of the private sector and the significant participation of family-owned
institutions.

6   Case Studies

Following are three cases of family-owned institutions. The first presents the
Cruzeiro do Sul Group, one of Brazil's largest educational groups, offering 562
undergraduate programs to 202,000 students and employing 6,000 individuals, including 3,550 members of the faculty. The Cruzeiro do Sul Group operates ten HEIs in four states and the federal district of Brasilia. The institution is
headquartered in São Paulo.

The second case is Dom Bosco University Center in São Luís do Maranhão
(UNDB). Don Bosco enrolls 3,300 students, employs 313 individuals of whom
129 are professors. The institution offers 9 undergraduate courses. Don Bosco
was founded by two women from the northeast of Brazil.

The last case is Toledo University Center (UNITOLEDO) in Araçatuba that
enrolls 4,800 students, employs 276 individuals including 166 professors. It currently offers 26 undergraduate courses. UNITOLEDO's founder is considered to
be a pioneer in higher education in the state of São Paulo.

The founding of these institutions is intertwined with the 1960s in Brazil and
the 1968 university reform. In all three cases, these institutions have proved to
be sustainable and profitable, allowing family members to live off of the profits
they generate. Not all FOMHEIs in Brazil are as viable.

In each case, part of the revenue the institution generates is invested in
scholarships. In 2018, Cruzeiro do Sul Group offered scholarships to 8.8 percent
of their students. At UNITOLEDO scholarships were granted to 11.6 percent of
the student body. UNDB has not defined a scholarship program. The three
institutions invest 1–3 percent of their earnings in professional development
programs for faculty. The investment may vary with the national economy and
the number of incoming students each year.

The three institutions all participate in MEC's Student Financing Program
(FIES). Cruzeiro do Sul Group funds 4.5 percent of their students through the
program; UNITOLEDO funds 10.8 percent; and UNDB funds 30.1 percent.

Due to the consolidation in the educational market, many families that
own small and medium-sized HEIs are in financial difficulties, in some cases

leading to bankruptcy. This has been an opportunity for educational groups like these three to acquire FOMHEIS in crisis.

6.1 *Cruzeiro do Sul Group*

The Cruzeiro do Sul Group began with seven friends from rural São Paulo who met as students. The friends were studying to become elementary and high school teachers. Although the Cruzeiro do Sul Group has grown to encompass ten HEIs and benefit from foreign investment, it is still controlled by two of the original founding families.

Cruzeiro do Sul opened in 1965 offering primary education, preparatory courses for the admission tests at federal universities, and a technical business course. In 1966 the school opened in the neighborhood of São Miguel Paulista, at the time located in the outskirts of São Paulo, with 200 students. The young friends recognized potential for population growth in the neighborhood due to urban expansion and economic development.

In 1969, the friends met federal deputy, Manoel Bezerra de Melo, a Catholic priest who founded Mogi das Cruzes University in 1962 and who had strong ties to the region, especially in the São Miguel Paulista neighborhood. He advised the friends to open a college, an opportunity Bezerra de Melo anticipated would grow due to the university reform of 1968.

To launch their college the group borrowed the equivalent of approximately US$1,200 with two cars as collateral. They invested family funds as well. At that moment, the region hosted a small population with no opportunities for higher education.

Amid ambiguity in the legislation regarding requirements and procedures of opening a college, the group started the process. The founders met with representatives of the National Education Council (CNE), an agency of the Ministry of Education in Brasilia, and sought consulting support to guide them. They filed their application with CNE 1969 and opened in 1970.

In 1972, the college was authorized as the Accounting and Administration College of São Miguel Paulista. Only 10 students applied for the 180 places authorized by the MEC in 1973. The founders then launched street campaigns, handing out leaflets and talking to people at local fairs. As a result, the 180 spots were filled.

The institution was authorized to offer new courses every two years by the MEC. From the outset, the bureaucracy at the Ministry of Education stymied family investment in higher education. The LDB and ensuing legislation from 2016 to 2017 had a pivotal role in changing the dynamics of higher education by allowing greater autonomy to HEIs subsequent to positive results on institutional evaluations carried out by the government. Delays persisted and led to complaints from families investing in new HEIs since the MEC could take up to five years to authorize new institutions and new courses.

Several of the original founders realized there were expansion opportunities in the private higher education sector due to the LDB. They began working with politicians, the church, and members of the Ministry of Education to petition a change from college to university status that would allow for greater administrative and academic autonomy. At that time petitioning change of status required lobbying and political influence; networking was key for acquiring university status. The efforts led to the creation of Cruzeiro do Sul University in 1991. In 1998, the owners bought Geraldo Resende and Paulista de Artes College beginning an expansion process that has continued. The expansion was made feasible through bank loans and the institution's own resources. The owners of Cruzeiro do Sul University purchased institutions with existing campuses. It was a common practice to buy the administration of an institution and rent the buildings from the former owners.

Until 2001, the university was administered by different families, but it became clear that it was necessary to professionalize governance and management which led to the departure of some of the original founders. Ultimately, Hermes Ferreira Figueiredo and Gilberto Padovese were left in charge of the institution.

The children of the two partners took positions within the university and the process of professionalizing management began. An educational consultant firm was hired to install the new governance model that included a board of directors with participation of the two founders. The university deanship and other management functions were then occupied by individuals who were not family members. It was decided that only one member of each of founding family could have a management role at the university provided that they demonstrated the professional abilities needed for the position. Fábio Figueiredo, Hermes Ferreira Figueiredo's son, assumed oversight of administrative functions and Renato Padovese, from the other family, over academic functions. Other members of both families left positions they had held at the university.

In 2002 the university began investing in distance education. In 2007, the owners acquired Módulo University Center and their campus on the coast of São Paulo state. In 2008, they bought Distrito Federal University Center, located in Brasília.

In 2012, Cruzeiro do Sul received capital from the private equity fund, Actis Capital, that allowed for additional expansion through the acquisition of other institutions. The investment amounted to approximately US$100 million, or 37 percent of all Cruzeiro do Sul shares. Actis Capital sold their shares in 2017 to

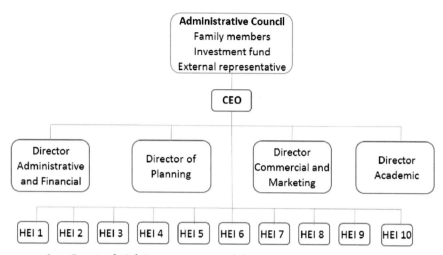

FIGURE 6.2   Cruzeiro do Sul Group organizational chart. (Source: Institutional Development Plan; Cruzeiro do Sul Group, 2018)

the Sovereign Fund of Singapore, that subsequently acquired a further 6.5 percent of Cruzeiro do Sul, resulting in control of 43.5 percent of the group. The fund's investment was approximately US$175 million. The other 56.5 percent is controlled by the Figueiredo and Padovese families.

In Brazil, educational groups arise from one or more families acquiring HEIs and forming a for-profit partnership with the aim of entering the educational market with professional management, long-term planning and financial goals. These amalgamations have the advantage of lower costs due to scale and the centralized administrative offices. Cruzeiro do Sul operates marketing, human resources, registrar functions, technology and information departments as a single, centralized unit (Figure 6.2).

The Cruzeiro do Sul Group will continue to acquire other educational institutions and will likely launch an IPO on the stock market. The Figueiredo and Padovese families remain in control of the institution after having professionalized the management structure and adopted standard practices for corporate businesses. Investors in the group also have decision-making power. The next challenge will be to balance financial interests and the institution's original essence that was shaped by founding friends who were teachers.

6.2   *Dom Bosco University Center (UNDB)*

In 1957, Maria Izabel Rodrigues, ultimately the chair of UNDB's administrative council, was invited by her friend, Maria de Lourdes Mendes, to partner in the establishment of a school. In 1958, the two teachers founded Little Thumb Kindergarten in São Luís, Maranhão, in northeastern Brazil. Family resources were combined with a bank loan that was approximately US$4,500 to purchase furniture, create a library, and assemble a classroom for 30 students.

A third collaborator, Maria Amelia Mendes, became a teacher and coordinator at the school. Mendes had studied pedagogy in Bahia where she learned teaching techniques through music and theater. She was part of Little Thumb until 1970, when she retired.

Since the 1960s, members of the Rodrigues family have participated in the city's education council and one relative was even involved in the state government. Maria Izabel Rodrigues's mother was a teacher and teaching coordinator in the public education system of São Luís. In 1960 she became the secretary of education for the city.

It was unusual for women to establish an educational institution in the 1950s in Brazil. Sexism was a significant influence in a society that was very conservative at the time, especially in the northeastern region. The teaching model they followed was also unusual for the time. The three female teachers established a model that favored student engagement in the learning process. Since its inception, learning at UNDB has involved music, theater, games, and group interaction.

Having achieved positive results with Little Thumb, the three Maria's—Maria Izabel Rodrigues, Maria de Lourdes Mendes, and Maria Amelia Mendes—were able to expand into a primary school that became the Dom Bosco School.

The school was inspired by Dom Bosco, a 19th century Italian priest in Turin, who worked with the education of young people through a series of playful activities. Dom Bosco was the founder of the Salesian congregation that operates primary, secondary and higher education institutions and social programs targeting youth at risk in more than one hundred countries. According to Dom Bosco's teachings, teachers must express interest and affection for their students and care for young people with learning difficulties. Dom Bosco provided essential inspiration for the school's pedagogical model.

The Dom Bosco School began with 30 students, even though 50 students applied at the time. In 1980, Maria de Lourdes, one of the founding members, decided to follow a different professional path. As a result, Maria Rodrigues became the sole owner of the school and her daughters, Maria Ceres and Elizabeth Pereira, began working at the institution as teachers. Over the years, the founder, her daughters, and five grandchildren would work at the school.

During the 1990s, parents at Dom Bosco School encouraged Maria Rodrigues to establish a higher education institution. In 1998 they were accredited as a college and were able to fully operate by 2002. The college was established as a for-profit institution, like the school. Since its inception, the institution has obtained top results in the evaluation processes conducted by the MEC, becoming one of the best HEIs in the state of Maranhão.

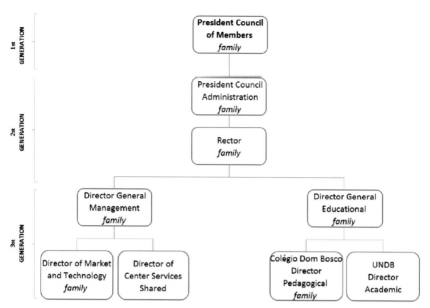

FIGURE 6.3   New UNDB organizational chart. (Source: Institutional Development Plan;
              UNDB, 2018)

In 2013, a consultant was hired to develop a structure for governance and management. The founder, her daughters and grandchildren participated in the process. A new management model (Figure 6.3) was implemented in 2015 and led to the creation of UNDB's administrative council. The council decided that UNDB's overall profit should be aimed at 30 percent of the earnings before interest, taxes, depreciation and amortization (EBITDA), and all managerial decisions should be aligned with achieving this goal.

According to the new model the family retains control of the business. The next steps were to consolidate the school and the college and to be recognized nationally for the development of an innovative academic model. In September 2018, the institution became a university center which allows for more autonomy and academic independence in the development of new programs as well as administrative flexibility.

6.3   Initiatives of the Toledo Family: UNITOLEDO University Center

UNITOLEDO maintains the tradition established by its founders to this day. In 2019, the rector was the great-grandson of founder, Antonio Eufrásio de Toledo, whom he honors by maintaining close relationships with students and pursuing the mission of transforming people's lives. UNITOLEDO is one institution among the many established by this one family.

Antonio Eufrásio de Toledo's story is somewhat typical of FOMHEIs in the countryside of Brazil. He was born in 1901 in the small town of Cambui in the state of Minas Gerais. He was born into a family of teachers and married Maria do Carmo Leite, also a teacher. He studied engineering and became a teacher in Cambui. He founded a school in Paraisópolis and later another in the city of Ouro Preto. The financial resources came from local donations since they were located in small towns and the local community was interested in opening schools to stimulate real estate development and attract families with children who would be potential tuition-paying students.

In 1949, Antonio Eufrásio decided to establish himself and his family in the city of Bauru because he saw an opportunity to establish yet another school. Bauru had already emerged as an agricultural and industrial city. Antonio Eufrásio founded a technical college where he offered courses in chemistry and structural engineering. Resources again came from local donations combined with family funds and bank loans.

In 1950, Antonio Eufrásio founded the Toledo Teaching Institute in Bauru that gave rise to one of the most significant ventures in the countryside of the state of São Paulo. In 1951, the institute launched the College of Law of Bauru. Ultimately, Antonio Eufrásio de Toledo led the administration of the following HEIs in the state of São Paulo:

- Toledo Educational Institute (ITE) in the city of Bauru, founded in 1950, an institution that spawned other HEIs in the countryside of the State of São Paulo.
- Lins University Center (UNILIS) in the city of Lins. Founded in 1958 as the Structural Engineering Technical School, it became the College of Engineering of Lins in 1964. In 1969 Antonio Eufrásio transferred the management and ownership of the institution to 30 professors.
- Toledo Prudente University Center (Toledo Prudente) in the city of Presidente Prudente, founded in 1961. The institution remains under the control of a relative of Antonio Eufrásio de Toledo.
- Toledo University Center (UNITOLEDO) in the city of Araçatuba, founded in 1966.
- College of Medicine of São José do Rio Preto (FMRP) in São José do Rio Preto, founded in 1968. Antonio Eufrásio de Toledo was responsible for the construction of the campus in cooperation with doctors and the city's government. In 1994 the institution became a public state college.
- São Manuel Institute of Higher Education (IMES) in the city of São Manuel, founded in 1972. In 1979, the administration was transferred to the city government.
- Botucatu Integrated Colleges (UNIFACS) in the city of Botucatu, founded in 1979.

The HEIs were founded with the benefit of land and buildings donated by the city government with support from local entrepreneurs, bank loans, and family resources. In Bauru, Araçatuba and Presidente Prudente, the institutions are still under the ownership of the Toledo family. In the other cities, the campuses were transferred to governmental entities or local communities. Antonio Eufrásio believed that his children could assume the management of all of the institutions he created, but that did not occur.

Antonio Eufrásio's son, Maurício Leite de Toledo, was a city councilor in Bauru (1964–1968) and federal deputy (1971–1974) where he presided over the education committee of the chamber of deputies. Maurício de Toledo was responsible for the expansion of the family's institutions. Federal deputy, Ulysses Guimarães, was also instrumental in the growth of the family's holdings. The political intervention by Guimarães occurred when Brazil needed to expand higher education enrollment. The state of São Paulo, the richest in Brazil, was able to coordinate the founding of HEIs throughout the state. Starting in the 1960s, some institutions under control of the Toledo family were donated and transferred to new ownership.

6.4   *UNITOLEDO*

UNITOLEDO was founded in Araçatub in 1966 with bank loans and donations from the private and public sectors. Antonio Eufrásio was the first rector. Maurício Leite de Toledo assumed leadership of the institution in 1975 although he had been involved with its management since its founding. The institution has approximately 6,000 students and 260 teachers.

The experience of Maurício de Toledo as a politician and educational manager positively influenced his administration of UNITOLEDO. He was the rector until he died in 2004. He had one son, Antonio Afonso de Toledo, who participated in the management of the institution, but died in 2000. Bruno Toledo, one of Antonio Alfonso's sons, assumed leadership of the administrative board at the age of 24, the role previously held by his father and grandfather. He became the rector of UNITOLEDO at age twenty-nine.

The other family members do not interfere in governance or management of the institution. An important characteristic of FOMHEIS is the frequent lack of professional preparation provided to successors assuming leadership positions and this has proved to be a problem for the administration of a complex organization. In the case of UNITOLEDO, this was evident when management passed from Antonio Eufrásio to his son, Maurício, and from Mauricio to his son, Afonso. The administration was based on the experiences of the three men and on family traditions without a well-defined governance model. In 2001, Bruno Toledo began to study educational management at São Marcos University in São Paulo and, as a result, strengthened UNITOLEDO's management structures, especially with regard to financial sustainability.

The professionalization of management took place in a context of heightened competition for students among different HEIs and it became clear that the institution needed to have a solid, long-term financial plan. Bruno Toledo began a process to manage UNITOLEDO's financial resources, cash flow, and the cost of each undergraduate degree more efficiently. Likewise, he began to establish criteria and a management system for student scholarships.

In recent years UNITOLEDO has been concerned with maintaining financial equilibrium while investing in projects to improve academic activity. For Bruno Toledo, the priority is to invest in areas that are aligned with institutional mission. He adheres to his great-grandfather's belief that higher education can transform lives through the achievement of an advanced qualification and workforce preparation that empowers youth and gives them the possibility of shaping and realizing dreams.

In 2010, the institution launched a strategy for enrollment growth and a process to improve the design and structure of governance. The institution has made progress (Figure 6.4) in management as well as in academic and financial planning. The academic results, as measured by the Ministry of Education, have improved since 2016. In 2018 the institution scored 5, the highest possible grade in institutional evaluation. The institution's goal is to maintain a balance between financial sustainability, academic quality, and inclusive teaching.

UNITOLEDO is now a reference for academic innovation and has joined the Conceive, Design, Implement, Operate (CDIO) movement that has influenced

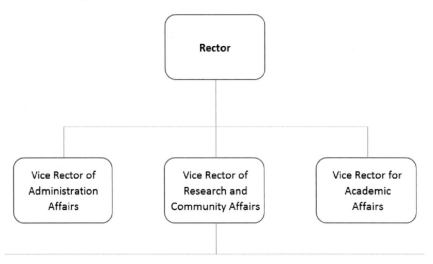

Undergraduation Coordinators

FIGURE 6.4   UNITOLEDO organizational chart. (Source: Institutional Development Plan; UNITOLEDO, 2018)

the reform of engineering education. The institution has invested in professional development for faculty and staff through successful collaborations with Finland, Denmark, the United States, Chile and Mexico. UNITOLEDO also created the Center for Academic Innovation and Administrative Training (NIFA) and has invested in laboratories, internationalization strategies, and infrastructure.

UNITOLEDO is on the way to becoming a benchmark for higher education in the state of São Paulo and in Brazil. UNITOLEDO hopes to remain true to Eufrásio de Toledo's dream of transforming people's lives and forming citizens with the capacity to shape their local communities in a thoughtful and collaborative way.

7   The Future of FOMHEI's in Brazil

The expansion of the Brazilian private higher education system occurred in a context in which three factors are particularly important—families realized the benefits of investing in higher education; politicians interested in increasing their electoral base supported these initiatives; and changes in legislation favored the creation of private HEIS.

The three cases presented in this chapter differ from institutions that pursued IPOS. The cases reveal the diversity of family trajectories as they built higher education institutions.

The three cases show significant differences. Some families advanced by pursuing private equity investments as in the case of Cruzeiro do Sul Group. The expansion of this educational group's business required corporate governance practices similar to companies that operate with budgets of millions of dollars. In the case of UNDB, it became clear that it was necessary to move to professional governance in order to establish management parameters and define the role of each family member. The institution has become an important reference for family-owned institutional governance by creating clear parameters for institutional dynamics and a board of directors that plays a key role in making corporate decisions.

UNITOLEDO was born out of Antônio Eufrásio's pioneering vision that influenced the institution's management and educational standards. Throughout the development of institutional projects, the commitment to transforming people's lives has remained unchanged and defines the leadership of the rector, Bruno Toledo. The institution continues to improve systems and processes for better governance and management. Although UNITOLEDO has not yet solidified its management model, it has produced respectable academic results as measured by MEC and has become a sustainable institution that invests in academic quality.

In recent years, the educational market has prioritized investment in distance education that grew 139 percent from 2009 to 2017 in the private sector. Undergraduate distance tuition averages US$910. HEIs that offer distance education and have reasonable MEC evaluations can open distance education centers. There are currently more than 15 thousand distance education centers in Brazil Many families understand that investing in distance education can help increase enrollment and improve financial performance. Some educational groups that invest in distance education evolved from family-owned institutions such as the Maringá University Center, controlled by two families with more than 10 thousand students in traditional courses and more than 100 thousand in distance education courses.

Brazil is likely to confront a dilemma in coming years. The expansion of higher education has been largely supported by institutions with a self-sustaining financial model dependent largely on student fees. That cannot generate a system adequate to meet the national need to train people with the skills and abilities to keep pace with the fourth industrial revolution. This does not mean that private higher education, FOMHEIs, or profit-reliant institutions are not necessary. Being a for-profit institution is sometimes the only option for survival in the regulatory and legal context of Brazilian education. The risk lies in focusing solely on financial models that satisfy the objectives of shareholders or making compromises to survive in a competitive environment. In general, family-owned companies have been more successful in achieving a balance between financial viability and a sound education. Even though profit to the owner families is legal according to Brazilian law, it is the institution's academic quality that determines their survivability.

In a highly competitive environment that lacks adequate resources coupled with a great deal of uncertainty in regard to the direction of a new government's educational policies, FOMHEIs may struggle to remain financially viable while maintaining academic quality. The future of family-owned institutions in Brazil will depend on the professionalization of management and governance, on the HEI's ability to participate in national and international networks, and on the implementation of institutional projects that promote innovation.

References

Capelato, R., & Garcia Reis, F. J. (2017). Panorama sobre a educação superior no Brasil e o impacto do financiamento estudantil na expansão das matrículas. In C. Rama

(Ed.), *La Universidad privada en America Latina y el Caribe* (pp. 69–82). Montevideo, Uruguay: Magro Editores.

Consultoria, K. P. M. G. (2018). *Fusões e Aquisições – 1º. Trimestre de 2018*. Retrieved from https://home.kpmg.com/br/pt/home/insights/2018/06/fusoes-e-aquisicoes-10-trimestre-de-2018.html

Corbucci, R., Kubota, L. C., & Meira, A. P. (2016). Evolução da educação superior privada no Brasil: da reforma de 1968 à década de 2010. *Revista Radar, 46*, 7–12. Retrieved from www.repositorio.ipea.gov.br/bitstream/11058/7066/1/Radar_n46_evolução.pdfCovac, J. R., & Coimbra, B. C. A. (2013). Maximização de resultados operacionais por meio da eficiência regulatória da educação superior. In D. C. Silva (Ed.), *Competitividade na gestão jurídico regulatória das entidades privadas do ensino* (pp. 123–141). São Paulo: Editora Ensinamento.

Cunha, L. A. (2007a). *A universidade crítica: O ensino superior na república populista*. São Paulo: Editora UNESP.

Cunha, L. A. (2007b). *A universidade reformada: O golpe de 1964 e a modernização do ensino superior*. São Paulo: Editora UNESP.

Garcia Reis, F. J. (2018). Sistemas de ensino superior inovadores e competitivos. In F. J. Garcia Reis (Ed.), *Inovar para transformar*. São Paulo: Editora Cultura.

Martins, C. B. (2009). A reforma universitária de 1968 e a abertura para o ensino superior privado no Brasil. *Revista Educação e Sociedade, 30*(106), 15–35. Retrieved from http://www.scielo.br/pdf/es/v30n106/v30n106a02.pdf

Ministério da Casa Civil da Presidência da República do Brasil. (1996). *Lei de Diretrizes e Bases da Educação Nacional (LDB), Lei 9.394*. Retrieved from http://www.planalto.gov.br/ccivil_03/Leis/L9394.htm

Morhy, L. (2003). *Universidade em questão* (Vol. 1). Brasília: Editora UNB.

Schwartzman, S. (1980). A crise da universidade. *Revista de Ensino Superior, 10*. Retrieved from https://www.revistaensinosuperior.gr.unicamp.br/artigos/a-crise-da-universidade

Schwartzman, S. (1988). *Brasil: Oportunidades e crise no ensino superior*. Retrieved from http://www.schwartzman.org.br/simon/pdf/oportun.pdf

CHAPTER 7

China: A Publicly Listed Private Higher Education Initiative

Kai Yu

1   China Education Group

China Education Group Holdings Limited was established as a holding company through which its subsidiary companies in China offer education management services to private education institutions. The holding group company became a publicly-listed company in December 2017. Its shares are listed on the Hong Kong Stock Exchange.

China Education Group operates mainly in the higher education sector but also maintains vocational schools for students age 15–18. By January 2019, it operated seven private education institutions including three bachelor-granting universities, one junior college, two technical colleges, and one vocational secondary school with a student enrollment of around 145,000.

The company was founded by two pioneers of private education in China, Yu Guo and Xie Ketao. Yu founded the institution that later became Jiangxi University of Technology in 1994 and Xie founded the Guangdong Baiyun University in 1989. Sharing the same vision for private higher education in China, Yu and Xie joined forces in 2007 to jointly manage the schools. Under joint management the institutions pursued cooperation with government organizations, education institutions, education exchange associations and private enterprises to improve student training and education, course design and content, applied learning programs, student enrollment and employment, and management know-how. Through their joint endeavors the overall competitiveness of the schools has been enhanced.

To expand the school network and to improve more schools by applying the company's successful model of management, the organization accepted investment from four investors including the International Finance Corporation of the World Bank, the Singapore Government Investment Corporation, the Chinese private equity firm Greenwoods, and Value Partners of Hong Kong. The company became a publicly-listed higher education group in Hong Kong in December 2017.

© KONINKLIJKE BRILL NV, LEIDEN, 2020 | DOI: 10.1163/9789004423435_007

The company is owned and ultimately accountable to its shareholders. The two founders of the company retain the majority of stock. Despite the involvement of its founders, China Education Group operates as an independent entity. Company management conducts executive and financial operations independently of the owners and a board of directors oversees the company's activities. The board of directors currently consists of seven members including four executive directors and three independent, non-executive directors. The board of directors sets the overall strategic direction for the company and appoints the chief executive officer. Therefore, China Education Group is a company largely owned by the two founding individuals but operating under a modern governance structure that meets the standards of a publicly-listed company.

2 The Context of the Higher Education System in China

Education is considered "the true religion of the people" and has always played an important part in Chinese tradition. Learning has always been highly valued and respected.

China is the world's largest higher education market in terms of student numbers, followed by India and the United States. Total student enrollment in higher education in China reached 37 million in 2016. The higher education participation rate stood at 41 percent. This figure is high compared to most developing countries but still falls behind many developed nations. Another useful figure is the acceptance rate to higher education based on the national university entrance exam. In 2017, 75 percent of the individuals who sat the exam entered a university. It is worth noting that high school education for students aged 15–18 is not compulsory and many students drop out of school at the age of 15. Increased participation in high school, promoted by central government policy, will lead to increased demand for higher education.

China's higher education can be divided into public and private sectors. China has about 3,000 higher education institutions of which 740 are private. Public higher education institutions are established and operated by national or local governments and their major source of funding comes from public expenditures on education, while private higher education institutions are established and operated by non-governmental institutions or individuals, and their major source of funding comes from school operations. There were about 260 independent colleges in China in 2017, often classified as private schools despite being formed by partnerships between a public university and private sponsors.

The Ministry of Education sets educational policies nationwide and also sponsors approximately 100 public universities. The remaining public universities and colleges are sponsored and administered by provincial governments. All private universities and colleges are supervised by provincial governments as well. Public and private higher education institutions are subject to the same governmental regulations for admissions and accreditation. For example, for the normal degree and junior college diploma programs, both public and private universities and colleges have to admit students based on the national entrance exam and admission is regulated by the government based on quotas.

The total revenue to Chinese private higher education has increased steadily from RMB69.6 billion (US$10.1 billion) in 2012 to RMB95.4 billion (US$13.9 billion) in 2016 and is expected to increase further to RMB139.0 billion (US$20.2 billion) by 2021. The total number of students enrolled in private higher education in China increased from 5.3 million in 2012 to 6.3 million in 2016 and is expected to increase to 8.0 million by 2021. Currently, 22 percent of students in higher education in China are studying at private institutions. This is expected to increase to 24 percent.

A major concern for higher education in China is the employment prospects of university graduates. It is becoming more difficult for graduates to secure a job. The proportion of recent graduates who are counted among the unemployed grew from 35 percent in 2005 to 45 percent in 2016. Markets increasingly demand graduates with professional skills, while in the previous environment when the higher education participation was low, graduate employment was not a problem.

Universities in China have been accustomed to theoretically oriented teaching instead of applied learning. More recently, many public and private universities have reoriented towards more applied education. Educational authorities at both the national and provincial levels have also promoted the development of applied education in universities. Compared to public research universities, most private higher education institutions conduct little research and emphasize applied learning oriented to the employment of their graduates.

The Chinese government has invested heavily in improving access and quality for basic and secondary education and is achieving very encouraging results. China has achieved universal access for primary and junior secondary and the participation rate for high school, including academic and vocational tracks, reached 88 percent in 2017. In higher education and vocational education, however, there is still a need for more affordable and quality education services offered by reliable education providers. The private higher education industry in China experienced rapid growth while the relevant government authorities endeavored to complete a regulatory framework.

2.1   The Nature of Private Universities in China

Although there were always scholars in ancient China, modern higher education in the country was introduced in the late 19th century influenced by the West. By 1947, China had established 207 universities including 107 governmental, 79 private, and 21 missionary institutions. The founding of the People's Republic of China (PRC) in 1949 marked a turning point for the nation as well as for its higher education system. Existing institutions were dismantled and systematically re-established with private and confessional institutions transformed or merged into public ones.

China adopted the Reform and Opening-up Policy in 1978 and some landmark actions were taken in regard to higher education including again permitting the establishment of private institutions. In 1999, amid the Asian financial crisis, the central government decided to massively increase university enrollment to help boost the domestic economy through increased private expenditure on higher education, construction of new campuses, increased employment of teachers and staff, improved productivity of the labor force, and delayed entry into the labor market for the university-age cohort. The establishment of private universities and so-called independent colleges (institutions established as a partnership between a public university and private sponsors) to absorb demand were encouraged during this time. In 2017 there were 741 private higher education institutions (HEIs) in the country including private universities offering four-year bachelor's programs, private junior colleges offering three-year junior college diploma programs, and independent colleges offering four-year bachelor's programs. In the same year, around 22 percent of the students in higher education in China were studying at private HEIs.

The education authorities classify and report higher education institutions as public, private, or independent colleges and do not define private institutions by the nature of the founder (individual, family, or professional corporation). Although there has been no systematic study, it is believed that most of the private HEIs are established and managed by private individuals. Because the schools are founded by individuals, it is not uncommon for relatives of the founder to engage in activities of the school. As almost all private higher education schools were established after 1990 and most of them after 2000, most of the founders are still managing the schools, but as time goes on more founders are, or will be, retiring and in many cases passing the management on to the next generations. In other cases, selling the school is an option.

Private education in China is usually referred to as Minban (民办), literally "run by the people." Although the Chinese phrase Sili (私立) represents "privately established" more precisely, it is not used often to refer to private higher educational institutions in China despite being frequently used to refer to private institutions in other countries. These institutions were traditionally referred to as schools "run by social force" (社会力量办学, Shehui Liliang Banxue) as they were administered under the state council's Rules for Social Force-Run Schools (社会力量办学条例, Shehui Liliang Banxue Tiaoli). Although Minban institutions generally receive no state subsidies they are tax-exempt and enjoy certain legal privileges applicable to public institutions.

The establishment of private institutions was encouraged after 1992 as the Chinese government gradually established a framework to govern public and private higher education. The Private Education Promotion Law (民办教育促进法, Minban Jiaoyu Cujin Fa) of 2002 established conditions for their operation. The law was amended in 2016 to categorize private schools into two different groups—for-profit and non-profit. Private schools in both groups are encouraged but are subject to different regulations such as entitlement to tax and land incentives, subsidies and freedom on deciding the tuition fees, etc.

Private HEIs initially served to supplement opportunities offered at public institutions by meeting unmet demand for higher education and often enrolled those who failed to gain admission to public institutions. As a result, public esteem for private HEIs is usually lower than for public HEIs. Subsequently, private institutions usually do not compete with public institutions because they are serving different markets and different prospective students.

A burgeoning middle-class presents vast opportunity for higher education and has become a key area for investment in China. A report by Deloitte (2016) refers to the "golden age of the Chinese education market." There has been a rapid increase of private capital flowing into the education industry. According to Deloitte, investment in the Chinese education industry in 2015 was more than double the amount invested in 2014. Mergers and acquisitions in the education industry increased by 165 percent year on year and initial public offerings (IPOs) increased by 76 percent from 2014–2015.

In 2018 there were over 740 private higher education institutions, and thousands of private vocational and technical schools, most founded, sponsored, and operated by individuals. Because the ownership and management has been fragmented, there is significant room for improvement in efficiency and instruction quality at many of these institutions. With many of the original sponsors of higher education institutions expected to retire over the next decade, China's fragmented private higher education industry is expected to undergo a wave of consolidation.

Student enrollment at institutions of higher education is subject to admission quotas set by government authorities. In provinces where student enrollment in higher education is low, the demand for higher education services generally exceeds supply. The admissions quota tends to be high creating growth potential and incentives for providers to expand services in these regions.

Another feature of the higher education sector in China is that there are now high barriers for entities wishing to establish new institutions. One barrier is the requirement to own land and buildings. Elsewhere in the world, it is common for universities to operate with leased land and buildings, but in China land and building ownership are often prerequisites for obtaining a university license. This has implications for capital expenditure and for the time needed to prepare the license application. Therefore, acquisitions offer a more efficient opportunity for market entry.

The acquisition activity in private higher education in China has reached record highs and the momentum continues as higher education groups compete for market share. As the industry consolidates and competition heats up, the larger players with stronger balance sheets are expected to step up their acquisitions of existing schools to further enhance the competitiveness of the group and their schools.

Private education groups normally evaluate schools based on their location, degree level, size, and subject areas; extensive research is done to identify schools with the greatest growth potential. For private universities to stand out, they usually need to earn a respectable reputation by focusing on career-oriented education.

Acquired schools can usually benefit from increased enrollment, size, and programmatic diversity. Taking course development as an example, a newly acquired school may establish new programs with the resources and experience of other schools in the education group, hence reducing the time and cost for course development at the new school. The success of these acquisitions will depend on the educational group's ability to leverage their resources to help the acquired schools meet changing market needs.

3   The Case Study

China Education Group's mission is to pioneer excellence and innovation in education. As an educational service provider, the group is committed to providing industry-leading higher education to students in China through student-centered teaching strategies and methods. The group integrates education and research to cultivate practical and workforce-ready graduates from a broad range of programs and who are prepared to excel in a technologically driven world.

The group was formed in 2007 by combining two prestigious private universities—Jiangxi University of Technology and Guangdong Baiyun University. The two founders, Yu Guo and Xie Ketao, were both engaged in commercial and industrial businesses before founding education institutions. The two institutions quickly became important private higher education institutions in their respective regions. The two schools were promoted to four-year undergraduate university status by the Ministry of Education (MOE) in 2005 and with an eye to greater competitiveness and synergies, Yu Guo and. Xie Ketao joined forces in 2007.

Yu Guo and Xie Ketao are vice-chairmen of the China Association for Private Education. Yu Guo was the only representative from the private education industry at the National People's Congress in the late 1990s where he promoted the promulgation of the Private Education Promotion Law that laid the foundation for the rapid development of private education in China.

Jiangxi University of Technology is located in Nanchang, Jiangxi. It enrolls 36,000 students making it the largest private university in the country; it was ranked number one in terms of overall competitive strengths in the Private University and College Ranking of China for nine consecutive years from 2009 to 2017. Guangdong Baiyun University is located in Guangzhou, Guangdong with 26,000 students. It was ranked number one in terms of competitive strengths among private universities and colleges in Guangdong province by the Guangdong Academy of Social Science for 12 consecutive years from 2005 to 2014.

The universities offer over 120 bachelor's degree programs in almost all major disciplines. In addition to recognition in the rankings, the two universities have received numerous awards from the government recognizing their achievement in education including the "First Class Award of Education" from the Guangdong provincial government to Guangdong Baiyun University and the "First Class Award of Education" from the Jiangxi provincial government to Jiangxi University of Technology. The group's education model to improve student innovation and entrepreneurship has been recommended by the state council as a successful example to all provincial education departments and national key universities.

3.1   *The IPO*

China Education Group raised US$ 420 million in its IPO, making it one of the largest IPOs in the Hong Kong market in 2017. Three months later, in March 2018, the group acquired two vocational schools in Zhengzhou and Xi'an. Zhengzhou School is China's largest vocational secondary school with 24,000 students. Its size is equal to that of the next five largest schools combined.

Meanwhile, Xi'an School is China's largest technical college with 20,000 students.

Although vocational schools cater to the 15 to 18-year-old age group, they are more like higher education institutions than traditional high school in that students focus their study in programs like computer science, electronics, arts, design, etc. Teaching resources are shared between vocational schools and higher education institutions. Looking forward, the group intends to expand in both the vocational and higher education sectors and create synergies among the schools in both sectors.

As a publicly-listed company, the company's stock prices change day to day but this has little impact on the daily operations of the group or its educational institutions. The group's mission is to pioneer excellence and innovation in education and to ensure more students have access to high-quality education. Operations are not influenced by short-run stock performance.

In any industry, integrating and aligning acquired organizations to objectives poses immense challenges. In fact, a large majority of mergers and acquisitions fail to achieve their hoped-for benefits. Some estimates put the success rate at less than 20 percent. China Education Group has a proven record of promoting its schools to be the top players in their respective categories. China Education Group is well positioned to improve the management of many more private higher education institutions in China.

3.2   Competitive Strengths
The following competitive strengths contribute to China Education Group's success and differentiate it from its peers.

3.2.1   Operating Well-Respected Private Higher Education Institutions
The two founders, Yu Guo Guo and Xie Ketao, were pioneers in private education in China. Jiangxi University of Technology and Guangdong Baiyun University were both among the first private bachelor's degree-level universities approved by the MOE in their respective provinces. Guangdong Baiyun University was behind the historic launch of the Association of Universities (Colleges) of Applied Technology in China and has been a leading force in promoting communication and cooperation among the member universities.

China Education Group's bachelor's degree programs and reputable vocational programs have fueled its continuous growth and enabled it to have a diverse student body to lower market risk. The large student body shows the popularity of these schools among students and reflects the quality and reputation of the group's education services, granting it a competitive edge over its peers.

3.2.2   Large-Scale Benefits

The group enrolls students across all 31 provinces, municipalities and autonomous regions in mainland China. In particular, the Jiangxi University of
Technology enrolled 36,000 students as of August 2017 and was the largest private university in China in terms of student enrollment as of that date. The
Guangdong Baiyun University enrolled 26,000 students as of August 2017.
The majority of students in the two universities are full-time, on-campus students admitted on the basis of the national university entrance exams. There
are additional part-time students in continuing education courses as well.
Through the technical school and universities, the group is able to offer a
variety of education programs and cater to different academic and vocational
needs of its students.

The schools in the group have a long history of inter-school cooperation
and sharing arrangements that have helped the group to implement comprehensive, efficient, and centralized management. Leveraging experience
accumulated over years, the group is well-positioned to implement centralized management functions in curriculum development, student recruitment,
career services, international courses, teacher training, etc. For the purpose
of implementing the above functions, the group's central administration
includes over 60 individuals with various professional backgrounds including
education management, information technology, legal compliance, business
administration, accounting, and finance.

3.3   *Elements of Success*

The private higher education industry has high entry barriers and early entrants
with an established brand name have better opportunities. China Education
Group has been able to extend its program offerings, amplify its academic
strengths, and further enhance its reputation and competitive advantages.

The success largely hinges on the quality of education and offerings that
China Education Group provides through its school network. The combination
of its universities and technical school cover higher education degrees in many
major areas. Its universities offer 80 bachelor's degree programs in economics,
law, education, literature, science, engineering, medicine, management and
arts and 32 junior college diploma programs in 11 junior college diploma disciplines categorized by the MOE. According to statistics published by the MOE
in 2016, the degrees offered by China Education Group cover areas where 97.7
percent of undergraduate students and 91.9 percent of junior college students
in China are enrolled.

Furthermore, the group has partnered with a number of overseas universities and colleges in the United States, United Kingdom, Australia, and South

Korea to offer exchange and joint-education programs. These programs are designed to add a global perspective for its students.

By 2017, the group's schools had established cooperative relationships with over 30 overseas universities and educational institutions. For example, Jiangxi University of Technology initiated cooperation with the University of Derby in the United Kingdom in 2017 to offer joint-education programs in environmental art design and clothing and costume design. Guangdong Baiyun University has cooperated with Western Sydney University in Australia in bachelor's and master's degree programs for students in translation and commerce majors. The group also admits international students to diversify its student base. With the implementation of the "One Belt, One Road" national strategy, more foreign students will be interested in studying in China.

In addition to comprehensive offerings and international education programs, the group's team of experienced and dedicated teachers and its research capacity have further solidified its brand. Approximately 59.6 percent of its faculty members have a master's degree or higher and approximately 9.3 percent of faculty members hold doctoral degrees. Some of the faculty members have been involved in authoring and publishing textbooks covering a variety of subjects. The group's focus on scientific research and innovation differentiates it from other, lower-ranked private higher education institutions. The group has also obtained 1,142 patents in China.

The group has also developed a series of workplace simulation training programs to provide students with a replicated work environment. As of August 2017, Jiangxi University of Technology had established over 10 simulation training centers and numerous laboratories on the campus. In view of its focus on the education of applied technology, double-qualification teachers are of great importance for the realization of its educational goals. "Double-qualification teacher" refers to full-time teachers with the title of lecturer or above and certain professional qualifications or industry experience. By August 2017, the group had 1,195 double-qualification teachers representing 33.9 percent of the total number of teachers. Its schools also emphasize cooperation with relevant enterprises in terms of research and development.

3.3.1   Strategic Geographical Locations and Cutting-Edge Practical
          Curriculum

The locations of the group's schools were strategically planned. Prior to the IPO, the schools were either in the Pan-Yangtze River Delta Economic Zone or the Pan-Pearl River Delta Economic Zone. Undergraduate students in these two regions accounted for 33 percent of the total number of undergraduate students in China in 2016. Consisting of only eight provinces, municipalities and autonomous regions, these two economically vibrant regions in China also accounted for approximately 43 percent of the total GDP of China in 2016. As a result of favorable economic policies, well-developed infrastructure and rapid urbanization, these two regions continue to attract domestic and foreign enterprises and create job opportunities for the large inflow of the labor from other regions. Approximately 46 percent of all university graduates with a bachelor's degree in China were employed in these two regions in 2016.

Guangdong Baiyun University and Baiyun Technician College are located in Guangzhou, Guangdong province, one of China's most developed provinces, with a GDP of approximately RMB8.0 trillion (US$1.16 trillion) in 2016. Guangdong province is among the locations most preferred by college graduates in China for post-graduation employment due to ample opportunities and relatively high starting salaries. Guangzhou has also been reviewed as the best city for commercial activities in mainland China five times by *Forbes*, due to its ability for rapid economic development and to promote innovation. Guangzhou attracts many enterprises, including tech companies, presenting abundant employment opportunities.

Jiangxi University of Technology is located in Nanchang, Jiangxi province, in the vicinity of Zhejiang province and Guangdong province, that are among the most developed provinces in China with high GDP rates. Nanchang was named one of the 10 most dynamic cities in the world in 2006 by *Newsweek* magazine. The group has been cultivating the private higher education market in Guangdong province and Jiangxi province and has fostered positive relationships with local government and employers. Its deep understanding of the private higher education market in those regions and its position as a market leader are of great value for its high success in graduate employment.

The group has partnered with a number of enterprises to provide students with internship and training opportunities as well as potential employment. Built upon its strong relationships with over 400 enterprises, the group aims to closely cooperate with them for mutual benefit in terms of production, education, and research. Specifically, some of its enterprise partners provide equipment and facilities needed for teaching activities so that students can have opportunities to apply newly acquired skills. In return, the group provides enterprise partners with research and development support and high-quality graduates for their operations.

With a view to stimulating graduate employment, the schools provide comprehensive career counseling services for their students. Due to the emphasis on career services, the group's schools stand out among private universities and colleges in China with a high graduate employment rate. In 2014, 2015, and 2016, the initial employment rate of Jiangxi University of Technology was 88.3 percent, 88.4 percent, and 88.1 percent respectively; the initial employment rate of Guangdong Baiyun University was 96.2 percent, 96.6 percent, and 96.1 percent respectively and for Baiyun Technician College, it was 99.3 percent, 99.4 percent, and 99.4 percent respectively. In contrast, China's overall initial employment rate for higher education graduates in the same years was approximately 77.5 percent, 77.7 percent, and 77.9 percent.

3.4   *Business Strategies*
The group's vision is to become a leading global education group providing high-quality education services to a significant number of students. In the short term, it will continue to solidify its position as a renowned, large-scale private higher education provider by optimizing pricing and increasing the student base of its existing schools including the development of its new campus in Guangzhou. It will also actively seek acquisition and business cooperation opportunities to further expand its existing and sizeable school network. In the medium to long term, the group will consider diversifying its revenue sources through leveraging its large student capacity, providing high value-add international programs, establishing online courses and expanding its business beyond China. To achieve these goals, it plans to pursue the following business strategies.

3.4.1   Develop a New School Campus to Increase Capacity
The group is developing a new campus for Guangdong Baiyun University. The new campus is located in Baiyun district in Guangzhou. The construction of the new campus is expected to proceed in phases. The group expects the new campus to be fully developed around 2021. Once fully developed, the new campus is expected to occupy an area of 498,000 m² and accommodate approximately 26,000 students.

3.4.2   Further Enhance the Competitiveness of Its Students and Curricula
The quality of the group's education and the image of its brand are crucial to its business growth. The group intends to continue enhancing its ability to provide quality higher education and maintain its high employment rate. The group plans to further solidify its competitive advantages in the private higher education market and maintain its leading market position to upgrade its national brand to an international education brand for competitive potential in the global market.

3.4.3   Expand the School Network
With its capital raised through the IPO and future debt-raising capacity, the group is in a net cash position and intends to further expand its school network

to extend its geographic coverage and increase market penetration in the private higher education industry. The group plans to add suitable universities, junior colleges, and technical schools to its school network through acquisition, cooperation, or other means.

Based on the group's market research and analysis there are an estimated 200 education institutions in the PRC that are within the group's potential acquisition target. The group has a target of acquiring 51 percent to 100 percent equity interest in these institutions.

The group's successful operating history and its established premium school brands afford it significant competitive advantages for network expansion. Given the competitive landscape, a considerable number of schools aiming to improve their education quality and achieve economies of scale will be willing to join a school network operated by an education group with a strong brand and advanced management system. The group plans to optimize the management, operations, curriculum, and pricing strategy of the acquired schools helping them to improve. With the group's extensive operational experience in private university management, it will also consider the feasibility of converting acquired junior colleges into private universities to offer bachelor's degree programs.

The group intends to integrate newly acquired schools into the school network and incorporate them into its centralized management system to improve operating efficiency, increase their size, and optimize their pricing strategies. The schools have sufficient talent reserves including experienced senior or middle-level management as well as teachers and administrative staff who are available for immediate dispatch to new schools to help improve management and teaching capabilities quickly. Moreover, the group's comprehensive program offerings covering a broad range of disciplines and extensive experience in education program design and implementation will enable it to expand discipline coverage in new schools and effectively enhance educational quality.

Newly acquired or joined schools could immediately benefit from the group's broad student recruitment network covering all provinces, municipalities and autonomous regions in China that will improve enrollment qualitatively and quantitatively. In terms of graduate employment, the group will share its employment information and resources with all schools within its network. The close relationship with over 400 enterprises will significantly benefit the newly-acquired or joined schools. The group's teaching management system and administrative information system could also be adopted by new schools and could implement online management of teaching affairs, dormitories, student recruitment, and tuition payment. The adoption of these systems will improve management efficiency and lower the operating costs of newly- incorporated schools.

To support the expansion plan, the group operates a head office in Hong Kong and offices in Shanghai and Guangzhou to identify, assess, and evaluate potential targets and implement its investment plan. The group has also established a management department to take charge of the post-acquisition integration and management with its extensive internal support systems and resources.

3.5   *Post-IPO Acquisitions*

In March 2018, China Education Group acquired two schools in Zhengzhou and Xi'an in China. Although the market expected these initiatives, these two acquisitions came earlier and were more substantial than anticipated. The two acquired schools were Zhengzhou City Rail Transit School, China's largest private vocational school with 24,000 students and Xi'an Railway Technician College, China's largest technical college with 20,000 students. The largest and second largest technician colleges in China are both operated by China Education Group. Zhengzhou is in the heart of Central China and Xi'an is in the heart of Northwestern China. The regional economies are growing rapidly and there is significant demand for quality education.

In June 2018, China Education Group acquired two additional schools in Guangzhou. The two acquired schools, Guangzhou University Songtian College and Guangzhou Songtian Polytechnic College, have solid educational foundations. The former is a fully accredited university at the bachelor's degree level with 8,700 students while the latter is a vocational college with 3,300 students. Upon completion of the two deals, total student enrollment for China Education Group is expected to reach 132,000.

Guangzhou University has more than 90 years of history in education and is a key comprehensive university supported by the Guangdong provincial government and Guangzhou municipal government. The two higher education institutions have built a strong academic reputation and their graduates are in high demand and valued by business enterprises. The initial employment rate of graduates of Guangzhou University Songtian College was 95.6 percent in 2017. For Guangzhou Songtian Polytechnic College, the initial employment rate was 100 percent for graduates of 10 of the 17 professional programs it offers, while the overall employment rate for all graduates was 98.4 percent.

Guangdong province, where the two acquired schools are located, has promising development prospects for higher education. Guangzhou City, situated right at the heart of the Pearl River Delta, is where Cisco, Huawei, GAC

Group, Qualcomm, Foxconn, Microsoft, and GE have launched projects and their presence has spurred demand for high-caliber talent. China Education Group's strategic deployment in the city will not only help address the demand for quality higher education in the region, but also enable the group to capture strategic development opportunities in the Guangdong–Hong Kong–Macao Big Bay Area.

China Education Group integrates newly acquired schools into all of its management and services such as IT, finance, and course development. Taking course development as an example, the group as a whole, offers over 300 programs covering virtually all the popular programs in China, so it can contribute new programs to a newly acquired school by leveraging existing resources and experience, reducing time and cost. Thus, merged entities benefit from increased enrollment size and programmatic diversity.

With an excellent 30-year track record in education, the group has continued to deliver on its mission statement—to pioneer excellence and innovation in education and to ensure more students have access to high-quality education. The inclusion of the new schools in the group's network mirrors the highly effective and well-paced strategic advancement the group has achieved and its confidence in the potential of education development in the regions. The group will empower all its member schools, enabling them to share resources and reap the benefits of synergies, thus enhancing their capability to nurture talent. More students will be able to receive high-quality education and highly skilled human capital will benefit companies and local economic development.

3.6   Challenges

Private higher education in China, as elsewhere, is highly regulated and developments in the sector are usually sensitive to regulatory changes. Still, China is usually characterized as low risk in that the demand is strong while supply is limited. Tuition is charged upfront and therefore there is limited financial uncertainty and students are usually mature and present less risk.

One challenge faced by many private higher education schools is the transition of ownership and management. As many founders are reaching the age of retirement, ownership and management transition is becoming a pressing issue. Where a second generation is interested in taking over, passing ownership and management to the next generation is an obvious choice, but a smooth handover is key. But if the founders consider exiting from ownership, there are still opportunities within China Education Group as it has the resources and expertise to take over.

3.6.1   Regulatory Environment

In general, private higher education in China, including China Education Group, faces challenges stemming from continued growth in the regulatory environment, enrollment quotas, and fee level restrictions.

The regulation of private education in China is undergoing major change with the introduction of the Private Education Promotion Law 2016. Under the new law, all non-compulsory private schools need to choose for-profit or non-profit status and are subject to different policies accordingly. For-profit schools are expected to be subject to tax and land fees although the new law also provides room for the government to introduce tax and land incentives for these institutions. For-profit schools will have the discretion to set their own tuition fees. Non-profit schools enjoy more tax, land and subsidy incentives, but are subject to greater scrutiny and operational restrictions. Since China Education Group only operates non-compulsory post-15 schools, all of China Education Group's schools are eligible for for-profit status under the new law and would benefit from more flexibility under the new regulation.

3.6.2   Student Quotas

Student demand is one of the main drivers of private school expansion in China. The majority of the students in China Education Group's universities and junior colleges are following the normal degree or junior college programs and are subject to admission quotas set by the relevant education authorities. A wide array of factors is generally taken into consideration by local education authorities in allocating admissions quotas including the capacity of the school, the quality of education, the school's reputation, regional economic and educational conditions and most importantly, the supply and demand of higher education in the region. China Education Group carefully selects regions in China with high unmet demand for higher education and enters these regions only where its schools have high potential for student quota growth.

3.6.3   Fee Level Restriction

According to the current regulations, fee levels at private higher education schools are administered by provincial governments. Different provincial governments have implemented different policies. In some provinces fee levels for private educational institutions are liberalized, granting institutions considerable autonomy; in others there are governmental restrictions. Because private education institutions may incur increased costs in the transition to for-profit status, these institutions may expect to increase fee levels. According to the Private Education Promotion Law 2016, for-profit private schools have discretion in regard to fee levels. It is not yet clear how the market or government will respond to fee level changes after the transition period.

4   Conclusion

In China, business models for higher education are beginning to shift away from an emphasis on student quantity and focus instead on improving the quality of their services. Education institutions are focusing on differentiating themselves through quality of instruction to attract students. According to the latest statistics, the proportion of recent higher education graduates who are among the unemployed has grown year on year from 35 percent in 2005 to 45 percent in 2016. The labor market increasingly demands graduates with professional skills while most public universities in China continue to focus on academic research. Private universities are earning their reputation by focusing on career-oriented education.

In China, there are currently over 740 private higher education institutions and thousands of private vocational and technician schools. Most of the private schools are founded, owned, and operated by individuals. In fact, most of these schools were established since 2000 and many of the original founders are approaching retirement and considering an exit, some by selling the school. There are abundant acquisition opportunities in the market.

In a slower-growth environment, more companies rely on mergers and acquisitions as an engine for driving growth. In fact, other industries, including healthcare, banking, automobile, and electronics manufacturing, have faced similar circumstances and responded with a wave of mergers and acquisitions across these sectors. While situations vary, the objective of business mergers is generally similar to what people hope to see in higher education—continued growth and impact, greater efficiency, greater economies of scale, better value, improved competitiveness, and, in some cases, improved chances for long-term survival.

Another feature of the higher education sector in China is the extremely high entry barriers set for the creation of new schools. One prominent example is the government's requirement to possess land and buildings. This has implications for the capital needed and for the time required to pursue licensing. It is therefore difficult for newcomers to enter this market.

The acquisition activity in higher education in China has reached record highs and the momentum continues as companies compete for market share. With significant support from stock and private equity investors, awareness has grown about the potential of the industry and the number of educational companies has soared; industry leaders have begun to emerge. There are eight education providers currently listed on the Hong Kong Stock Exchange and five of them offer higher education. There are eight more applying for listings in Hong Kong and four of them provide higher education. China Education Group pursued a public listing in Hong Kong in December 2017. Looking to the future and with access to international investors, China Education Group will capitalize on its best-in-class education and its financial and management capacity to improve the educational quality and operational efficiencies at more higher education institutions in China.

References

Deloitte. (2016, May). *Golden age of China's education industry: Seize the momentum.* Retrieved from https://www2.deloitte.com/content/dam/Deloitte/cn/Documents/technology-media-telecommunications/deloitte-cn-tmt-golden-age-of-the-chinese-education-market-en-160713.pdf

Kwong, J. (1997). The reemergence of private schools in socialist China. *Comparative Education Review, 41*(3), 244–259.

Li, F., & Morgan, W. J. (2008). Private higher education in China: Access to quality higher education and the acquisition of labour market qualifications by low-income students. *Education, Knowledge & Economy, 2*(1), 27–37.

Lin, J. (1999). *Social transformation and private education in China.* Westport, CA: Greenwood Publishing Group.

Lin, J., Zhang, Y., Gao, L., & Liu, Y. (2005). Trust, ownership, and autonomy: Challenges facing private higher education in China. *China Review, 5*(1), 61–81.

Mok, K. H. (1997a). Privatization or marketization: Educational development in post-Mao China. *International Review of Education, 43*(5–6), 547–567.

Mok, K. H. (1997b). Private challenges to public dominance: The resurgence of private education in the pearl river delta. *Comparative Education, 33*(1), 43–60.

Mok, K. H., & Wat, K. Y. (1998). Merging of the public and private boundary: Education and the market place in China. *International Journal of Educational Development, 18*(3), 255–267.

Wu, H. (2009). Prospects of private education in China. *Chinese Education & Society, 42*(6), 40–60.

Yan, F., & Levy, D. (2015). China's new private education law. *International Higher Education, 31*, 9–10.

Yang, R. (1997). Private higher education development in China. *International Higher Education, 9*, 8–9.

Zha, Q. (2006, March). The resurgence and growth of private higher education in China. *Higher Education Perspectives, Special Issue*, 54–68.

CHAPTER 8

Colombia: The Complex Reality of Family Universities

Gabriel Burgos Mantilla

This chapter provides a description and analysis of FOMHEIs, family-owned or managed institutions, in Colombia. The chapter offers information about the origin and status of the Colombian higher-education system with statistical data and information about the nature of private institutions. This is followed by three case studies of family-owned higher education institutions— Corporación Universitaria Rafael Núñez located in Cartagena de Indias and Barranquilla, Corporación Universitaria del Meta (UNIMETA) in Villavicencio and Universidad Piloto de Colombia with campuses in Bogotá and Girardot. In Colombia there are 52 family universities that represent 18 percent of the total 292 higher education institutions and 27.5 percent of non-religious private institutions.

The chapter concludes with an analysis of the current situation of these institutions within the Colombian higher education context and finally the challenge of transferring leadership to a new generation.

1 Historical Context

Colombian universities were first established during the Spanish colonial period between 1550 and 1810. They were founded and governed by the Roman Catholic Church with authorization from the Spanish crown. The earliest universities were the Universidad Santo Tomás, Colegio San Bartolomé, Universidad Javeriana, and Colegio Mayor de Nuestra Señora del Rosario.

The dominance of the Roman Catholic church continued through much of the 19th century. Lay institutions exclusively under state supervisions were established slowly over the course of the century—Universidad de Cartagena and Universidad de Cauca (1827), Universidad Nacional (1867) in Bogotá, and Universidad de Antioquia in Medellín (1871). However, following the defeat of the radicals in the revolution of 1885, the conservative party restored control over education to the Catholic church. In protest, the radicals founded the law school, Externado de Derecho, in 1886 that today is the Universidad Externado de Colombia.

© KONINKLIJKE BRILL NV, LEIDEN, 2020 | DOI: 10.1163/9789004423435_008

During the second decade of the 20th century the strict control over education by the conservative regime began to loosen and greater independence evolved at lay universities in two stages. The first stage saw the creation of the Universidad Republicana in 1913, the reopening of the Externado de Derecho in 1918, and the creation of Universidad Libre in 1923. All of these institutions were private. The liberal party came to power in 1930 led by President Alfonso López Pumarejo (1934–1938) and amendments to the Constitution eliminated the monopoly of the Catholic church over education and allowed the state to regain control over public universities and schools. The Catholic church reacted by fortifying the Universidad Pontificia Javeriana in Bogotá in 1934 and founding the Pontificia Universidad Bolivariana in Medellín in 1938.

The liberal party lost power in 1946 and the conservative regime returned authority over education to the Catholic church. In response, lay, non-confessional universities were established in what may be seen as a second stage of higher education evolution. The institutions created during this period were the Universidad de Los Andes (Uniandes), Universidad de Medellín, Universidad Santiago de Cali, and the Universidad Autónoma de Bucaramanga (originally created as the Instituto Caldas).

This was the state of Colombian higher education until the rectors of public universities and elite private institutions of higher education, entreating the reestablishment of normalcy, created the Colombian Association of Universities (ASCUN) in 1957 to represent university perspective and concerns to the government.

A period of expansion in Colombian higher education followed in which the first family-owned institutions were created. The University of America in 1956 was established by Dr. Jaime Posada, former minister of education, in Bogotá and the Autonomous University of the Caribbean in 1967 by lawyer and ex-magistrate, Mario Ceballos Araujo, in Barranquilla. Posada had been instrumental in the creation of ASCUN.

This same period saw other changes in higher education including the development of graduate studies and three new modes of delivery—evening classes aimed primarily at working adults, distance education seen as a solution for expanding access for those whose opportunities were limited due to geographic or financial circumstances, and online or virtual education that began to transform distance education.

Contemporary higher education in Colombia is defined by the recognition of university autonomy in the Constitution of 1991, Law 30 of 1992 that organizes the Colombian higher education system, and the creation of the Vice-Ministry of Higher Education.

In 2002 the state established the *Registro Calificado*, a system that requires all institutions to undergo an evaluation in order to be listed in the national registry and recognized legally as a degree-granting institution (Law 1188, 2008). In addition, a system of voluntary accreditation provides an endorsement of a higher level of quality.

2   Colombian Higher Education: Categories and Statistics

According to statistics published by the Ministry of Education, by 2018 there were 292 institutions of higher education in Colombia that fell into four categories—*universidades* (universities); *instituciones universitarias* (university institutions) and *escuelas tecnologícas* (technological schools); *instituciones tecnológicas* (technological institutions); and *institutos técnicos profesionales* (professional technical institutes). The distinctions are confusing, even in Colombia.

Universidades conduct scientific or technological research, education for the professions and academic disciplines, and the production and transmission of knowledge and culture. They offer programs at the undergraduate and graduate levels including professional and technical specializations, master's degrees and doctorates in accordance with the requirements specified in Law 30 of 1992. There are 85 institutions in this category with 31 public, 53 private, and one in a special category created for institutions with a special purpose and supervised by an entity other than the Ministry of Education, such as a military school.

Instituciones universitarias or *escuelas tecnológicas* are those authorized to offer vocational and academic programs in professions, disciplines, and specializations. Like universities, they offer programs at the undergraduate and graduate levels and professional and technical specializations. They may pursue authorization from the Ministry to offer master's and doctoral programs. In total, there are 128 institutions in this category—17 public, 99 private, and 12 special regime.

Instituciones tecnológicas can offer and develop training provided in shorter cycles. Students can complete a first cycle of study in a professional technical program with the option to continue and reach the level equivalent to a university professional after fulfilling all requirements required by law. These institutions can offer professional technical programs and technological programs at the undergraduate level and some professional and technical specializations at the graduate level. There are 49 institutions in this category—five public, 38 private, and six special regime universities.

Institutos técnicos profesionales are those that offer training programs oriented to employment with a specialization in a particular field. They can offer undergraduate, professional technical programs, and graduate-level technical specializations. There are 30 institutions in this category with nine public and 21 private institutions.

Nationally there are 62 public institutions, 211 private, and 19 operating in a special regime category. In 2017 the Ministry recorded 2,446,314 students enrolled in higher education almost evenly divided between the private and public sectors—50.7 percent in the public sector and 49.3 percent at private institutions. The size of Colombian private higher-education institutions varies considerably with enrollments between 2,500 and 10,000. Although some institutions have grown by expanding distance and virtual offerings, enrollment at individual institutions remains much smaller than at some of the large private institutions in other Latin American countries such as Brazil, Mexico, or Argentina.

3 Private Universities

According to Colombian legislation private higher education institutions can only be constituted as foundations or non-profit civil corporations (Law 30, Article 98, 1992) and are established for the public good; assets cannot be considered shares or capital or provide private benefits. Assets cannot be distributed among the members of a family that might make up the governing body but must be reinvested in the improvement of the institution's activities. In Colombia, private higher education institutions, according to their origins and control, are classified into four groups—corporate, business, religious, or family institutions.

Corporate universities are developed by business owners or stakeholders who seek to replicate the model of the non-profit research-oriented North American private university. This group includes the Universidad de Los Andes, Universidad EAFIT, Universidad Autónoma de Bucaramanga, Universidad del Norte, Universidad ICESI, Colegio de Estudios Superiores de Administración (CESA), Universidad de Ibagué, Universidad Autónoma de Manizales, and others.

Business universities were founded in the 1980's following the expansion boom in Colombian higher education. Their main objective is to offer academic programs based on market demand and make a profit. Examples are Politécnico Grancolombiano and Fundación Universitaria del Área Andina).

Religious universities are institutions affiliated with the Roman Catholic Church or other faiths. This group includes the Pontificia Universidad Javeriana, Pontificia Universidad Bolivariana, Universidad de San Buenaventura, Universidad Santo Tomas de Aquino, Corporación Universitaria Minuto de Dios, Universidad de la Sabana, Corporación Universitaria Adventista, and others.

Family-owned or managed universities (FOMHEIS) are set up by a family or by family groups. The fundamental characteristic of this type of institution is the dominance of family members in the management and administrative bodies of the institution. This group includes the Universidad de América, Universidad Autónoma del Caribe, Corporación Universitaria Rafael Núñez, Corporación Universitaria del Meta, Universidad Piloto de Colombia, Corporación Universitaria Remington, Universidad EAN, and others.

4   Differences between Family Companies and FOMHEIS

A family business is one in which "a single family owns the majority of the capital and has total control; the members of the family are part of the management and make the most important decisions" (Gallo & Sveen, 1991).

A family university in Colombia cannot be totally conformed as part of a family business because it is not *owned* by a person or a family group. As in a commercial society, there is a maximum authority for management and governance that is usually referred to as the *sala general* or *asamblea* (general board) made up of a members who annually review the financial results of the previous year, the projections for the next year, and make decisions that require board approval. In addition, there is another administrative body designated by the general board that is usually called the *consejo superior, junta directive,* or *consiliatura* that meets at least once a month for management and academic administrative purposes.

These two authoritative bodies develop and operate under statutes that they have established themselves in keeping with the autonomy awarded to all higher education institutions in Colombia. The exercise of autonomy requires compliance with two conditions. The first refers to the makeup of the general board where there must be at least one representative of the faculty and one representative of the students (Decree 1478, 1994). The second condition is that the creation of the institution and changes to the statutes are presented to the Office of Inspection, the entity responsible for compliance with existing laws and regulations on education. The aims and objectives of this office are monitored and controlled by the Vice-ministry of Higher Education.

There are some similarities in the nature of a family business and a family university. "Family" is reflected in the fact that members of the family maintain control by making decisions about institutional operations, designating the highest level of management, and controlling the succession of leadership and generational transitions.

FOMHEIs in Colombia are private higher education institutions that, like all private institutions, are created as a non-profit foundation or civil corporation (Law 30, Article 98, 1992). As explained above they are created as organizations for the public good and cannot distribute profits to the family involved with the institution. In the event that the institution earns a profit, it should be reinvested in the improvement, development, and growth of the institution. These institutions are privileged with special tax status that exempts them from taxes that would be charged to a private company in Colombia.

FOMHEIs are distinguished from other Colombian private institutions as they are operated by a family group that dominates the institution's governing body and thus exercises control over the management of the institution with authority to modify its statutes, including the determination of who makes up the general board and board of directors, how often they meet, how members are selected, the quorum required for decisions, and other critical aspects of institutional management.

4.1   Characterization of the FOMHEIs

Thirty-five percent of family universities (18 institutions) are multi-campus and operate in different cities. In Colombia, 75 percent of family universities are located in three major cities. There are 27 family institutions in Bogotá, seven in Medellín, and five in Bucaramanga. Following the pattern of the Colombian national system, family institutions are concentrated in major urban areas. This limits access for rural populations and smaller municipalities to traditional classroom education.

According to data published by the Ministry of Education at the end of 2017, 1,204,524 students were registered in the private higher education sector, with 349,070 students or 29 percent of private enrollment in one of the 52 family universities. This accounts for 14 percent of the total student population.

Research is not a distinguishing feature of family universities. In 2017 COL-CIENCIAS, the national science foundation of Colombia, indicated that only six percent of national research groups have connections to the FOMHEIS.

Three case studies of FOMHEIS follow and reflect the characteristics of this sector. Each case study includes a brief historical overview, family involvement, the nature of its holdings (size and scope of each institution), governance, and its place in the larger context of Colombian higher education system.

5   Corporación Universidad Piloto de Colombia (UNIPILOTO)

UNIPILOTO developed from a student movement in the school of architecture of a private Colombian university in the 1960s. A group of students supported by political leaders of the time, successfully established the institution on September 14, 1962. It started academic activities in a large house in Bogotá with a degree program in architecture. The first students graduated in September 1970. UNIPILOTO earned official status as a university in 1972.

According to the rector, Angela Bernal (Private interview, February 6, 2019), the founding members were reduced to a group of 17 people who wrote and signed the statutes of incorporation on December 12, 1994. Eight members of the group remained active and participated in the highest level of management as "founding members." The other four members of the governing board do not belong to the founding generation but were designated as substitutes to represent the founding families. The founders of UNIPILOTO maintain control of the institution and have approved a protocol for selecting replacements for members who have retired or are deceased.

Four of the founding families continue to be represented in management and dominate senior administrative roles:

- The Bernal family. Two members—Jose Angel Bernal Arraiz and Stela Medina de Bernal—participated in the founding of UNIPILOTO. Following Jose Angel Bernal Arraiz's retirement, he designated his daughter, Angela Bernal Medina, as his representative on the general board and board of directors, together with his mother, Stella Medina de Bernal. The daughter occupies the role of rector and the mother the role of director of academic records and control.
- Family Sánchez. Jorge Sánchez Puyana, a founder, is a member of the general board and the board of directors. Three of the members of the next generation are also involved with the institution.
- Family Cifuentes. José Maria Cifuentes Páez, a founder, is president of the general board and board of directors. His three children hold key positions within the university.
- Family Farfán. Jairo Alfredo Farfán Barreto is a founder and vice president of the general board. Two of his daughters hold key positions in the institution.

Two other founders, Orlando Gómez Quintero and Carlos Hernández Campo are members of the general board and board of directors and involved in the leadership of the institution.

UNIPILOTO has evolved to become a medium-size university in the Colombian context. It offers 27 programs at the undergraduate and graduate levels in the cities of Bogotá and Girardot. In the second half of 2018 it reported a total enrollment of 9,195 students. The programs are taught mainly on campus with only two virtual graduate programs. The university's tuition falls at a mid-point between a traditional large, private and a recently created university that has not attained institutional accreditation.

5.1   Family Involvement

As mentioned above, eight of the original group of students that created UNIPILOTO remain active and participate on the highest governing body as founding members. Another four members were appointed by the founders and act on behalf of their families. The founders of UNIPILOTO maintain control of the institution and have approved a protocol for replacing themselves based on recommendations made by the family member who dies or retires. There are members of a second generation—children or nephews—in management positions. The fact that some authority has passed to a second generation has not caused conflict or tension and has been a fluid transition.

The transition of management to the second generation has been addressed in meetings and documents prepared to regulate this process, but the founders have resisted approving and implementing anything officially. However, according to Ángela Bernal, the current rector and a second-generation family member, this is a priority issue to be resolved by the remaining founders.

5.2   Governance Structure

UNIPILOTO's highest governing body is the *sala general* (general board) made up of 12 members—eight founders and four members appointed by founders who are no longer on the board. The governing board elects the seven members of the *consiliatura* comprised of the president, the vice-president, four members of the general board, and the rector. The four members and the rector are the only ones who participate and vote during deliberations and decision-making. The *consiliatura* appoints the rector, the secretary general, the *síndico* (trustee) and others who are part of the academic administration including the vice-rectors, deans of the faculties, and program directors. The academic councils include the rector, the vice-chancellors, deans of faculties, administrative personnel of the academic programs, and representatives of the faculty, students, and graduates.

In accordance with the statutes, each member of the general board recommends the person who is to succeed him or her in the event of voluntary retirement or any incapacity that prevents continuing service. The nominee must be approved and ratified by a majority of the board.

6   Corporación Universitaria del Meta (UNIMETA)

On November 9, 1982, Rafael Mojica García, Nancy Leonor Espinel Riveros, and Ramiro Mojica García convened in Villavicencio to sign the Articles of Incorporation for Corporación Universitaria del Meta (UNIMETA). The institution received legal recognition in 1985 from the Ministry of Education. For 30 years its founder and rector was Rafael Mojica García.

UNIMETA is a small university in the context of Colombian higher education. It offers 25 undergraduate and graduate programs in Villavicencio. By the second half of 2018, it enrolled 2,671 students. Tuition in 2018 was comparable to costs of other private institutions operating in the same city.

6.1   Family Involvement

Rafael Mojica García was born 1944. He graduated from the Universidad Jorge Tadeo Lozano in Bogotá in 1970 with a degree in economics and taught at universities in that area. He became rector of the Universidad Cooperativa de Colombia, later vice-rector of the Universidad de los Llanos, and subsequently retired to start his own university project, the Corporación Universitaria del Meta (UNIMETA).

Rafael Mojica García served as rector of the institution from its founding until April 2016. Mojica García did not have any children so delegated control of the institution to his brother, Ramiro Mojica García, and two nieces, Leonor and Claudia Mojica Sánchez. Rafael Mojica García supported Claudia's education through graduation with a doctoral degree from Universidad de Salamanca in Spain. At the end of his life, Mojica García made changes to the institution's statutes ensuring that his nieces and brother held the majority of votes on the highest governing body of the institution. He designated his niece, Leonor, as rector.

Leonor Mojica Sánchez became the legal representative and rector of the institution in January 2016 and the other niece, Claudia Lucía Mojica Sánchez, became a member of the general board and vice-rector for administration and finance. Leonor Mojica Sánchez's husband holds a senior position in leadership as well.

6.2   Legal Status and Governance

The university is legally constituted as a non-profit civil corporation. The highest governing authorities are the *sala general*, the governing board and the highest management and administrative body, and the rector. The rector is the legal representative and highest academic and administrative authority of UNIMETA. In addition, several councils supervise academic activities, research, and teaching in accordance with the statutes and regulations of the institution. These include the *consejo superior*, the managing board of the institution.

The *sala general* is composed of five members—three are family members. All board members vote and decide appointments of other institutional authorities including the chairman of the governing board, rector, statutory auditor, and two representatives on the higher council. The *consejo superior* is made up of eight members—the chairman of the governing board, rector, representative of the deans, faculty, students, and two members appointed by the governing board.

As specified in the bylaws, each member of the governing board designates a person to succeed him or her in case of absence or disability. This nomination must be ratified by a majority of the board.

7   Corporación Universitaria Rafael Núñez (CURN)

CURN was established in the 1980s by Miguel Henríquez Emiliani and initiated activities in the city of Cartagena in 1987. In 1991, the campus moved to a colonial house within the historic walled section of the city. It received legal recognition from the Ministry of Education in 1985.

In the context of Colombian universities, CURN is a medium-size university offering 22 undergraduate and graduate programs in Cartagena and Barranquilla. In 2018, 5,357 students were enrolled. Tuition in 2018 is average for similar institutions in locations where the two CURN campuses are located.

7.1   *Family Involvement*

Miguel Henríquez Emiliani, founder and principal of the institution, led the institution from its founding until 2012 when he was replaced by his son, Miguel Ángel Henríquez Lopez. Carmen Lopez de Henríquez, the founder's wife and his children—Miguel Ángel, Viviana, and Vanessa—work for the institution although the first generation only participates in the general assembly. The second generation maintains control, not only of the general assembly, but also of relevant management positions within the institution such as the rector's and registrar's offices. Other members of the second generation, including some related by marriage, hold key positions within the organization.

Miguel Henríquez Emiliani was born in 1940. He graduated in law from the Universidad de Cartagena in 1972 and subsequently taught in the law school. He was politically active in the parliament of the Department (equivalent of a state) of Bolivar and as secretary of the government of Bolivar and Cartagena. Explaining why he decided to create a new institution, he states:

> From the moment I started to teach at the Universidad de Cartagena I had the idea to start my own institution out of love for teaching and the education and training of new professionals. Not only because of the importance of the development of competences, but also to cultivate new leaders who can contribute to development for their families and the region and, in this way, improve and transform quality of life. Noticing that many potential students remained outside of the system of higher education and noticing the frustration that this caused them and their families, I decided to make my dream come true and create more opportunities for access to higher education and the labor market. (G. Burgos, private interview, May 30, 2019)

Henríquez Emiliani chairs the general assembly; together with his wife and three children they hold a majority on the general board. His son, Miguel Angel, is rector of the institution and chairs the board of directors. His daughter, Viviana, is secretary general of the institution and of the general board and board of directors. His other daughter, Vanessa, is director of international relations of the institution. In this way, the second generation controls the university while other members of the family also hold key positions in the institution.

7.2   Legal Status and Governance

Legally incorporated as a non-profit, the highest governing bodies are the *asamblea general* (general assembly) and the higher, academic, research and faculty councils.

The general assembly is made up of eight members—the founder and seven members appointed by him of which five are family members. It is the highest governing body of the corporation. According to institutional statues, when the founder dies, the members of the assembly appoint new members or their successors by absolute majority.

The *consejo superior*, the highest administrative body, elects the rector who is the legal representative of the university. The *consejo* is composed of the rector, three members elected by the general board, the vice-chancellors, a representative of the students, and a representative of the faculty.

7.3   Challenges and Perspectives

According to a 2016 study by the Superintendencia de Sociedades in Colombia, 70 percent of the companies in the country are controlled by families who seldom succeed past the second generation. Only 30 percent continue as family businesses through a second generation and then only 13 percent of family businesses remain in the family by the third generation. In the Colombian economic environment these companies not only worry about generational succession so that the family can maintain control, but also constant fluctuations in the market. These circumstances demand different managerial capacities from those of the past.

Ministry of Education data at the end of 2017 show that 25 percent of higher education institutions were universities controlled by families with 349,070 students distributed among 52 FOMHEIs, 14 percent of national enrollment. This evidence indicates that family universities occupy an important place in the education of Colombia's young people.

The consistent challenges for FOMHEIs in Colombia are quality, control, and coverage. Quality requires improving current standards for academic programs and institutional processes. One way to demonstrate the achievement of quality is to obtain institutional and program accreditation which is a voluntary process. This requires planning and allocating economic resources to professional development for faculty, student scholarships, international outreach, alliances with the industry, and more. Unfortunately, private universities in Colombia depend on student fees to sustain operating budgets, a reality that limits discretionary resources for other purposes. There are not, as in some other countries, individuals or businesses inclined to make philanthropic donations to support institutional development.

Although there is a new system of long-term educational credit that subsidizes tuition for low-income students and at times in the past the national government has allocated resources to support private institutions, neither program represents a significant contribution to the budgets of Colombian private institutions.

More elaboration of government protocols is needed to oversee the administration and control of FOMHEIs and their transfer to a second generation; to define the participation of family members in institutional administration; and to guarantee their economic stability and growth in the long term.

Globalization and the development of new technologies have led to a significant number of international institutions offering academic programs online at competitive prices in the Colombian market. On the other hand, larger Colombian institutions have increased their online programs and are offering them throughout the country. This situation means that the FOMHEIs must make efforts to incorporate information and communication technologies to compete in quality and price with these new offers.

8   Conclusion

FOMHEIS are a reality in Colombian higher education, governed by national legislation that limits comparisons with similar institutions in other countries.

In most cases, FOMHEIS in Colombia have been created by individuals active in higher education and politics, responding to the needs and opportunities created by the massification of higher education in the country. They represent a younger segment of Colombian higher education as 66 percent were created after the 1980s and their sustainability has not been truly tested as most founders remain involved in governing bodies.

The majority of FOMHEIS in Colombia are still in the hands of their founders who continue to have an active role in the leadership of their institutions. A second generation is only beginning to assume authority. That process has advanced gradually and without major crises. There have been no mergers or acquisitions, a common occurrence in commercial family businesses.

The future must focus on economic sustainability given the threat of competition from domestic and foreign institutions offering online programs. The unique system of succession allows the family to retain the original vision and character but without clear rules for the responsible administration of resources or roles for members of the family to contribute to growth and quality.

FOMHEIS in Colombia have been important to expanding access to higher education for young people from a "less-favored" population through scholarships, grants, and other strategies.

Reference

Gallo, M. A., & Sveen, J. (1991). Internationalizing the family business: Facilitating and restraining factors. *Family Business Review,* 4(2), 181–190.

CHAPTER 9

Ethiopia: Inside the Black Box of Family-Owned Private Institutions

Wondwosen Tamrat

Private higher education (PHE) is the fastest growing segment of higher education across the globe (Altbach, 1999, 2016). In spite of variations in enrollment size, the presence of private higher education institutions (PHEIs) in every corner of the world is evident (Levy, 2015, 2018; Altbach, 2016). Within the context of PHE there are various forms of proprietorship including family and individual ownership that is growing in different national contexts. In general, family-owned or managed higher education institutions (FOMHEIs) appear to thrive in contexts where for-profit institutions are permitted, but they are also emerging in countries with no prior history of for-profit higher education (Tsamenyi, Noormansyah, & Uddin, 2008).

The African continent has experienced the surge of global private higher education with record growth during a period of the last three decades. Since the end of the 1990s, the period when the expansion of the private higher education sector began in earnest, Ethiopia joined the list of countries with a significant number of PHEIs, assuming a leading position in Sub-Saharan Africa in terms of the number of institutions and enrollment. The principal roots of growth are found in the aspirations of an emerging middle class and the resulting demand for access that exceeded what the government can provide in the public sector (Tamrat & Levy, 2017).

The beginning of a full-fledged private higher education sector in Ethiopia is marked by the establishment of the first family-owned institution in 1998. Since then, family-owned or managed higher education institutions (FOMHEIS) have grown steadily, overshadowing other forms of PHEIs in the country. Ethiopia can be considered a country that epitomizes the influence of this form of higher education provision on the continent, although little research exists about the specific nature of these FOMHEIS (Altbach, 2015; Tamrat, 2018a).

This study aims to address the research gap through an exploration of FOMHEIS, operational features, and governance challenges. The first section of the chapter presents the study design followed by a brief overview of the higher education context in Ethiopia, major findings, and conclusions of the study.

The study used a survey questionnaire and interview as primary data generation tools. The questionnaire was administered through Ethiopia's Higher Education Relevance and Quality Agency (HERQA). Interviews were also held with six FOMHEI leaders and two division heads of the HERQA. Secondary data was obtained from the Ethiopian Ministry of Education and relevant publications.

1   Higher Education in Ethiopia

Higher Education in Ethiopia refers to "education programs offered as undergraduate degrees for three, four or more years after completing secondary education and specialized degrees such as master's and PhD programs" (Higher Education Proclamation, HEP, 2009, 4977). Modern higher education dates back to the founding of the University College of Addis Ababa (now Addis Ababa University) in 1950, the first higher education institution in the country. Little was achieved over the next four decades in terms of altering the elitist orientation of the system comprised at its peak of only two universities and fewer than twenty colleges offering diploma and degree programs to a student population that did not exceed 40 thousand. The gross enrollment ratio (GER) at the national level by the 1990s was only around one percent, far below the then Sub-Saharan (SSA) average of three to five percent. This situation began to change when the government embarked on a scheme of expansion early in the new millennium, setting forth many changes and challenges.

The Ethiopian higher education sector has experienced unprecedented expansion over the last two decades. The number of higher education institutions in the country exceeds 180, two-thirds of which are privately owned. The number of students at the undergraduate and postgraduate levels has risen above 860,000 while the number of annual graduates has reached 160,000 (MoE, 2017). GER has grown beyond 10 percent, surpassing the regional average of 8 percent for the first time. The Ethiopian government plans to boost the figure to 15 percent during the 2019–2020 academic year (MoE, 2016).

Despite the increase in enrollment, the number of students in the private sector has declined since the early years of the sector's expansion. In 2001, 41 percent of total higher enrollment was captured by the private sector (MoE, 2002) compared to 14 percent in 2017 (MoE, 2017).The decrease has been the consequence of the government's aggressive expansion of the public system and a litany of regulatory requirements imposed on the private sector (Tamrat, 2008; Tamrat & Levy, 2017). It is worth noting that participation of women in private institutions continues to exceed that of the public sector. More than 50 percent of the regular and extension program enrollment at private HEIS are women while the participation of women at public institutions still remains below 40 percent (MoE, 2017).

2   The Genesis of PHE in Ethiopia

Ethiopia's long history of education is closely linked with centuries of religious education offered by the Ethiopian Orthodox Church and Quranic schools. As embodiments of Orthodox Christianity that began in the fourth century and of Islam in the seventh, church and Quranic schools represent a core component of the country's educational history. Non-government schools outside the religious domain were introduced much later and included privately-owned schools run by individuals, missionary schools, and community schools organized by foreign communities residing in Ethiopia.

Menelik II and Haile Selassie I were active promoters of individually and family-owned schools. Though identified as government schools, the establishment of the Menelik II School (Ecole Imperiale de Menelik)in 1908 and Ras Teferi Mekonen School in 1925 in Addis Ababa had features of privately-owned schools, especially in their formative years. Menelik II personally funded his school. The same was true of the Teferri Mekonen School that was financed from Haile Selassie's private coffers until it was formally transformed into a government school in 1942 (Dagne, 1976). In addition to his personal contributions, Emperor Haile Selassie repeatedly encouraged members of the nobility to follow in his footsteps.

> The crying need of our people is education without which we cannot maintain our independence. The proof of real patriotism is to recognize this fact. Those who possess the means should establish schools and forward the cause of education in every way ... I have built this school to make a beginning and to set an example which I appeal to the wealthy among the people to follow. (Ministry of Education and Fine Arts, 1961, p. 7)

Following this national appeal many regional feudal lords committed to building, financing, and administering private schools that sprouted in different parts of the country.

Haile Selassie's government assumed responsibility for setting legal directions for private schooling. The first legal endorsement of private education came when the Ministry of Education and Fine Arts was given the jurisdiction over private institutions through a proclamation issued in 1943 (Ministry of Pen, 1943). In 1944 another proclamation was issued to bring mission schools under the aegis of the Ministry (Ministry of Pen, 1944). These legal regimes served as the basis for the operation and control of private schools until another proclamation that detailed regulations on establishing and operating non-government schools was issued three decades later (Ministry of Education and Fine Arts, 1973). In the meantime, privately-owned schools thrived and played a significant role in the development of education in the country until they were closed by the Dergue, the socialist military government that toppled Emperor Haile Selassie in 1974 (Provisional Government of Ethiopia, 1975). The proclamation issued by the Dergue banned all forms of private investment in education with the exception of missionary and community schools. At the beginning of the Dergue period there were 1,502 private schools enrolling more than 200,000 students covering 30 percent of primary and secondary participation; however, after private schooling was outlawed, enrollment in private schools declined to 6 percent by 1995 (World Bank, 2005).

Even during the Haile Selassie period when private ownership of schools was promoted, there were no privately-owned higher education institutions in the country with the exception of Asmara University (now in Eritrea), founded in 1958 by a missionary congregation from Verona, Italy. This institution was given a charter by the government ten years later (Imperial Government of Ethiopia, 1968) and eventually became part of the public system.

In contrast with most of the region where the emergence and rapid growth of PHE was unplanned and caught governments by surprise, the beginning of PHE in Ethiopia was planned and promoted by the government (Tamrat & Levy, 2017). Cognizant of the limitations of the public sector in addressing increasing social demand for education at all levels, the country's 1994 education and training policy paved the way for private investment in education in general. This was further consolidated by the Council of Ministers Regulations Number 206/1995 that provided the legal framework for "Licensing and Supervision of Private Educational Institutions" (Transitional Government of Ethiopia, 1995). Concurrently, the Ethiopian Investment Regulation (1996) and the Investment Incentives Amendment Regulation (1998) offered incentives to potential investors in the sector. Higher education proclamations issued in 2003 and 2009 further developed the legal framework that governed how private higher education institutions were to be established and run. One major outcome of these policies has been an unprecedented number of privately-owned schools and higher education institutions. Against this background, the following section examines the growth and profile of FOMHEIs in Ethiopia.

3   Family-Owned HEIs: Looking inside the Black Box

The key objective of this research is to identify features of FOMHEIs in Ethiopia. The outcomes of the survey are summarized below under the following sub-themes—the establishment and history of FOMHEIs; their geographic distribution; enrollment and graduation patterns; program focus; faculty profile; ownership and governance patterns. The classification of these subthemes is partly influenced by Kinser's (2006) typology that classifies for-profit higher education along the dimensions of degree status, geographic dispersion, and ownership.

3.1   Establishment History and Capital Outlay
The impressive growth of FOMHEIs in Ethiopia has been driven by the increasing demand for higher education and economic policies introduced by the government after the overthrow of the socialist Dergue that had restricted private investment in almost all forms. The absence of any legal restrictions in regard to the ownership has contributed to the many types of PHEIs that have appeared across the country.

The data collected in this study revealed that among 133 accredited PHEIs in the country, 121 (91 percent) are family-owned, established as limited private companies (PLCs). This includes four PHEIs that have attained university status. Another five (3.7 percent) are for-profit institutions owned by shareholding companies and the remaining seven (5 percent) are run as non-profit entities by religious groups and non-governmental organizations (NGOs). Most of the early family-owned institutions grew out of small language schools and training centers while those that came later were established as colleges and university colleges. The history indicates that there has been a veritable explosion of FOMHEIs since 2010 with 88 (66 percent) of all PHEIs in Ethiopia having been established between 2011 and 2018.

The 121 FOMHEIs collectively administer a capital of nearly 3.7 billion Ethiopian birr (US$123,223,655) that has grown by 224 percent from the original capital investment of 1,490 billion birr (US$49,675,028).

The overwhelming majority of Ethiopian PHEIs were established by limited private, for-profit companies. The other form of proprietorship is a share company that resembles publicly traded higher education models elsewhere (Kinser, 2007) although corporate ownership of PHEIs is rare in Ethiopia. The dominance of the for-profit model might suggest that higher education is viewed as a profitable business, but higher education offers only limited security and financial return compared to other private investment options such as banks, insurance companies, etc. where the involvement of investors is more common.

Non-profit institutions are quite distinct in terms of the motivation for their creation, ownership patterns, nature of programs offered, and facilities deployed. Most of this type are established by religious entities, foundations or NGOs whose primary focus is undertaking charitable and development-oriented activities and contributing to local development (Tamrat, 2018b). The fact that most non-profit institutions depend on financial backing from their founders limits the number of students they can enroll and programs they can offer. Operating mostly within their own buildings spares these institutions a range of challenges and burdens required of for-profit institutions.

3.2   *Enrollment Patterns*

It is not easy to obtain accurate enrollment or graduation figures from PHEIs due to limited available information and underreporting, but according to estimates obtained from HERQA, FOMHEIs cover nearly 95 percent of overall enrollment in the private higher education sector. The majority of graduates from the private sector are from FOMHEIs; the non-profit institutions constitute only 5 percent of PHEIs in Ethiopia and enroll only a limited number of students (Tamrat, 2018b).

FOMHEIs exhibit significant differences in terms of size and program focus. The institutional array ranges from those that accommodate a limited number to those that enroll tens of thousands of students. Most institutions are small and concentrate on providing programs demanded by the labor market. There are very few FOMHEIs that undertake research; the majority functions as teaching institutions with little participation in knowledge generation. These institutions are less highly regarded by the public than public institutions with a significant number of FOMHEIs perceived as low prestige institutions that operate "at the lower end of the academic pecking order" (Altbach, 2015). Some are, in truth, diploma mills indulging in various fraudulent activities to maximize financial gain (Tamrat, 2017). These differences are usually influenced by experience, social acceptance, location, educational goals, mode of operation, and ethical standards.

3.3   *Geographical Distribution*

FOMHEIs in Ethiopia are distributed across the whole country but 50 percent are still found in Addis Ababa. Encouragingly, a good number of FOMHEIs have extended their services across various regions through distance education. In fact, bigger, pioneering institutions based in Addis Ababa operate in the provinces mainly through satellite centers. Since these institutions rarely establish campuses outside the capital, expansion is most often undertaken by local investors in the regions.

Out of the nine states and two city administrations in the country, the two most popular regions for FOMHEIs are Amhara and Oromia that together host 25 percent of the total number of FOMHEIs. This is not surprising given the size and population of the two regions. While the Amhara region has 18 institutions, Oromia hosts 16 FOMHEIs. Tigray and Southern Nations, Nationalities and Peoples Region follow with 13 (9.8 percent) and 11 FOMHEIs (8.3 percent) respectively.

3.4 *Programs on Offer*

Ethiopian FOMHEIs overwhelmingly focus on market-oriented fields of study despite some diversification into other fields. The main program areas offered include business related subjects such as accounting, finance, management and leadership; medicine and health sciences including medicine, nursing, public health, clinical laboratory; computer and natural science; engineering and technology including civil engineering, construction management, surveying, automotive and electronics; agriculture and life sciences; social sciences and humanities including sociology, social anthropology and journalism. Table 9.1 shows program areas offered at the bachelor's and master's levels by FOMHEIs.

The number of institutions providing education at the bachelor's level exceeds the total number of FOMHEIs, indicating that a significant number of institutions are offering many degree programs. Many institutions are involved in providing courses in business and economics, a characteristic the Ethiopian

TABLE 9.1   Program areas of FOMHEIS

Program	No. of institutions	
	BA	MA
Engineering and technology	16	1
Natural and computational science	39	2
Medicine and health science	43	9
Agriculture and life science	11	1
Business and economics	84	14
Social science and humanities	17	1
Total institutions offering degree area	210	28

PHE shares with similar institutions elsewhere on the continent. On the other hand, a distinct feature of Ethiopian FOMHEIS is the fact that a substantial number of them are also involved in medicine and health sciences which is less common in this sector.

Postgraduate education is a recent development and only a small number of FOMHEIS offer it. Beyond the areas of business, economics, medicine, and health sciences, only a handful of institutions offer programs at the graduate level. The majority of institutions that offer education at this level run post-graduate courses as well as undergraduate programs.

Altogether the programs run by FOMHEIS (including distance education) are offered on more than 950 campuses across the country (Table 9.2).

TABLE 9.2   Number of campuses

Program	No. of campuses		Total
	BA	MA	
Engineering and technology	45	3	48
Natural and computational science	71	2	73
Agriculture and life science	51	4	55
Medicine and health science	109	17	126
Business and economics	559	53	612
Social science and humanity	33	4	37
Total	868	83	951

The most popular field of studies, business and economics, is offered on 559 campuses at the bachelor's level and 53 campuses at master's level. With the exception of business and economics, the participation of FOMHEIS in master's programs is limited to a few institutions. Bachelor's level programs in fields such as natural science, computational science, agriculture and life science are also limited to a few institutions.

3.5   Faculty Size and Mix

The 121 FOMHEIS identified in this study reported employing over 2,000 full-time academic staff (Table 9.3).

The highest concentration of faculty is found in business and economics, more than double the staff in medicine and health science, the next most popular program. The majority of faculty in FOMHEIS holds master's degree

TABLE 9.3   Size and qualification of full- time faculty at FOMHEIS

Program	Instructors			
	BA	MA	PhD	Total
Engineering and Technology	45	125	11	181
Natural and Computational Science	69	197	4	270
Medicine and Health Science	162	364	41	567
Agriculture and Life Science	1	7	7	315
Business and Economics	287	888	89	1264
Social Science and Humanities	8	37	4	49
Total	472	1618	156	2246

(72 percent) with only a small percentage holding a PhD degree (7 percent). Recent improvements in the share of faculty with master's degrees are encouraging compared to the earlier years when a serious challenge to higher education quality was that most of professors had only a bachelor's degree (Tamrat, 2010). However, the limited number of qualified staff available to FOMHEIS is still far below the national requirement that 70 percent of the faculty holds a master's and 30 percent hold an earned PhD.

3.6   Ownership Patterns

Public institutions in Ethiopia are established by the Council of Ministers and funded by the government. Private institutions are considered business entities and must comply with provisions in commercial law or other relevant laws that govern associations, business organizations, and cooperatives. Accordingly, ownership of PHEIs is structured as sole proprietorship, limited private company (PLC), and shareholder companies. PHEIs must have a business license to operate regardless of ownership and must fulfill all other requirements of law. In order to operate as academic institutions, PHEIs must also meet requirements to secure accreditation from the HERQA.

Ethiopian FOMHEIS are currently owned by a variety of proprietors including former college and university teachers or officers, entrepreneurs, medical doctors, nurses, and businesspeople. Unity College (now Unity University) was the first private higher education institution established in 1998 by an entrepreneurial medical doctor. While there are a few institutions run by non-government organizations such as religious ones, corporate ownership is non-existent.

Interview participants identified two types of motivations that encourage participation in this market—those who joined the sector with sincere motivation to contribute to society and those who were drawn to the sector for potential profit. Although most of the interviewees did not deny the appeal of financial gain, none identified their primary purpose as profit. Rather, most stated that they were mainly driven by social commitment. Yet, administrators at the FOMHEIs and division heads at HERQA hold a different view. They contend that despite the initiatives of a few entrepreneurs with genuine social motives, the sector is dominated by profit-seeking businesspeople who are less concerned about quality education or building long-lasting institutions. The president of one family-owned institution commented,

> When I joined the institution, I tried to create some [management] systems, but this did not go well since it came in conflict with the hidden motives of the owners. To this day I have not been able to distinguish between the owner's inherent motives and the practical needs of the institution. I created appropriate structures thinking that it would be better for the institution. However, this was perceived negatively since it would take away power from the owners. Owners repeatedly turned down or changed decisions made by important organs like the Academic Senate and did whatever they chose. We've now reached a stage where we're handling daily activities rather than envisioning long-term goals for the institution. (Private interview, June 2018)

Most respondents argued that FOMHEIs that focus on profit are characterized by poorly organized administrative systems, lack of transparency, excessive commercialization, high staff turnover, and abuse of power that have consequences for their reputation. Respondents accused owners of diverting income from FOMHEIs to other businesses they own. There were two interviewees who questioned whether private ownership could produce successful institutions in an environment supervised by a lax regulatory system. A leader in one family-owned institution argues,

> Given the Ethiopian context, it does not matter who owns [an institution]. What matters most is the strength of the regulatory body. Of course, individual owners have reportedly abused their power resulting in poor delivery of services by exploiting the weak regulatory body in Ethiopia. Though very small in number, the non-profit institutions too could abuse their independence unless they are better regulated. (Private interview, July 2018)

3.7 *Governance*

The governance framework adopted by public universities in Ethiopia is dictated by the higher education proclamation of the country that stipulates the presence of structures such as governing and advisory bodies, academic units, administrative, and technical support units where membership and selection are dictated in the proclamation (FDRE, 2009). These forms of governance are not necessarily required of PHEIs, but the higher education proclamation imposes general regulations that suggest the need for private institutions to have governing bodies and decision-making procedures making clear the rights and obligations of the academic community along with procedures for handling grievances. However, these general expectations have not been supported by specific policies or legislation. Hence, institutional owners have considerable latitude with the level of administrative control they wield. Sole proprietorship and PLC ownership provide more leverage to individuals and families that own the business, allowing a high degree of flexibility and the concentration of power with the proprietor. The shareholder model of ownership, on the other hand, operates more like a publicly-traded company with greater levels of accountability to shareholders and limits the power of institutional leadership. The findings of this study indicate that most FOMHEIS owners are directly involved in managing their institutions since they are not legally prevented from doing so.

In the 70 percent of the FOMHEIS set up as PLCs, owners are directly involved in the management of their institutions. Only a limited number of owners in shareholding companies assume senior positions (Table 9.4). The

TABLE 9.4   Number of owners participating in managing their institutions

Type of ownership	# PHEIs	Owners participate	# owners	Owners assuming position in the institution	Institutions where owners do not assume formal positions	No response
PLC	121	94	305	230	16	19
Investor-owned company	5	2	3,210	65	3	–
Religious or NGO	7	NA		NA	NA	–

NA = NOT APPLICABLE

type and level of owner involvement includes participation as board members (8 percent), CEO or managing director (44 percent), or as president or dean (25 percent). Although these institutions claim to have set up boards, interviewees admitted that board influence is, in most cases, nominal and rarely functional. Hence, the tradition of managing FOMHEIs with a strong board comprised of family members (Altbach, 2015) appears to be rare when there is no legal requirement for a board as part of institutional governance.

An owner in any of the top positions usually acts as a chief executive officer of the institution exercising the ultimate decision-making power. Both the academic and business division heads of the institution are accountable to him or her. Lower positions appointed by proprietors or their relatives may sometimes have little significance although they can be highly relevant in terms of controlling key resources like finance and property.

All respondents admitted that the individual or family ownership of higher education institutions has implications for institutional success or failure. Positively viewed FOMHEIs are identified as having dedicated leaders with altruistic motives, a strong academic background, and commitment to the creation of management systems with mechanisms for participatory decision-making. Owners in these institutions go beyond profits and satisfying the requirements of regulatory bodies; they use their autonomy to take risks and innovate to lead the institution towards specific goals. Decisions are made with little red tape; institutional assets are managed properly, and a healthy working environment is created for employees who are expected to develop a sense of commitment and stability. Owners usually subscribe to institutional regulations and create mechanisms that would allow their institutions to operate effectively, even during their absence.

FOMHEIs led by profit-driven owners were, on the other hand, identified with a lack of accountability or direction in their governance system. Family members and relatives with limited qualification and experience assume senior positions beyond their capacity (Tamrat, 2018a). The owner is usually the senior manager and meddles in almost every institutional matter with little regard to the contribution of other units or members of the institution. A respondent from the regulatory agency noted,

> I know some higher education institutions that are run by one ethnic group or one family (father, son, daughter, and other extended families) from top (the dean) to bottom (the guard at the gate). These higher education institutions are not only beset by academic and administrative governance problems ... but also are prone to academic and administrative malpractice. The very principle these higher education institutions

are built on is the nearer the relationship to the owner, the more reliable the person will be when making decisions regarding the financial and material resources of the institution. (Private interview, July 2018)

The limited research on the governance of Ethiopian PHEIs corroborates many of the above observations. Privately-owned higher education institutions are considered to be weak in promoting participatory governance and collective action in both academic and administrative matters (Assefa, 2008; Tizazu &Tamrat, 2010). Most staff at PHEIs contend that the system of governance at their institutions does not involve them in selecting institutional leaders, making financial decisions or even in establishing their associations. They also feel that in addition to excessive profit motives, power is concentrated in the office of the president and criticism of institutional policies and practice is rare (Assefa, 2008).

Most interviewees in this study were concerned about the governance system at FOMHEIs that are run like businesses without sufficient involvement from critical stakeholders. However, not all owner-leaders believe this should be a source of concern. An owner-managing director in one of the FOMHEIs had the following to say:

> An owner is logically committed to the institution he owns much more than a salaried employee who may have short-term interests and a brief stay at the institution. The owner's concerns with regard to the financial and governance aspects of an institution should not be viewed in a negative way as these remain the key areas which can determine the life or death of a given organization. The owner should naturally be more concerned about these critical aspects than anything else. (Private interview, June 2018)

Despite reservations about the nature of governance at FOMHEIs, none of the interviewees suggested the need for eliminating these types of institutions, acknowledging their contribution to meeting the demand for access to higher education in Ethiopia and the need for the participation of a multitude of higher education providers. Nevertheless, respondents emphasized the necessity and urgency of addressing many concerns if this form of ownership is to thrive.

3.8   *Generational Transition and Other Challenges*
The benefits and challenges of a family-owned organization can be complicated by the additional layer of family relationships (Tsamenyi, Noormansyah, &

Uddin, 2008). This unique characteristic makes family ownership an opportunity and a threat. Family ownership and commitment to the business can add value provided that the company responds to the concerns of investors, enhances organizational performance, and guarantees organizational growth (Zahra et al., 2008; Berrone, Cruz, &Gomez-Mejia, 2012). On the other hand, the unrestrained control that an individual or family wields could be a source of problems if it allows for abuse of power and leads to organizational failure (Altbach, 2015; Tamrat, 2018a).

The Ethiopian private higher sector is young and still in the hands of first-generation proprietors. Yet the issue of generational transfer appears to be a concern shared by most of the respondents. The culture of an institution is considered by respondents to be a critical factor that could determine whether a FOMHEI will survive. An owner related his experiences of grooming his children for their future leadership role by guiding their academic preparation, coaching their participation in institutional meetings, and assigning them to positions that would help them acquire management experience. In a similar vein, a shareholder-president at one of the family-owned institutions emphasized the need for proper future planning,

> The challenges of transferring individual family-owned institutions from one generation to the next occur due to lack of practices in regards to institutionalizing the business. In general terms, inadequate planning, lead time, insufficient on-the-job training, lack of understanding of the business culture are some of the challenges. Individuals intending to transfer their family-owned business must train the next generation. There should also be a legal framework that supports the continuity of a family business with due consideration to risks coming from interference by family members. (Private interview, June 2018)

A non-owner leader shared a similar perspective and noted that his institution might face serious challenges due to lack of owner attention to succession,

> The owner has not trained his children enough. They don't have the required skills, qualities, or experience to run the institution in the future. He doesn't know how to mentor them. If anything happens to him, I am afraid there will be no one to lead the institution. I don't even see anyone who's ready to substitute for me if I choose to abdicate my position. The staff turnover in the institution is extremely high. Most of those working for us on permanent basis are cleaners and security guards. (Private interview, June 2018)

While emphasizing the need for having an institutional culture that limits individual domination, the viability of the family-ownership model itself was questioned by respondents. It was suggested that the best way to ensure the generational transfer of FOMHEIS is either by adopting a different business model such as a shareholding company structure or through a regulatory intervention that can restrict the excessive powers of owners or make them more accountable if they do not create mechanisms to ensure the sustainability of their institutions. Evaluating the profile of owners before approving the creation of an institution and strict follow-up to ensure compliance with regulations were suggested to mitigate challenges related to transferring FOMHEIS to the next generation. A respondent from the regulatory agency stated,

> I think there is a need for revising HERQA's regulations on FOMHEIS. Institutions can only transfer to the next generation if they have developed a strong and functional management system. Excessive family interference in the governance of an institution should be prevented legally. An institution should not be exclusively dependent on a single individual who does everything. The previous history of owners should be checked before allowing the institution to operate so that the right kind of individuals and families can invest in the sector. HERQA should encourage responsible institutions and discourage owners who abuse the system. Healthy competition should be promoted in order to sustain the life of FOMHEIS in the future. (Private interview, July 2018)

4   Conclusion

Despite their increasing growth, FOMHEIS and their ownership have received little scrutiny that would contribute to understanding the factors that determine their success or failure (Altbach, 2015). While the need for deepening our understanding of FOMHEIS through further research is warranted, the results of this exploratory survey provide some insights about the features and operational dimensions of Ethiopian FOMHEIS that account for the fastest growing segment of private higher education in the country.

The foregoing analysis has highlighted the demand for higher education that continues to encourage wider private participation. Moreover, the absence of regulation related to the governance of FOMHEIS has permitted the excessive involvement of owners at various management levels of the institutions without mechanisms for restraint. With few changes, FOMHEIS will continue to dominate the Ethiopian private higher education scene in the years to come.

It was also possible to discern that in addition to sharing key features consistent with PHEIS elsewhere, FOMHEIS are shaped by the background, commitment, and motives of the family or individual owner's influence that cannot be overemphasized (Altbach, 2015; Tamrat, 2018a). This is especially evident in the ways in which FOMHEIS are governed and the mechanisms in place to facilitate their continuity across generations. In this regard, the findings of this survey underscore the detrimental influence of proprietors who indulge in extensive managerial interference, offer limited transparency, and demonstrate little accountability, but focus instead on maximizing returns on their investment (Akpotu & Akpochafo, 2009; Omuta, 2010; Mwebi & Simatwa, 2013; Barsoum, 2014; Oseni, 2015; Tamrat, 2018a).

As can be seen from the findings of this study, though concluding whether the FOMHEI model is successful or unsuccessful is difficult, FOMHEIS can face unique operational challenges due to the additional layer of familiar relationships. Hence, any discussion of institutional effectiveness or the survival of FOMHEIS must address the issue of how to ensure good governance that balances the benefits to family owners with the academic interests of students and faculty along with how to develop effective strategies for leadership transfer from one generation to the next. This balance may not be best left to individual proprietors in contexts where private interests can conflict with the interests of the institution. This may call for legislative interventions that can guarantee effective management, greater accountability, and generational transfer without excessive infringement on private ownership.

References

Akpotu, N. E., & Akpochafo, W. P. (2009). An analysis of factors influencing the upsurge of private universities in Nigeria. *Journal of Social Sciences, 18*(1), 21–27.

Altbach, P. G. (Ed.). (1999). *Private Prometheus: Private higher education and development in the 21st century.* Boston, MA: Boston College Center for International Higher Education and Greenwood Publishing Company.

Altbach, P. G. (2015). Universities family style. *International Higher Education, 39,* 10–12.

Altbach, P. G. (2016). *Global perspectives on higher education.* Baltimore, MD: The Johns Hopkins University Press.

Assefa, T. (Ed.). (2008). *Academic freedom in Ethiopia: Perspectives of teaching personnel.* Addis Ababa: Forum for Social Studies.

Bae, K., Kim, S., & Kim, W. (2012). Family control and expropriation at not- for-profit organizations: Evidence from Korean private universities. *Corporate Governance: An International Review, 20*(4), 388–404.

Barsoum, G. (2014). *The challenges of private higher education in Egypt, Working paper 833*. Dokki: Economic Research Forum.

Berrone, P., Cruz, C., & Gomez-Mejia, L. R. (2012). Socio-emotional wealth in family firms: Theoretical dimensions, assessment approaches and agenda for future research. *Family Business Review, 25*(3), 258–279.

Dagne, H. G. (1976). Non-government schools in Ethiopia. In M. L. Bender, J. D. Bowen, R. L. Cooper, & C. A. Ferguson (Eds.), *Language in Ethiopia* (pp. 339–370). London: Oxford University Press.

Federal Democratic Republic of Ethiopia (FDRE). (1996). *Investment Proclamation No.37, Negarit Gazette*. Addis Ababa: FDRE.

Federal Democratic Republic of Ethiopia (FDRE). (1998). *Investment Incentives Council of Ministers Regulations (Amendment) No. 36. Negarit Gazette*. Addis Ababa: FDRE.

Federal Democratic Republic of Ethiopia (FDRE). (2003). *Higher Education Proclamation 351*. Addis Ababa: FDRE.

Federal Democratic Republic of Ethiopia (FDRE). (2009). *Higher Education Proclamation 650*. Addis Ababa: FDRE.

Gosaye, S. (2000). *Demand and development trends of private primary schools in Addis Ababa* (Master's thesis). Addis Ababa University, Ethiopia.

Imperial Government of Ethiopia (IGE). (1968). *Charter for the University of Asmara*. Addis Ababa: IGE.

Kinser, K. (2006). From main street to wall street: The transformation of for-profit higher education. *ASHE Report Series, 31*(5), 1–155.

Kinser, K. (2007). Dimensions of corporate ownership in for-profit higher education. *Review of Higher Education, 30*(3), 217–245.

Levy, D. C. (2015). Private higher education: Patterns and trends. *International Higher Education, 50*, 7–9.

Levy, D. C. (2018). Global private higher education: An empirical profile of its size and geographical shape. *Higher Education, 76*(4), 701–715.

Mekuria, G., & Mengistie, L. (1996). The role of NGOs and the private sector in social service delivery. *Ethiopia Social Sector Study Report*, n.p.

Ministry of Education (MoE). (1994). *Education and training policy*. Addis Ababa: MoE.

Ministry of Education. (2002). *Education statistics annual abstract*. Addis Ababa: MoE.

Ministry of Education. (2016). *Education statistics annual abstract*. Addis Ababa: MoE.

Ministry of Education. (2017). *Education statistics annual abstract*. Addis Ababa: MoE.

Ministry of Education and Fine Arts. (1961). *Education in Ethiopia*. Addis Ababa: MoE.

Ministry of Education and Fine Arts. (1973). *Non-government schools regulation*. Addis Ababa: Berhanena Selam Printing Press.

Ministry of Pen. (1943). *Negarit Gazette, order no 1.* Addis Ababa: Ministry of Pen.

Ministry of Pen. (1944). *Negarit Gazette, order no 3.* Addis Ababa: Ministry of Pen.

Mwebi, B., & Simatwa, E. M. W. (2013). Expansion of private universities in Kenya and its implications and completion rate: An analytical study. *Educational Research, 4*(4), 352–366.

Omuta, G. E.D. (2010). *The place of private participation in higher education: A periscope on private universities in Nigeria.* Benin City: Center for Population and Environmental Development.

Oseni, M. (2015). Effectiveness and desirability of private higher education in Nigeria. *Journal of Educational and Social Research, 5*(1), 151–158.

Provisional Government of Ethiopia, PGE. (1975). *A proclamation to provide for the public ownership of private schools* (Negarit Gazeta, 35th year No. 3). Addis Ababa: PGE.

Tamrat, W. (2008). *The anatomy of private higher education in Ethiopia.* Addis Ababa: St. Mary's University College Press.

Tamrat, W. (2010). Faculty profile in the undergraduate programs of Ethiopian public universities. *The Teacher, 3*(6), 1–11.

Tamrat, W. (2017, December 2). The scourge of unscrupulous private higher education institutions. *University World News.*

Tamrat, W. (2018a). Family-owned private higher education institutions in Africa. *International Higher Education, 95,* 23–24.

Tamrat, W. (2018b). A glimpse of non- for profit private higher education institutions in Ethiopia. *The Teacher, 8*(16), 1–9.

Tamrat, W., & Levy, D. C. (2017). Unusual in growth and composition: Ethiopian private higher education. *International Higher Education, 90,* 19–21.

Tizazu, G., & Tamrat, W. (2011). The status of private provision of higher education in Ethiopia. *Proceedings of the 9th national conference on private higher education institutions in Ethiopia.* Addis Ababa: St. Mary's University College.

Transitional Government of Ethiopia. (1995). *Licensing and supervision of private educational institutions* (Council of Ministers, Regulation No. 206). Addis Ababa: TGE.

Tsamenyi, M., Noormansyah, I., & Uddin, S. (2008). Management controls in family-Owned Businesses (FOBs): A case study of an Indonesian family-owned University. *Accounting Forum, 32*(1), 62–74.

UNESCO. (1988). *Ethiopia: Higher education development of university education.* Paris: UNESCO.

World Bank. (2005). *Education in Ethiopia: Strengthening the foundation for sustainable progress.* Washington DC: World Bank.

Zahra, S.A., Hayton, C., Neubaum, D. O., Dibrell, C. & Craig, J. (2008). Culture of family commitment and strategic flexibility: The moderating effect of stewardship. *Entrepreneurship Theory and Practice, 32*(6), 1035–1054.

CHAPTER 10

India: Symbiosis—An International University

Vidya Yeravdekar

This chapter presents a comprehensive discussion of the dramatic growth of family-owned or managed private universities in India. It utilizes the case of Symbiosis International University to extrapolate key themes of this phenomenon as well as to contextualize the significance and realities of private universities (many of which are family-managed) within the Indian higher education system. The specific context of the Indian higher education system is well-suited to an examination of the expansion of family-managed universities that seems to be a global trend. Most importantly, the Indian higher education system is growing very rapidly in terms of enrollment and number of institutions. It is also significant that privatization is experiencing a phenomenal ascent within the Indian higher education system and this has supported the modernization of the system. In particular, private institutions have contributed to the push towards internationalization.

The case of Symbiosis International University presents an opportunity to gather information, perspective, and a broad-level understanding of family-managed institutions in India including aspects related to evolution, operational realities, the challenges of functioning in a developing country, and making future predictions. Symbiosis, a leading family-managed institution, grew from, and continues to be rooted in, the Symbiosis Society, a highly reputed educational trust that dates back to the 1970s. The university has earned a solid reputation for achieving academic excellence, pioneering internationalization, and bringing skills-acquisition to the forefront of higher education in India.

1 The Indian Higher Education System

The Indian higher education system has undergone remarkable transformation in response to globalization and related phenomena in recent decades. The trends of "massification," privatization, and diversification of higher education are related in many ways to the government's goal of linking India with the global knowledge economy (Agarwal, 2017). These patterns of growth have occurred rather precipitously in response to the urgent need to educate a very

© KONINKLIJKE BRILL NV, LEIDEN, 2020 | DOI: 10.1163/9789004423435_010

diverse and ever-expanding base of young people desiring postsecondary education, all without adequate strategic planning. While the system is experiencing unprecedented growth and diversification, there are systemic challenges that prevent it from meeting the full range of the needs of the economy and the individual student.

The discussion of privatization of Indian higher education rests heavily on the phenomenon of family-managed institutions, since a considerable segment of private institutions fall into this category. This study utilizes the definition of family-managed institution according to Altbach (2005) stating that a family-managed higher education institutions is an academic institution "established by an individual or family group in which family members remain directly involved and generally dominant in the administration, governance, financial control, and/or direct ownership of the institution" (p. 10). In addition to Symbiosis International University, other prominent family-managed institutions in India include DY Patil Deemed to be University, SRM University, Vellore Institute of Technology (VIT), Lovely Professional University, Bharati Vidyapeeth, MIT World Peace University, Amity University, and Galgotia University.

Private institutions in India are those institutions that are established and managed by non-governmental organizations and are for the most part, self-financing. The majority of private universities in India are categorized as "deemed-to-be" universities. On the recommendation of the University Grants Commission (UGC), the central government, through the Ministry of Human Resource and Development, bestows the status of deemed-to-be university on institutions that demonstrate a consistent track record of academic excellence. These universities enjoy the academic status and privileges of a university.

The concept of private higher education institutions as it is understood in India is in many ways distinct, if not unique. In India, the ideal of education for collective good is a very prominent aspect of the ancient cultural legacy. It is also a core development requirement as India moves ahead on the path towards a knowledge-based economy aligned with long-term nation-building planning and policy goals. Indian private institutions are not "owned" by individuals or families, they are governed and managed by non-profit trusts or societies. The trust is a legally-recognized body—not individual(s)—that holds ultimate decision-making authority. The vision and mission of the trust is to guide the planning and operation of the institution. The trust is the custodian of the institution and individual members of the trust hold authority in relation to the institution only in the context of their custodianship. In the spirit of guardianship or custodianship the trust generates surplus, not profit, that is channeled back into the institution for further development. The participating members of the trust (trustees) receive salaries for their contribution based on the guidelines of the trust. In India, for-profit universities are not permitted because education is still considered a non-profit or charitable enterprise and therefore cannot generate profit. The surplus cannot be distributed to the trustees.

Privatization of higher education in India has been driven by a very compelling demand for accessible higher education rather than public policy. The origin of private institutions can be traced back to the 1970s when the public sector within the Indian higher education system was constrained by limited funds and an inability to establish a sufficient number of mass-access institutions. Several states allowed the operation of self-financing colleges to facilitate mass enrollment and catered to the rising demand for professional education. Growing industrialization and expansion of the manufacturing sector in the 80s further emphasized the importance of linking employability and skill development with higher education.

According to the 2016 "All India Survey on Higher Education" report of the Ministry of Human Resource and Development, as many as 34.2 million students were enrolled in institutions of higher education in 2014–2015. Of this number, nearly 22 million students (65 percent) were enrolled in private institutions that were mainly self-financing.

In India, an institution of higher education can only be established as a society under the Society Registration Act of 1860 or as a trust under the Maharashtra Public Trust Act of 1950. An institution of higher education can be created by having it registered as a society or a trust, after which it can operate as a standalone institution once it has the approval of the Statutory Council or a college affiliated to a public state university. The most recent data on higher education institutions, by category, operating currently in India can be seen in Table 10.1.

A university-level institution that has operated successfully for five years can apply to the Ministry of Human Resource Development (MHRD) to receive the status of a "deemed to be university" under Section 3 of the UGC Act or apply to a state government for the status of a private university under state legislation. Nineteen Indian States have established a Private Universities Act or Guidelines such as the Gujarat Private Universities Act 2009 and Assam Private Universities Act 2007. These institutions rely on student tuition for operating revenue. Therefore, the source of funding becomes very important. Often, the people who manage these enterprises are members from the same family or close confidants and associates of the founder and his family. This is how "family-managed" institutions are established in India.

With the world's second largest population, India is home to the world's second largest higher education system with over 35 million students, 800

TABLE 10.1   Higher education institutions in India 2016–2017

Universities	Total
State universities	384
Deemed to be universities	123
Central universities	47
Private universities	296
Institutions under special state legislature act	3
Colleges	41,435

SOURCE: DATA ADAPTED FROM UGC ANNUAL REPORT 2016–2017,
ACCESSED SEPTEMBER 6, 2018.

universities, and 41,000 colleges. India has overtaken the United States in total enrollment, even though only 24 percent of the age group participates in post-secondary education.

The government of India, through the Department of Higher Education in the Ministry of Human Resource development (MHRD), formulates all policies related to higher education. The University Grants Commission (UGC), a statutory body established in 1956 by Parliament and modeled on the UGC of United Kingdom, is responsible for the coordination, evaluation, and maintenance of standards for higher education in India. The UGC, funded through MHRD, is also responsible for establishing central universities across India and for recognizing "deemed to be universities" run by privately funded trusts and universities established by the 28 state governments across India.

A host of reforms and financial investment could transform the country into an advanced knowledge economy. Investment in the higher education sector is likely to increase as well. As developing a skilled human resource base gains prominence on the national policy agenda, it is expected that developing higher education infrastructure will become a key focus area.

The origin of Symbiosis must be understood in the context of strengthening in the private sector, the economy in general, and in higher education in particular during the late 1970's. This was a time when the Indian public higher education system was impacted by cuts to public expenditures and rising demand for career-oriented higher education. In order to address this situation, several states authorized self-financing colleges that primarily offered professional education. During the 1980s, as the knowledge economy and globalization gained prevalence, Indian policymakers began to emphasize the importance of linking employability and skills acquisition with higher education. States in the south and west were at the forefront of economic development in India, so it is not surprising that Karnataka and Maharashtra took the first steps towards privatization within higher education in the country.

2   The Symbiosis Story

S. B. Mujumdar, a professor of botany at Fergusson College, one of India's oldest colleges established in 1885, was enjoying a quiet afternoon during the Diwali Festival of Lights holiday when he noticed a young girl passing something through the window of the boy's hostel where he was the warden. He observed this incident repeatedly for a week before entering the hostel to find out what was going on. He saw a frail young man lying on the bed. When he questioned the young man, the boy started weeping profusely. He told the warden that he was a student from Mauritius and was suffering from jaundice. He had become weak and could not even walk a few steps. All his fellow students had gone home, as it was Diwali vacation. His sister, also a student at the Fergusson College, brought him home-cooked food daily and passed the lunch box through the window of his room as girls were not allowed to enter the boys hostel.

This incident was pivotal. Mujumdar discovered that foreign students in Pune faced many problems related to language, accommodation, home sickness, etc. He decided to form an organization dedicated to the welfare of foreign students to provide them with a "home away from home" (Mujumdar, 2007). Influenced by his study of botany, he named this organization Symbiosis, meaning two different organisms in close proximity that result in a relationship of mutual benefit. With friends and students, Mujumdar registered Symbiosis as a society under the Society's Registration Act and as a trust under the Maharashtra Public Trust Act. For the purpose of registration of the trust, every member had to pay Rs. 250 (US$3.40). Prof. Mujumdar fell short of one member to qualify as a trust so included his wife, Sanjivani Mujumdar, as a member and trustee and paid the fee to the Trust Office. Thus, the Symbiosis Society was established with six members and the amount of 1500 Indian Rupees (US$20.53). The trust later became the sponsoring society of the Symbiosis International University.

The justification for establishing educational institutions was to promote international understanding through quality education. Mujumdar believed that education would be the best medium to promote international understanding between foreign and Indian students.

The Symbiosis International University germinated from the Symbiosis Society established in January 1971 in Pune, Maharashtra. The one-acre plot in central Pune and adjoining areas on which the Symbiosis Society was founded remain the nerve center of Symbiosis. The society is an educational trust formed with the singular goal of improving the living and educational experience of international students in Pune. On many levels, the setting up of the society was groundbreaking at the time. In India there just wasn't much of a place to ensure that international students had a safe and rewarding experience. Far too often, international students faced prejudice and disorientation as foreigners living and studying in India.

As rector and professor at Fergusson College, Mujumdar observed the challenges closely and established an organization grounded in the institutional and the local communities that would ensure that the student experiences inside and outside the classroom exceeded their expectations (Mujumdar, 2007).

Altbach (2015) notes that, "Many of the best-known and respected universities that are either family-owned or that stem from family roots ... are established because the founder was guided by sense of philanthropy or social mission—a visionary thinker with ideas about education ..." (pp. 11–12). The Symbiosis Society reflects this. The society was ideologically grounded in the values of intercultural understanding and cooperation—*Vasudhaiv Kutumbakam* (The world is one family.) and the intent of the initiative rang true to students from the beginning. International students and later, the academic community of Pune, came together to ensure the welfare of international students. The society also sought to change the mindset of local people, indeed all Indians, to encourage open-mindedness and inclusivity that encompassed international students. The society continues to work at the levels of collective action and individual awareness to enhance the lives of international students. It has grown, building on its success and the requirements of the local international student community, rather than being influenced by external factors.

The organization has always been guided by the overarching goal of having students from varied cultural backgrounds share a common platform and providing an environment that would promote a multicultural experience. The contemporary ideas of global citizenship and intercultural understanding have been the cornerstones of Symbiosis since its inception.

Symbiosis shares many characteristics that are typical of family-managed institutions in general. Although the chief criterion for this category is centralized management, family-managed institutions can be divided into two categories. There are those that emerged during the "higher education boom" and rarely figure in the prestige hierarchy. In this scenario, the family management aspect and financial arrangements are often kept opaque. There is a second category of higher-quality and reputable institutions that were established before the boom (Altbach, 2015). In India, the vast majority of family-managed institutions were set up at the beginning of the millennium when private institutions were proliferating. Symbiosis belongs to the latter category.

2.1   Symbiosis: Ideas and Development

Symbiosis was founded to solve a very real problem. It has grown less along a planned trajectory, but along a largely unforeseen path, responding to the emerging requirements within the realm of higher education. At the outset, by virtue of being headquartered in Pune, it has benefitted infinitely from a cultural legacy that values and upholds education as the worthiest of human endeavors. It has also benefitted from a vast pool of talented and educated men and women who call Pune home—a stable, peaceful political environment, an effective judicial apparatus, and modern urban-civic infrastructure. The Maharashtra state government has been proactive with respect to education, especially higher education. It is no wonder that Maharashtra was one of the states to herald the wave of privatization that began in the 1980s. The close involvement of the state government has contributed to putting the state at the top of the higher education map in India. The organization has been fortunate in receiving the backing and goodwill of people from diverse backgrounds. Symbiosis has grown as an organization deeply entrenched in the educational and cultural ethos of the city of Pune (Mujumdar, 2007).

The first three institutes that were established reflect the rationale behind Symbiosis as well its institution building strategy from the time of inception to the present. The majority of government-owned and managed institutions in India have offered curriculum and pedagogy oriented more towards policymakers than to student requirements. Educators in the public sector are changing for the better, but this wasn't the case in the past. The educational model within the public sector is often criticized for not being sufficiently responsive to students or aligned to labor market needs. Dynamism and innovation have been lacking.

The setting up of the English Language Teaching Institute of Symbiosis (ELTIS) in 1972 was groundbreaking as it institutionalized teaching the English language in a way that was quite radical for the time. It offered English as second language to Indian as well as international students. Even though it may not seem much of a leap, it was an approach ahead of its time. The ELTIS has been successful because it responded to a very real, but ignored problem—that international students struggle with English and that becomes an obstacle to their educational success and living experience.

The Symbiosis Law College followed in 1977. This marked a shift to a mainstream educational institution for both international and domestic students.

Until then, Symbiosis mainly addressed the experiences of international students. It is not possible for an organization to be grounded successfully in the social milieu without being more broadly responsive to the needs of local people. By diversifying into new academic areas and including more students, Symbiosis was able to generate more resources and solidify its organizational foundation. This diversification allowed Symbiosis to provide international students with better support.

As Symbiosis expanded, it strengthened its organizational stature and means to serve student needs. Self-sufficiency through resource building has been central to the institutional ethos of Symbiosis. The Symbiosis Law College and the Symbiosis Institute of Business Management (SIBM), established in 1978, were among the first institutions in India to offer evening classes. It was a step towards an educational goal of lifelong learning. The SIBM and law college are ranked by India's National Institute Ranking Framework among the top management and law schools in India.

The most important reason why Symbiosis has succeeded in receiving accreditation and the regulatory nod for its many unique offerings is because the senior management has made every effort to contract the best experts to develop and deliver programs, hire competent teachers, and oversee ongoing quality management. Mujumdar's position as a well-liked and respected member of the academic community undoubtedly contributed to Symbiosis's success in attracting thought leaders as well as subject and industry-experts from a number of disciplinary realms. The close involvement of expert and experienced advisors ensures that programs benefit from their insights and that teaching and non-teaching staff keep working to improve the student experience.

Mujumdar (2007) states that Symbiosis reflects sociologist Herbert Spencer's concept of "progressive differentiation" whereby the growth of the entity occurs with increasing complexity in both structure and function. Symbiosis has grown steadily, diversifying organizational structure and functionalities. By 2002, Symbiosis had established a solid reputation for academic excellence.

Symbiosis institutes offer highly specialized programs in fields as diverse as law, management, computer science, mass communication, international business, humanities, social science, telecom, healthcare, and information technology. Four of the Symbiosis institutes are affiliated with the University of Pune, a respected public institution. At that time, this affiliation offered students much reassurance as it verified that these institutes met the stringent standards of the university—a degree from University of Pune represented prestige. However, this was a period when many changes were taking place in the Indian economy that necessitated a corresponding shift in the skills required by the labor market.

Career-focused education and career-preparedness skills were becoming increasingly important. Only an academic culture attuned to the needs of students and industry and capable of innovation could respond to these nationwide and global changes. Although affiliation to the University of Pune brought recognition to the Symbiosis institutes, it was becoming clear that it was a mixed blessing. The rigid, outdated rules and protocols typical of public universities posed an obstacle to modernizing curriculum and pedagogical practices. A common challenge to colleges affiliated with a large public university in India is that self-determination and autonomy become compromised. The university mandates administrative and academic decisions related to student intake, assessment, curriculum, and hiring practices. It became clear that a greater degree of self-governance was required for Symbiosis to remain in step with the transformative forces at play in India and across the globe.

The Indian government announced an educational policy whereby institutions formally affiliated to a public university could apply for a "deemed university" status. Three of the institutes met the criteria required by the University Grants Commission. Mujumdar and other members of the Symbiosis Society worked together to ensure that the institutes were strong candidates for inclusion in the deemed university category. Many public officials were consulted. A committee of experts, from the University Grants Commission (UGC) and later another team from the All India Council for Technical Education (AICTE) visited the Symbiosis institutes to examine their strengths as potential candidates. Both committees made positive recommendations and Symbiosis was awarded the "deemed to be university" status in 2002.

2.2   Symbiosis: Institutional Culture and Management Principles

The Symbiosis leadership has always elevated the vision of academic excellence through international understanding and cooperation as a guiding principle. Chester Barnard, in *The Functions of the Executive* (1938) proposed the concept of "organization man." According to this concept, the most important single contribution required of the executive is loyalty, not the loyalty of employees to their supervisors, but the loyalty of the executive to the guiding principles and the motivation that led him to embark upon the entrepreneurship voyage (Mujumdar, 2007).

The concept of organizational culture allows an educational organization to perform by helping to identify potential ways to improve management and enhance operational strategies (Lacatus, 2013). A university's culture is essentially about core beliefs, values, and norms. In other words, it is about its self-identity. Institutional culture is complex and multidimensional because it includes and intersects with scores of social concepts such as diversity, equality, hierarchy, and centralism. The idea of university culture has assumed even greater significance in recent times because universities are pressured to respond to rapid socioeconomic and technological changes. The postindustrial society presents unrelenting stress to higher education institutions to adapt and evolve in relation to the ever-changing environment.

The senior leadership at Symbiosis has maintained that universities are more than degree-granting bodies; they are multifaceted organizations and a distinctive institutional ethos is crucial to success. Whereas academic freedom and operational autonomy are basic values, transformations in socioeconomic conditions must be acknowledged because they shape the purpose of the university. The university's resilience in adapting to these changes will determine how well it does in the years to come.

At Symbiosis, the mission of achieving international understanding and cooperation reflects the ideological identity of the organization. It is very much a student-centered mission. The university's core objective is to educate students who will emerge as responsible global citizens and agents of peace, harmony, and goodwill. The fact that Symbiosis believes so strongly in multiculturalism—the belief that diversity is an asset, in fact a resource in and of itself—has reinforced a culture of meritocracy at all levels.

Merit is the only consideration in hiring practices and admission policies. Symbiosis has been thoroughly inclusive and non-denominational in spirit as well as in practice. Intercultural understanding and cooperation are the cornerstones of the organization and leadership does not merely accept, but rather encourages, diversity of backgrounds, beliefs, and opinions.

At Symbiosis, transparency and accountability in decision-making and in operational guidelines are upheld through an intricate system of checks and balances at all levels. At the level of institutional leadership are three top committees—the managing committee of the Symbiosis Society, the general body, and the board of management of SIU. In accordance with the Symbiosis constitution the general body elects the members of the managing committee. The members of the managing committee are elected for a period of five years. Mujumdar is the founding director and president of the Symbiosis Society. The managing committee of Symbiosis Society is comprised of 11 members, of which five members are from the same family and the rest are experts from different fields. The committee functions democratically and all members function as equals. The committee members are drawn from diverse areas and form a rich pool of talent and expertise. Below these committees are standing committees, advisory bodies, academic councils, etc. The committees invariably are comprised of a diverse pool of experts, practitioners, and entrepreneurs who contribute knowledge, experience, constructive criticism,

and healthy skepticism. The leadership has always believed that advisors contribute to more than quality assurance; they ensure the ethical operation of
the organization. At the operational level there are directors, administrative
heads, and faculty members—a total of 2,930 people employed by Symbiosis.
The institution heads exercise complete operational autonomy in accordance
with clearly outlined institutional protocols.

2.3   *Financial Policies and Realities*

The university, as with all private institutions in India, receive no grants or
other financial support from the government. Moreover, India does not have
a culture of endowments built from the donations of philanthropists as in US
and UK. Indian private institutions are responsible for generating all their own
funds. At Symbiosis, a customer-oriented, resource building approach guides
the generation of funds. The tuition fees are announced publicly in advance
of each academic year. From the time of its inception, the university has had
a pragmatic approach towards revenue generation based on an economically
viable and fair fee structure. This necessitates a balance between the interests
of students and the institution. More importantly, it implies that it is the university's responsibility to ensure that students experience a full range of benefits
for the fees they pay. In other words, management must deliver on the promise of an excellent instructional system, top-notch infrastructure, and provide
appropriate curricular and extra-curricular resources. This is made possible by
surplus capital generated from tuition fees and reinvested in the university for
the purpose of enhancement and expansion. The university follows a tuition
policy that rejects charging "capitation fees" to students in excess of published
costs. The stand against donation fees ensures that students are admitted on
grounds of merit alone.

Upon its establishment, Symbiosis did not have any external sources of
funding. Mujumdar drew from his monthly salary to cover expenses incurred
for conducting events and cultural programs to promote international understanding. Several industrialists in Pune rejected his idea of Symbiosis, but Sangtani, a prominent philanthropist, was excited. Sangtani encouraged Mujumdar
and loaned the funds for the construction of the first buildings to create infrastructure for the educational institutes.

The policy of sound financial management rests on the mantra of 25:50:25
that is 25 percent of expenses are allocated to salaries, 50 percent to educational activities and 25 percent to surplus to be reinvested in development.
The director of every institute is advised to follow this mantra when developing annual budgets. This gives the department heads autonomy with almost
75 percent of their revenues and makes a 25 percent surplus mandatory. This

model initiated in 1970s has worked well and the accumulated surpluses have aided growth and expansion.

2.4   *Management Orientation and Structure*

In "Marketing Myopia," Theodore Levitt (1960) stated that industry is a customer-satisfying process, not a goods-producing process. He also demonstrated that a thoroughly customer-oriented management philosophy is important to achieving continued growth. As an organization in the realm of higher education, Symbiosis has put the goal of serving student's educational needs over short-term gains and this is the principle reason why the university has continued to grow (Mujumdar, 2007).

In *My Years with General Motors*, Alfred Sloan (1963) stated that a well-judged combination of centralization with decentralization is crucial to the success of the organization. Sloan's management approach to organizational development was based on processes that led to centralized planning of core and critical functions, while also granting the authority to make operational decisions to middle-level managers. The challenge of striking balance between centralization with decentralization at Symbiosis was addressed with the help of coordinating committees that resulted in dispersing wide-ranging powers to divisional managers and encouraged them to find their own efficiencies, but still maintaining central oversight. An important aspect of management at Symbiosis is decentralization with coordinated control. The institute directors, administrative and academic heads, and faculty members enjoy a fair degree of operational autonomy in accordance with the norms of probity. However, they are expected to make decisions and execute processes while being mindful of the overarching vision and goals of the organization set forth by the leadership.

Communication between senior management, institutional heads, and administrative and academic personnel is achieved through the appointment of committees. Every new venture, whether an academic conference or periodic upgrading of infrastructure, begins with setting up a committee. The committees are invariably composed of senior management, administrative personnel, technical experts, faculty members, and subject experts from outside Symbiosis.

At Symbiosis, the leadership emphasizes that an educational institution is a social entity. It is rooted in and receives sustenance from its immediate social reality. It believes in giving back to the society through community welfare-oriented projects. Leaders at Symbiosis consider social activists, political figures, and captains of industry important stakeholders and collaborators in its community-building initiatives. Symbiosis is grounded in the local and global community in spirit and practice. Although the triad of teaching, training, and research is the core focus, the organization maintains a commitment to the collective good.

2.5   *Growth and Stature*

Today, Symbiosis includes five K-12 schools, an autonomous college affiliated to the University of Pune, and 38 institutions in Pune and other cities in India within the sphere of Symbiosis International (SIU). Campuses are spread across five cities—Pune, Noida, Bengaluru, Hyderabad, Nashik, and Nagpur. These institutions offer programs in fields as diverse as management, law, health and biological sciences, information technology, humanities, engineering, design, media, telecommunications, geo-informatics, and languages.

The university counts among its proudest achievements the fact that the number of international students continues to increase. In 1972, 900 foreign students from 21 countries were studying at various colleges in Pune. The number of foreign students studying at Symbiosis increased to 2,200 by 2017. The university has academic collaborations with 60 foreign institutions.

The university was ranked amongst the top 50 universities in India by the National Institute Ranking Framework (NIRF) in 2018. It was also featured in the list of top 250 universities in Asia and the top 110 in BRICS by QS World University rankings in 2018. The university has been re-accredited by the National Assessment and Accreditation Council (NAAC) with a Grade A and a cumulative grade point average (CGPA) of 3.58 on a four-point scale. Symbiosis institutions in the fields of management, media, law, and computer science have been ranked consistently among the top ten in the country by various surveys. Symbiosis has over 38,000 students from all states of India and over 85 countries. Symbiosis epitomizes the motto of *Vasudhaiva Kutumbakam*—The world is one family.

A unique institution established by Symbiosis is the Symbiosis Institute of Management Studies (SIMS). It provides management education exclusively for defense personnel and their dependents. Another innovative institution is the Pune Police Public School (PPPS) that provides education to the children of police. The PPPS school is managed and operated by Symbiosis through an MoU between Symbiosis and Pune Citizen Police Foundation, another trust established for the welfare of police personnel and their families. Pune is a major center for police training and research in India. Symbiosis has also established the Dr. Ambedkar Museum and Memorial that houses the personal belongings and memorabilia of Dr. Babasaheb Ambedkar, the architect of the India's Constitution. The Symbiosis Afro-Asian Cultural Museum is also an important cultural center. All these institutions are funded by Symbiosis Society, a non-profit organization.

2.6   *Family Management*

Sanjivani Mujumdar, the founder's wife, was appointed a trustee of the Symbiosis Trust and Society at the creation of Symbiosis but was not involved in the
formal operations of Symbiosis. Sanjivani Mujumdar manages the Dr. Babasaheb Ambedkar Memorial Museum. Symbiosis International University is the
only university in India to have two museums. Sanjivani Mujumdar has created a public library on the premises of the Dr. Babasaheb Ambedkar Museum
where students from poor families are provided with books and reading spaces
so that they can study peacefully.

The Mujumdar daughters, Vidya Yeravdekar and Swati Mujumdar, were
kept at a distance from the operations of Symbiosis initially. As young women
they pursued careers of their choice. Yeravdekar, the elder daughter, became a
gynecologist and lived and worked in Oman. During her stay in Oman, she was
impressed with the robust Omani public health system. She returned to India in
1997 and wanted to introduce Symbiosis students and staff to some of the innovative ideas she had observed in Oman. She established the Symbiosis Centre
for Health Care in 1997. This marked the beginning of Yeravdekar's association
with Symbiosis. When Symbiosis received deemed university status, Yeravdekar
became more active in operational activities. She has played a very important
role in building excellence and contributing to the expansion of the university.
Her husband, Rajiv, was invited to establish the faculty of health sciences.

The younger daughter became a computer engineer and worked in the
United States. She returned to India in 2000 when the Symbiosis Centre of Distance Learning (SCDL) was going through an enrollment crisis. Prof. Mujumdar
asked Swati Mujumdar to assume management of the Centre, beginning her
association with Symbiosis. She later established the Symbiosis Open and
Skills University and Symbiosis University of Applied Sciences that offer skill-
based and distance education programs.

Both daughters work in the same way as any of the directors of Symbiosis
institutes. They report to the president of Symbiosis. Mujumdar incorporated
his daughters and son-in-law onto the board of management as a result of their
contributions to the development of Symbiosis.

Although the board of management of the Symbiosis Society includes
members of the family, there is a greater number of members who are not
from the family. Mujumdar has deliberately maintained this balance because
of his belief that an educational institution should be managed by professionals. He also believes that family members should be custodians of the trust
and society, not owners. This culture is instilled in all family members. They
get paid a salary for the services that they render as do other professionals at
Symbiosis. They do not receive other benefits or perks. Although the trust is
doing exceedingly well and generates surplus, all surplus is invested back into

the development of Symbiosis and not appropriated by members or trustees of the Symbiosis society or trust.

2.7   Succession Planning and Legacy Issues

Mujumdar is an educational entrepreneur in India and one of the most respected educators in India. He has received the highest civilian awards, Padma Shri and Padma Bhushan, from the president of India for his contribution to education. It is expected that his daughters must not only maintain the standard of excellence that he has set, but also take Symbiosis to greater heights. Although they enjoy the benefits of a strong Symbiosis brand, they must create an identity based on their own achievements and merit.

Each of the daughters has created a niche for herself. Vidya is interested in the internationalization of higher education. She has been nominated twice as member of the University Grants Commission, the most important agency governing higher education in India. As pro-chancellor of Symbiosis International University, she has contributed significantly to policy formulation of higher education in India. Her husband, a medical professional and dean of the faculty of health and biological sciences at Symbiosis, has created a niche for himself as well in the area of health education and public health. He was nominated to the board of governors of the Medical Council of India, a statutory body for the establishment of uniform and high standards of medical education in India. His research is in the area of public health and he is frequently invited to contribute to policy formulation.

Swati, the younger daughter and pro-chancellor of Symbiosis University of Applied Sciences, has excelled in the specialized fields of skill development and distance education. She has established universities in skill development in Pune and Indore. She has also drafted policies for skill development education for the government of Maharashtra.

Although the second generation in a family-managed university has innumerable opportunities, the challenges they face may outweigh the them. These challenges include issues related to identity, being constantly scrutinized by the public, being compared with the founder and, above all, being criticized for the perception that they achieved their position by virtue of birth.

In truth, members of the family face the most difficulty in establishing their identity due to the frequent comparisons made between them and the founder. That said, the opportunity to bring innovation and professionalism to the organization is theirs and it is up to them to do what they can with the opportunities given to them.

With 108 family-owned businesses, India has the third highest number of family-owned business in the world. Indian family-owned businesses are generally more mature with 62 percent of India's 50 largest businesses having already been passed to the second or third generation (Explore the might, 2018). From neighborhood stores to influential business conglomerates families such as the Tatas, the Ambanis, the Birlas, and the Godrejs and their family-managed businesses have fueled the entrepreneurial spirit in India.

Family and business, two distinct institutions, operate in the same space as one entity with a mix of strengths and weaknesses. Indian family-owned businesses enjoy many advantages. They have an intimate knowledge of the opportunities and challenges as knowledge is passed from one generation to the next; they tend to be people savvy as a result of formal and informal networking; there tends to be more familiarity and trust amongst senior leaders; their distribution capabilities are strong due to size and the ability to scale; their brand stature is more likely to be robust because Indian culture equates a tightly-knit family system with positive attributes such as loyalty, trustworthiness, respect for tradition, and integrity. The challenges are generally related to succession planning, talent retention, and a conservative outlook.

Succession planning is certainly complex. The question is whether future generations will have the talent needed to manage the enterprise successfully. Inheritors are commonly pushed to acquire leadership and managerial capabilities through high quality education and training. As a result of formal qualifications and experience and informal know-how, they function as equals to the executives who report to them, but with additional leadership skill and vision to complement professional knowledge. They command the respect and confidence due to them as professionals, not because of hierarchy or family rank, but because of education and training.

An important skill is the ability to judge when to delegate control and to what degree. Family members must appreciate the difference between operational and entrepreneurial decisions. Many second and third generation family leaders in businesses realize that their role is not to override managerial and technical experts in conducting day-to-day operations, but to provide direction, ensure that the organization functions as a cohesive body and stays on a path that is in keeping with long-term mission and goals.

Future generations carry a huge weight and pressure to prove their competence and measure up to the stature of the founder. Many second and third generation family members prove themselves by raising capital, diversifying, infusing modern ideas and contemporary technology, embracing positive change, competing with multinational companies, and charting new courses. But there is the risk that as different generations take over, the possibility of splits and cracks within family leadership increases.

Many Indian family-owned businesses have dealt with legacy challenges commendably. After becoming the head of the Tata group, Ratan Tata, chairman of Tata Group between 1991 and 2012 and a member of the Tata family, brought about significant modernization and led the company to unprecedented success. The Birla group, led by Aditya Birla, who was grandson of legendary G. D. Birla, set up highly successful ventures in Southeast Asia and Egypt. He was succeeded by his son Kumar Mangalam Birla, who further expanded and modernized the Birla Group. Mukesh Ambani (son of Dhirubhai Ambani, and chairman and managing director of Reliance Industries) and Anand Mahindra (son of Harish Mahindra, and chairman of the Mahindra Group) are sterling examples of young inheritors (who inherited at the ages of 34 and 36 respectively) who have proved to be successful business leaders and have contributed to enhancing India's position on the global corporate scene (Chandran, 2008).

Transformation has been brought to Symbiosis by the second generation with greater emphasis on internationalization across academic programs, new delivery and services channels, promotion of public health, and skill development.

The Indian family system is different from family-run businesses in the West. The Indian family system is more united. In the West, children are likely to leave their families at the age of 18 and become more independent. The profession of the father is only rarely continued by the son or daughter. In a typical Indian family, the *karta* is a male member who is the breadwinner and head of the family. It is his responsibility to keep the family living close together as a unit, even after new generations enlarge the family. The values of the family are passed down from one generation to the next along with the family business or profession. Thus, a goldsmith will pass his trade to his children and a doctor will encourage his children to study and practice medicine. However, in India things are not as rigid as they used to be; increasingly children are less inclined to follow the father's path.

The founder of an organization not only creates it but nurtures it and sets certain institutional standards. Importantly, the founder creates a vision and strategy for the organization. The second generation carries forward this legacy, brings in innovation and professionalism, and maintains the values of the founder. The third generation is aware of the vision but may divert it towards a new direction. In India, there is a saying, "Kothi ki umar saath sal" (The age of a house is 60 years.), that means that a house remains intact for 60 years or up to the third generation. After 60 years, the house may need to be rebuilt. Therefore, to maintain the vision of the founder, an innovative and flexible model of governance needs to evolve for the future generation to carry the legacy forward.

As with any other organization, a family-managed university has challenges to sustain a vision and mission through leadership transitions. Whereas family-managed universities have certain advantages, these universities also have the burden of putting in place a solid ideological foundation, so that the core values that guided the establishment of the organization do not get lost as control passes to new generations.

3   Conclusion

In an increasingly globalized world apprehensions and anxieties emerge as to the future. As Altbach, Reisberg, and Rumbley (2010) have observed, an academic revolution has been afoot during the past half century. The transformations that have taken place are unparalleled in scope and diversity. Globalization will add layers of complexity to higher education in India and elsewhere. The challenges that come with massification have increased with more diversified demand for tertiary education and the increased participation of the private sector will make higher education a more competitive enterprise than it has been. The future of higher education may not be predictable, but it also holds myriad promises and a wealth of opportunities for everyone, institutions, and students at the "center" as well as those at the "peripheries" (Frank, 1978).

Symbiosis prepares itself for the future by being keenly attuned to trends and transformations in higher education in India and abroad. University leadership and senior faculty members are on committees and boards related to higher education at the national and international level and attend a large number of conventions and conferences to stay abreast of advances in higher education and bring them home to Symbiosis students.

Symbiosis has stayed in step with student and labor market requirements as well as advances in pedagogy and curriculum in India and abroad. This has been a key differentiator for the organization since its inception and it continues to drive success to the present day. At Symbiosis, senior management acknowledges the central role of universities in supporting the knowledge economy, promoting equitable social mobility, and preparing responsible global citizens. The university appreciates that higher education is fundamentally an instrument of collective welfare and that its multiple and diverse contributions to society must be fulfilled. An understanding of the emerging challenges and the broader roles of higher education in the globalized society are crucial to assessing where the university stands today and where it is headed tomorrow. Symbiosis, a university guided by a dedicated and dynamic leadership, is empowered to deal with new challenges and optimize opportunities in the years to come. Endowed with a unique historical legacy and a steadfast institutional ethos, the university is poised to scale greater heights. Family-management has proved to be the organization's top asset and there is every reason to believe that the future holds even more promise.

References

Agarwal, P. (2017). India's growth of postsecondary education: Scale, speed and fault lines. In P. G. Altbach, L. Reisberg, & H. de Wit (Eds.), *Responding to massification: Differentiation in postsecondary education worldwide* (pp. 75–87). Rotterdam, The Netherlands: Sense Publishers.

AISHE. (n.d.). *All India survey on higher education.* Retrieved from http://aishe.nic.in/aishe/reports

Altbach, P. G. (2015). Universities: Family style. *International Higher Education, 39,* 10–12.

Altbach, P. G., Reisberg, L., & Rumbley, L. E. (2010). *Trends in global education. Tracking an academic revolution.* Rotterdam, The Netherlands: Sense Publishers.

Barnard, C. (1938). *The functions of the executive.* Cambridge, MA: Harvard University Press.

Chandran, R. (2008, October 12). India's corporate empires grapple with succession. *Reuters.* Retrieved from https://www.reuters.com/article/us-india-conglomerates-succession/indias-corporate-empires-grapple-with-succession-idUSTRE49C01L20081013

Explore the might of family-owned businesses in India. (2018, May 3). *Moneycontrol.* Retrieved from https://www.moneycontrol.com/news/business/podcast-explore-the-might-of-family-owned-businesses-in-india-2562307.html

Frank, A. G. (1978). Dependent accumulation and *underdevelopment.* Basingstoke: Palgrave MacMillan.

Lacatus, M. L. (2013). Organizational culture in contemporary university. *Procedia – Social and Behavioral Sciences, 76,* 421–425.

Levitt, Theodore. (1960). Marketing myopia. *Harvard Business Review, 38*(4), 45–56.

Mujumdar, S. B. (2007). *Symbiosis: Biography of an idea.* New Delhi: Macmillan India Ltd.

Powar, K. B. (2012). *Expanding domains in Indian higher education.* New Delhi: Association of Indian Universities Publications.

Sloan, A. (1963). *My years with general motors.* New York, NY: Doubleday.

Sporn, B. (1996). Managing university culture: An analysis of the relationship between institutional culture and management approaches. *Higher Education, 32,* 41–61.

Yeravdekar, V., & Tiwari, G. (2016). *Internationalization of higher education in India.* New Delhi, India: Sage Publications.

CHAPTER 11

Japan: A Special Breed—Family-Owned or Managed Universities

Kazuhito Obara

Heredity in Japan means that a status held by parents or their occupation is passed on to their children or relations ensuring that successors obtain social power and authority. The concept of hereditary occupations is often criticized for its exclusive, feudalistic, and anti-democratic characteristic. This type of criticism is levied in the education industry.

When a fraudulent subsidy at Hokkaido Asai Gakuen University, a family-owned higher education institution, was reported in a newspaper article in November 2005, it startled the Japanese educational world and led to the accusation that the owner was using the university for his own purposes. In the educational industry particularly, ensuring transparency through fair, democratic governance and management throughout the process of decision-making is indispensable; FOMHEIs are no exception.

This chapter briefly introduces FOMHEIs in Japan in the context of laws, regulations, statistics, patterns of ownership, and their role in Japanese higher education. Tamagawa University, a private university in the Tokyo area, is introduced as a case study and carefully analyzed in light of its history, philosophy, mission, organizational structure, governance, succession, and challenges.

1   Overview of Private Universities in Japan

The Japanese higher education system is an example of a diversified mass higher education system in a highly industrialized country. It consists of various categories and types of institutions with diverse missions, functions, academic standards, prestige, status, and financing methods. Japanese higher education has reached universal access with more than 50 percent of the age cohort continuing to postsecondary education and the sector therefore represents a mature stage of development. However, the Japanese higher education system and the mode of its operation have been affected by significant new trends such as globalization, an aging population, and increasing international competition. Consequently, there have been radical reforms. In 2004,

© KONINKLIJKE BRILL NV, LEIDEN, 2020 | DOI: 10.1163/9789004423435_011

the National University Corporation Law extended the level of discretion and flexibility that universities should retain in the management of their assets. In response, national universities were incorporated and became national university corporations. An official evaluation system was initiated, and competitive resource allocation established. Internationalization is being promoted but institutions are struggling to strengthen international competitiveness. Universities continue to improve the quality of university education and develop human resources capable of playing an active role across national borders, but foreign students may experience difficulty in finding an institution that offers internationally recognized programs and degrees delivered in English.

Japanese universities are divided into three categories—national, originally created by the Japanese government, but subsequently established by national university corporations known as *kokuritsudaigaku houjin* and that enjoy the highest prestige; public universities, established by local or prefectural public entities or public university corporations known as *kouritsudaigaku houjin*; and private universities, established by incorporated educational institutions known as *gakko houjin*.

According to the Ministry of Education, Culture, Sports, Science, and Technology (MEXT), each private university has its own unique education and research activities based on its founding mission and vision and plays an important role both qualitatively and quantitatively in the development of Japanese higher education. Private universities are expected to serve public needs and to create attractive schools for the future but operating on financial resources acquired through their own efforts. They are expected to release and disclose official information.

Private universities in Japan account for about 77.1 percent of all universities and enroll about 73.7 percent of all university students. There are 603 private universities, 86 national, and 93 public universities. According to the Promotion and Mutual Aid Corporation for Private Schools of Japan, 491 private universities were able to fill only 80 percent of their enrollment capacity with eight filling less than half of their capacity. In fact, 39.6 percent of incorporated educational institutions that manage private universities have expenditures that exceed revenues. In other words, much of the private higher education sector is in a state of financial crisis prompting many changes to take place.

1.1   *Laws and Regulations*
In addition to articles addressing education in the Japanese Constitution, the Basic Act on Education, the School Education Act, and the University Foundation Standards, all incorporated educational institutions offering university-level programs have to comply with additional laws, regulations, and other

related acts. The Private School Act, Act on Subsidies for Private Schools, Accounting Standards for Educational Corporations, and Review Standards for the Act of Endowment were established specifically for the regulation of private universities.

The Private School Act stipulates rules related to the establishment and administration of incorporated educational institutions. This law was enacted in 1949 and designed for promoting "the sound development of private schools by taking into account their characteristics and features, putting a high value on their autonomy, and enhancing their public nature" (Article 1). It was revised in 2004 and 2014 in light of changing situations such as the decline in the birthrate, requirements for governance and accountability, the accreditation system, and so forth.

The law clearly defines the rules for managing and administering incorporated educational institutions. Those institutions need five or more trustees and two or more auditors as institutional officers where one of the trustees becomes the chairperson. The board of trustees determines the business of the institution and executes trustee duties. While the chairperson represents the institution and presides over its business, the other trustees administer the business of the institution by assisting the chairperson.

The Private School Act of the national government includes articles to assure transparency in hiring and firing leadership and teaching staff. Paragraph 7 of Article 38 is the most relevant to FOMHEIS where it is stated that the officers "must not include the spouse of any officer or more than one relative within the third degree of kinship of any officer." By prohibiting control over the board of trustees by relatives, the law attempts to eliminate arbitrary proceedings and instead aims to achieve democratic and appropriate management of incorporated educational institutions to ensure that public good take priority over family interests. The law contains regulations and punitive consequences constraining the activities of chairpersons and trustees to prevent corruption at their universities.

1.2   *Patterns of Ownership and Succession*

Family businesses and family succession are frequently criticized in Japan and it appears with some reason. In a national study comparing family businesses and non-family businesses, the Research Institute of Economy, Trade & Industry (RIETI) analyzed microdata comparing productivity and business objectives. The research findings (2008) show labor and overall productivity of family businesses to be significantly lower. The performance of *nisei* (second generation) companies run by immediate family or relations of the founder was inferior to both non-family businesses and companies run by the founder.

In its conclusion, the RIETI (2008) asserted that the dynamics of family businesses had a negative effect on market entry and exit strategies, competition, and inter-enterprise distribution. As a result, family businesses may seem unattractive, especially from the standpoint of national policy for improving productivity. However, it is also clear that the presence of family and relations of the founder in itself would not necessarily mean inefficient labor. What becomes crucial is for family businesses to avoid prioritizing private benefits and sacrificing corporate profits by taking into account the trade-off between family continuance and their long-term productivity and growth opportunities.

In contrast, Fujimoto (2010) focused on the reality that most of the small-to-medium-sized enterprises (SME) in Japan account for 90 percent of the 4,210,000 companies nationwide are actually family businesses where hereditary succession persists. He took up the positive aspects of hereditary succession, stating that it enables those in charge of managing their companies to pass on long-term perspective and to transfer operations in a way that supports the continuance of the business. Furthermore, he emphasized the merit of hereditary succession in avoiding time and effort needed to select and assign a replacement and train him or her. A family member successor grows up in an environment where his or her parent carries out the business. Growing up in such an environment leads to an unconscious "imprinting" of knowledge that supports a smooth transfer of leadership.

In his research, Fujimoto (2010) categorized successors in family businesses into two types. The first is a successor who attained his or her position from an authoritative executive and who has a record strong achievement and motivation and consequently, an intense desire to realize leadership. The second is the person who started at the bottom of the career and demonstrates affinity and fellowship with colleagues.

According to the Research Institute for Independent Higher Education (2018), FOMHEIS constitute approximately 40 percent of all private universities. There are two types ownership. One is where the chairperson also holds the position of president of his or her university. This type of ownership is preferred when stable management and finances become the top priority as decision-making is faster and smoother compared with non-FOMHEIS.

The other type is when the roles of chairperson and president are occupied by different people. If a FOMHEI is affiliated with a religious body such as a Buddhist, Christian, or Shinto-assembly or a newly-established-religious university, the owner may hold the post as a president rather than chairperson as the chair position is conventionally held by a person dispatched from the religious body and parent organization.

Although ownership is usually transferred to the next generation through heredity, there are some FOMHEIs that were not founded by families or FOM-HEIs that pass to non-family ownership. In these cases, new ownership is achieved by a takeover.

Heredity is still the most common way of transferring ownership of family businesses. In these cases, grooming and training a family successor is crucial.

2   FOMHEIs in the Higher Education Environment in Japan

FOMHEIs in Japan are incorporated educational institutions that are typically non-profit; therefore, unlike business enterprises studied by the RIETI, FOM-HEIs give less attention to productivity as a performance measure. For-profit FOMHEIs also exist, are more like business enterprises, and required to pay corporate taxes.

The prime concern of the founder and his or her family is the cultivation of a successor who is capable of maintaining the stability of the business and in certain cases, expanding it. In other words, the priority of FOMHEIs in the higher education environment in Japan is to protect the founding spirit and unique features. While national and public university corporations are required to protect impartiality and neutrality in the cause of education, incorporated educational institutions, protected by academic freedom, are allowed to develop more focused missions.

However, as Fujimoto's research indicated, if hereditary succession is controlled exclusively by the family, the successor may continue the pattern of concentrated authority at the expense of other objectives. Even while FOM-HEIs continue to lose market share in Japan, they may be motivated by the desire to maintain family control over the institution rather than to adapt to changing circumstances. In order to survive, FOMHEIs need next generation leadership that shares the original vision, philosophy, and commitment and devotes him or herself to good management and transparent governance.

3   Case Study: Tamagawa University

Tamagawa University is located in the Machida district of Tokyo. The location is designated by the Tokyo Metropolitan Ordinance as *bunkyo chiku* (a school zone). According to the Tokyo Metropolitan Ordinance, a designated school zone strictly prohibits buildings that spoil the surrounding environment or that corrupts public morals. The total area of the campus is 610,000 square meters, but the university also has facilities located outside the campus. The following facilities are located beyond the main campus—Hakone Research Facility for forestry and ecology, a 770,000 square meter laboratory for education on the natural environment in Kanagawa; the Teshikaga Research Facility dedicated to biological production and the environment in a subarctic climate; Teshikaga Research Field, 1,221,000 square meters of northern vegetation forests in Hokkaido; Kushi Research Field with 100,000 square meters to study the functional development of tropical vegetation in Kagoshima; and the Nanamio campus, a 320,000 square meter laboratory for education on ecological systems on Vancouver Island in Canada.

Tamagawa Gakuen encompasses both higher and K-12 education on one campus. There are currently 7,254 undergraduate students, 2,192 full-time distance education students, 633 part-time distance education students, 132 graduate students, and two certificate programs in the arts. In addition, there are 2,051 K-12 students. Tamagawa employs 305 full-time academic staff at the university, 130 full-time K-12 teachers, and 273 full-time administrative staff.

Tamagawa University is closely tied with Tamagawa Academy. A carefully coordinated and administered connection between the high school and university enables high school students to take advantage of the opportunity of early decision and advanced placement at the university. In fact, the university is planning to offer an early college program beginning in 2022 where high school students are offered the opportunity to take university subjects while in the twelfth grade. Moreover, interaction of academic staff and K-12 teachers has been intensive and active. Therefore, a culture that exchanges knowledge and information with the Tamagawa schools has flourished. In short, Tamagawa University and Academy have implemented a unified and consistent education program from K-16.

3.1   *Growth and Evolution*

In 1929, Kuniyoshi Obara established an incorporated foundation (*zaidan houjin*), Tamagawa Gakuen (*gakko houjin*), with a K-12 section known as Tamagawa Academy. The school (kindergarten, elementary school, middle school) began with 111 students and 18 teachers. Obara added a university section allowing graduates of Tamagawa Academy to enroll without requiring the examination required for entry into the imperial universities. In 1942, Tamagawa Gakuen established Koa Kogyo University that moved to Kimitsu, Chiba in 1946 and changed its name to Chiba Institute of Technology. In 1947, Tamagawa University was approved under the old system by the Imperial Order of University. In 1949, Tamagawa University was opened in accordance with a new system of the Acts of Colleges and established a college of humanities and a college of agriculture. The distance education division within the college of humanities was added in 1950. In 1951, Tamagawa Gakuen converted from an incorporated foundation to an incorporated educational institution under the Private School Act.

Tamagawa University established the college of engineering in 1962, the department of arts within the college of humanities in 1964, a master's program at the graduate school of engineering, and the women's junior college in 1967. In 1971, the university established the graduate school of humanities and a master's program in education, then added a doctoral program in education in 1973. The graduate school of agriculture with a master's program were established in 1977 followed by a doctoral program in agriculture. A certificate program in arts was added in 1979. The graduate school of engineering began to offer a doctoral program in 1980.

In 1987, the museum of education was established. The materials collected at the museum are diverse, ranging from the history of education in Japan, the arts, folklore, and archaeology to materials on Schweitzer, Kuniyoshi Obara, the history of Tamagawa, the John Gould bird series lithographs, a collection of Eastern Orthodox Church icons, and Italian art dating from the 17th to the 19th centuries. The museum encompasses more than 30,000 items in a diverse range of fields.

In 1996, the research institute in the area of brain science was opened. The university established the college of business administration in 2001 and the college of education and the college of arts in 2002. A department of liberal arts was incorporated into the college of humanities in 2003. As Tamagawa Gakuen expanded its higher education division, it closed the women's junior college in 2004 due to shrinking enrollments.

In 2005, the university established the graduate school of management and a master's program followed by the graduate school of education and a master's program in 2006. In 2007, the college of arts and sciences and a department of tourism and hospitality within the college of business administration were established. The university was officially accredited by the Japan University Accreditation Association (JUAA) and became an official member of the association. In 2010, the graduate school of brain sciences and its doctoral program were established. The college of tourism and hospitality was established as a separate entity in 2013 and the center for English as a lingua franca was established in 2014.

3.2   Philosophy and Mission

Education at Tamagawa University can be organized around twelve precepts—(1) zenjin (a well-rounded or liberal arts) education; (2) respect for individuality; (3) independent learning and autonomy; (4) efficient education; (5) education with scientific evidence; (6) appreciation of nature, (7) mutual respect between teachers and students, (8) Arbeitsschule (*rosaku* or elaboration and exertion); (9) coincidentia oppositorum (the unity of opposites); (10) pioneer spirit; (11) *juku* education (study of martial arts, traditional crafts and other specialized skills); and (12) international education.

What especially makes Tamagawa University distinctive is *zenjin* education. The founder regarded education in Japan as too narrowly focused because it concentrated heavily on preparation for entrance examinations. On the other hand, he believed a true education should fully and harmoniously incorporate values of culture and humanity.

A *zenjin* education is a value system owing much to German psychologist, Hugo Münsterberg, and neo-Kantian philosophers, Heinrich Rickert and Georg Mehlis. According to this value system, a person is divided into mind and body and defined by six values—truth (*veritas*), goodness (*bonum*), beauty (*pulchritude*), holiness (*sanctitas*), health (*sanitas*) and wealth (*copia*). The aim of a *zenjin* education is to "realize the optimal development of a human personality embodied in six values in a well-balanced, well-rounded, and harmonious way" (Obara, 2018). Thus, by uniformly and thoroughly developing these six areas of human culture, a unique person evolves who is a *zenjin*, a well-rounded person or a whole person who can carry out innovative and creative activities in a variety of fields.

The mission of Tamagawa University, described on its website, follows:

> The mission is to produce outstanding individuals who can contribute not only to Japanese society but to the world. To achieve these goals, students need to improve their knowledge and skills, cultivate healthy mind and body, and lift their spirits. People can always find dissatisfaction in any age. But someone must do the difficult work to improve the situation. People with the courage to start working in the most difficult, unappealing, painful, and disadvantageous situation with a smile are those who are worthy of becoming leaders in the 21st century. Tamagawa University is determined to cultivate those pioneers in life who will courageously take up challenges without fear of failure, even though unknown hardships are sure to come their way. To do that, the university has advocated the twelve precepts of education since its founding.

With the mission above, Tamagawa University is progressing towards the realization of a *zenjin* education and producing outstanding individuals who contribute not only to the Japanese society but also to the larger world.

3.3   *Governance and Structure*

The chairperson of a board of trustees of Tamagawa Gakuen typically supervises both the president and the school principal, although in the case of Tamagawa University, the same person holds all three roles concurrently, a tradition of Tamagawa Gakuen. The authority of the chairperson is clearly defined in the Operation Rules of Tamagawa Gakuen with procedures for delegation, should the chairperson decide to assign the roles of president and principal to others.

The president of a national university typically represents his or her national university corporation and manages the business of the institution. The chairperson of a public university corporation generally occupies the position of president. Thus, the notion that the same person holds multiple positions at a university and oversees academic activities as well as administration is common in Japan. The role and responsibilities of the president at Tamagawa is the same as that of other private universities. At Tamagawa, the president oversees three divisions—the higher education division, other divisions attached to the university, and the support divisions. The higher education division constitutes the six graduate schools, certificate programs, and eight colleges

The board of trustees has a permanent standing committee where the full-time trustees and the chairperson assemble on the occasion that a particular issue occurs such as an employment plan or an urgent operation plan. As the Private School Act prescribes in Chapter 41, incorporated educational institutions have a board of councilors. The board of councilors is convened only when the board of trustees refers matters such as the budget for the coming fiscal year, the business plan and schedule, or the settlement of financial accounts.

At Tamagawa Gakuen the final voting and decision body is always the board of trustees and the permanent standing committee. A dean's council, a K-12 council, and a corporate council vote and make decisions on the matters such as an annual events schedule or a recruitment plan for part-time lecturers or teachers. The chairperson (who is also the president and the principal) attends all of the above-mentioned meetings. In general, new trustees, including the permanent standing committee trustees, are appointed by the current board of trustees.

Deliberative bodies include the board of councilors, faculty meetings, internal staff meetings, and many committee meetings. Meetings are held to discuss and review matters such as the adjudication of student grades, curricula modification or restructuring, and other matters if the council requires further consultation or opinions. For those meetings, neither the president nor the principal is necessarily in attendance.

In short, the governance at Tamagawa Gakuen is carefully and clearly designed. The delineation of authority assigned to the chairperson, the president and the principal is clear so the organizational decision-making process at Tamagawa Gakuen is carried out harmoniously.

3.4   *Finance*

Table 11.1 summarizes Tamagawa's revenue and expenditures for the 2017 fiscal year. Most of the revenue was received from tuition fees (81.5 percent) and a MEXT subsidy accounts for 9.6 percent of income. The subsidy is a significant part of the budget.

Personnel account for 54.8 percent of expenditures. This is typical for most Japanese universities. In the 2017 fiscal year, the balance was an excess of expenditures over revenues, but the fiscal balance of Tamagawa Gakuen on a single fiscal year does not necessarily indicate the financial conditions of the institution over time. In fact, the 2016 fiscal year resulted in a positive balance of revenues over expenditures.

TABLE 11.1   Operating activities revenue/expenditure statement

Revenues from operating activities (in US$)

Tuition fees	138,594,889
Service fees	3,073,333
Contributions	1,990,694
Subsidy	16,273,157
Ancillary business revenues	3,649,778
Miscellaneous	6,525,676
Total: (A)	170,107,528

Expenditures from operating activities (in US$)

Personnel expenses	95,039,620
Education and research expenses	66,064,731
Maintenance expenses	12,302,213
Uncollected fees	29,880
Total: (B)	173,436,444
Total balance: (A) – (B)	−3,328,917

SOURCE: TAMAGAWA GAKUEN WEBSITE

In summary, Tamagawa Gakuen is an institution that is greatly affected by the number of students enrolled and this is a general characteristic of FOMHEIS, particularly those that do not have a medical school or a hospital since medical schools in Japan charge higher tuition fees and a university hospital brings in significant revenue. Tamagawa Gakuen's financial situation has remained strong, but it could be vulnerable to the continuing decline in the Japanese birthrate.

An office of compliance at Tamagawa Gakuen contracts auditors as required by the Private School Act. The office is charged with auditing the business and the status of the property belonging to the incorporated educational institution; preparing an audit report each fiscal year; submitting the report to the board of trustees and the board of councilors within two months of the end of the fiscal year; and attending the meetings of the board of trustees to express opinions on the status of the business or property of the institution.

3.5 Academic Units, Research and Outreach

The graduate schools cover areas of humanities, agriculture, engineering, management, education, and brain sciences. Distinctive characteristics of the different schools are noted below.

The graduate school of agriculture is noted for its studies of the honeybee, food sciences and research on growing vegetables with LED lights, and self-contained, circulation-type aquaculture. LED-grown lettuce is an entrepreneurial endeavor as part of the university's academia-industry cooperation program.

The graduate school of management is known for its program of staff development where first-year administrative staff enroll and attain a master's degree while working.

One distinctive characteristic of the graduate school of education is the International Baccalaureate research course in which students can acquire the certificate of teaching and learning (CTL) through completion of the course and the advanced certificate of teaching and learning through submission of a thesis. The university is currently planning to open an online course for the CTL. The graduate school of education also offers a professional degree program in teacher education that was established in 2008.

The graduate school of brain sciences is widely recognized for its vigorous research activities. It was adopted as the 21st Century Center of Excellence (COE) Program in 2002, as the Global COE Program in 2008, and as the Joint Usage/Research Center in 2017.

The college of humanities offers specialized teacher training and a course for either Japanese (*kokugo*) or English language middle and high school teacher certificates. The English certificate requires students to study in Australia for two semesters during their second year.

The college of engineering has attracted attention for various activities such as acquisition of certification by the International Organization for Standardization 9001 and superior results at the RoboCup World Competition and the World Green Challenge Solar Car Rally.

The college of arts and science offers education synonymous with a *zenjin* education. In this college, students are offered a wide range of academic subjects and allowed to decide their major (and minor) by their third year.

The college of tourism and hospitality is attracting students who wish to work internationally because the college requires students to study in either Australia or England for two semesters during the second year.

Finally, the distance education division in Tamagawa University has a long history. Although the number of students who enroll full-time is decreasing due to demographics in Japan, the demand for lifelong learning shows a relatively sharp increase.

Additionally, the higher education affiliated divisions represent six centers, three research institutes, and a museum. The multimedia resource center oversees the university libraries as well as multimedia facilities. The center for continuing learning offers approximately 70–80 lectures annually for local residents such as *sencha* (green tea), *kou* (incense burning) and so forth. The center for teacher education research mainly conducts research on teacher education and supports students preparing for the teacher appointment examinations implemented by the board of education of the prefectures and ordinance-designated cities. The center for international program supports both short-term and long-term study abroad programs, sending students to more than 20 affiliated schools in the U.S., England, Australia, and France. The center for English as a lingua franca is a unique feature of Tamagawa University, designing English classes that students in all of the colleges take. The center for adventure programs offers students and external organizations (including Machida Zelvia, a local professional soccer team) the opportunity to undertake outdoor challenges oriented to the development of social and physical skills.

The research institute contains centers such as the center of K-16 education research and the center of higher education and development. The brain science institute and the quantum ICT research institute recently separated and became independent. Both research institutes conduct activities overseas, initiating collaborative research with foreign university partners such as the California Institute of Technology in the brain sciences field.

Finally, the museum of education collects and possesses a wide range of items including works of Kuniyoshi Obara, the founder of Tamagawa Gakuen.

The higher education support division is comprised of two offices and two centers. The office of academic affairs contains the instructional and learning support division that provides workshops on topics such as academic writing and support to assist students with the correction of assignment papers. The office also manages the university's learning commons, a unique study space designed to promote individual and collaborative learning.

The office of university admissions coordinates visits to high schools, campus visits, entrance examinations, and enrollment management. Tamagawa University has established agreements with individual "designated" high schools that facilitate the automatic enrollment of their students based on a recommendation letter from the school principal and a transcript demonstrating the required level of achievement. These students are not required to take an entrance examination. Graduates of Tamagawa Academy who have achieved the minimum required grade-point average (GPA) are only required to have an admissions interview where they are evaluated for character, curiosity, and drive. Other candidates must submit results of a written admissions examination and may be required to comply with additional requirements.

The center for student affairs supervises the activities of university clubs, manages various university scholarships, and handles problems that arise with students.

Finally, the center for career planning and placement facilitates postgraduate employment students. It offers mock interview sessions, resume development, and on-campus information sessions with company representatives.

The office of alumni affairs takes charge of maintaining a connection with graduates of the university. Every year it holds a reunion, invites alumni as speakers, offers a career development seminar, and solicits a donation.

The healthcare center is a clinic where students, parents, academic, and administrative staff as well as local residents can receive services. It was built a year after the establishment of Tamagawa Gakuen and inaugurated a new facility in 2018.

A university press and a campus store contribute revenue to the university. Tamagawa University Press is widely recognized for its commitment to the education field specifically in early childhood and higher education. The campus store has been outsourced to Kinokuniya Bookstore, Inc. There are a variety of original university goods. Among the most famous and popular are Tamagawa honey ice cream and pure homegrown honey.

Several administrative offices are critical to effective management. The office of strategic planning plays a role in institutional research. It is expected to become a hub for all of data and provide a range of analyses for the board of trustees and the chairperson. The offices of general affairs, human resources,

and financial affairs are the heartbeat of Tamagawa Gakuen for the management and administration of an incorporated educational institution. Distinctive features of these offices are the campus security division that is outsourced
to Sogo Keibi Hosho Co ; a personnel management system called *yoin chosa*
that is annually conducted in order to review the needs of administrative staff,
including those who are part-time; and asset management that is outsourced
to several major financial institutions as part of risk distribution.

3.6   *Academic Promotion*
To become the next president of Tamagawa Gakuen the candidate will have
to hold an earned doctoral degree (preferably in education) and demonstrate
achievement in research and teaching so that he or she can meet the requirements to become an assistant professor of the university and progress to
professor.

An assistant professor is appointed for five years and may be reappointed
for three years. Assistant professors are not renewed unless they demonstrate
research achievements. To become a professor requires significant accomplishments, especially in research. Tamagawa Gakuen uses a point system for the
promotion of academic staff with specific points required for each ascension.

In addition to attaining the level of professor, a candidate for the presidency
must successfully complete two terms in a managerial position, first in the K-12
section and then in the higher education section as dean or in another responsible role. Managerial appointments are usually for two years with the possibility of reappointment. A designated successor to the presidency is expected to
have at least 4 years of managerial experience.

All incorporated educational institutions must comply with the Private
School Act and Tamagawa Gakuen is no exception. In accordance with Paragraph 7 of Article 38, the successor is allowed to become a full-time trustee as
well as chairperson. As a member of the board of trustees and the permanent
standing committee, the successor is involved with all decision-making. The
term of trustees is usually four years and may be renewed once. As a result, a
potential successor may be a full-time trustee for eight years. While a successor bears responsibility as a trustee, he or she also begins to do the work of
chairperson.

The first phase of leadership transfer is as a vice-president and vice-prin-
cipal. The term of office is four years with the possibility of immediate reappointment. However, a successor usually becomes the president and principal
after one term. The term of office as president and principal is four years and
renewable without a term limit. The current president and principal has been
in office for 24 years.

The decision to transfer leadership is made in consultation with the chairperson. A chairperson ordinarily resigns his or her position at the age of 80.

3.7 *Challenges Facing the University*

Private universities in Japan are facing various difficulties. The birthrate and consequently the-18-year-old cohort is constantly shrinking. Small-to-medium-size private universities are forced to compete with national and public universities in the same geographic area as well as better-known and more prestigious, large private universities where students enroll from all over the country. In addition, several national and public universities have begun to merge. The mergers cross boundaries between national, public, and private universities. National universities are allowed to seize control of other universities (national, public, and private) and if they seize control of private universities, those private universities benefit from public funding. In some cases, the private university might retain its name and identity even after the merger. A private university that is financially strong enough may seize control of other universities.

Private universities must raise tuition every year due to rising personnel expenses. A salary increase is unavoidable due to a traditional wage system that emphasizes seniority in Japan. Private universities are struggling to shift to an alternative wage system oriented to merit-based remuneration, but their effort has met with strong protests from workers as well as labor unions.

FOMHEIs have several unique challenges. Among them, how to cultivate a successor with the ability to assuage the voices against familiar succession by demonstrating his or her qualifications. Preparing a successor demands an enormous amount of time. Unlike Japanese small-to-medium-size enterprises where heredity is accepted as an immutable custom and executed to ensure the company's stability and continuance, different criteria are applied to FOMHEIs. Since FOMHEIs in Japan are expected to contribute to the public good by guaranteeing fair and impartial educational activities, those who wish to assume positions of leadership in FOMHEIs must prove themselves, otherwise academic and administrative staff will not accept them. A successor must win the trust of his or her subordinates.

The biggest challenge and concern for Tamagawa University is to develop leadership from the next generation who meets the qualifications discussed, who excels in teaching and research activities, and also demonstrates the expertise and skills necessary for the future development of Tamagawa Gakuen.

4 Conclusion

The number of FOMHEIs in Japan is gradually decreasing as a result of multiple environmental conditions. Fostering a successor fit for the post of chairperson requires an enormous amount of labor and time to transcend barriers and overcome challenges. Not only is it mandatory for a successor to hold a doctoral degree, but also to make steady progress as a scholar and professor. A shorter path will not prepare a successor to meet the many challenges that Japanese FOMHEIs face.

At a time when it is difficult for FOMHEIs to prepare the next generation to assume leadership, the number of those institutions is also in decline. FOMHEIs have been important actors in Japanese higher education. They are distinct from national and public institutions in terms of their philosophy and mission, academic opportunities, and their agility to respond to change.

Furthermore, the continuity and consistency of educational services offer important stability to these institutions. Family ownership handed down from parents to children reflects *isshisoden* (passing on knowledge). The vision of parents is inherited by their children who grew up within "the family business" and appreciate its contributions and challenges intimately.

References

Fujimoto, K. (2010). The motivation for successors to manage small-to-medium-size enterprises. *Keiei Senryaku Kenkyu, 4*, 227–238.

MEXT. (2012). *Higher education in Japan.* Retrieved April 22, 2019, from http://www.mext.go.jp/en/policy/education/highered/title03/detail03/__icsFiles/afieldfile/2012/06/19/1302653_1.pdf [in Japanese]

Obara, K. (2018). West meets East: A well-rounded education versus an angular education in Japan. *Espacio, Tiempo y Educación, 5*(2), 101–122.

National Institute for Educational Policy and Research. (2011). *Higher education in Japan.* Retrieved from https://www.nier.go.jp/English/educationjapan/pdf/201109HE.pdf [in Japanese]

Research Institute for Independent Higher Education. (2018). *The present state of governance and management of private universities and for improvement and reinforcement.* Tokyo: Association of Private Universities of Japan.

CHAPTER 12

Korea: Family-Owned Universities and Colleges—A Dark Future of Speculation?

Edward Choi

In South Korea (hereafter referred to as Korea), the presence of family-owned or managed higher education institutions (FOMHEIS) is significant. Upwards of 200 FOMHEIS, all non-profit by law, but of various institution types, may be found across the nation. A handful of these institutions are reputable and enjoy widespread national respect. Many are lesser known but are highly regarded within their local communities. These institutions provide invaluable socio-cultural and economic benefits locally in the form of employment and educational opportunities. However, most operate on the periphery and remain largely unknown to the general population although some even have achieved notoriety due to family-managed corruption. Their peripheral status can be explained by a typically rural base of operations, local focus, profit-driven owners who may engage in unethical business practices, negative public perception, a short history, financial instability, or government administrations critical of private enterprises. All of these characteristics warrant further discussion, especially as they handicap most family-owned institutions in their capacity to manage environmental change effectively.

The Korean higher education system is in the midst of significant restructuring that is transforming the higher education landscape and while challenges beleaguer all institution types, the survival of most FOMHEIS is at stake. Analyzing this risk is a key element of this chapter.

1   Korea's Higher Education System: Structure and Political Climate

Today, there are 432 higher education institutions in Korea. They are all non-profit by law and enroll 3.5 million undergraduate and graduate students (Korean Educational Statistics Service, 2017; Ministry of Education, n.d.). More than 70 percent of the college-bound population (Altbach, 2016) attend Korea's 320 private institutions. The private sector includes a mix of FOMHEIS and other types of institutions that might be sponsored by a large corporation (e.g., Pohang Iron and Steel Company) or a religious group. The remaining students attend public institutions operated by local municipalities or national universities sponsored and regulated by the Ministry of Education (MoE), the Ministry of Science and Technology (MoST), or the Ministry of Labor (MoL). Most institutions fall within the regulatory purview of the MoE. In the private sector, tuition payments constitute the bulk of total revenue and often account for up to 70 percent of the institution's budget (Grubb et al., 2009). Other revenue sources include alumni donations, direct assistance from the government in the form of grants, indirect government assistance in the form of tax breaks, and, in some cases, government funding for research (Kim, 2008; Weidman & Park, 2000). By contrast, public institutions receive most of their funding from local and national governmental bodies with tuition revenue only covering around 30 percent of the institution's budget (Kim & Kim, 2015).

Two institution types dominate the national landscape. Four-year universities constitute the first type with 189 institutions enrolling roughly 2 million students (Korean Educational Statistics Service, 2017). These institutions are comprehensive; offer bachelor's, master's, and doctoral degrees; and have a mandate to generate research. An additional 138 junior colleges enroll around 700,000 students (Korean Educational Statistics Service, 2017) and represent the second most common institutional type. These institutions link professional and technical fields to theory, design programs based on college-industry partnerships (Grubb et al., 2009), and offer only associate's and bachelor's programs requiring two to three years of study.

The Korean government exercises strong control over many aspects of institutional affairs without regard to institution type. Control mechanisms may be found in budget development, faculty salaries, admissions standards, faculty tenure requirements, student enrollment quotas, curriculum, and tuition (Byun, 2008; Grub et al., 2009; Weidman & Park, 2009; Shin & Koh, 2005). In recent years, these controls have intensified under a government reform initiative known as the University Restructuring Plan (URP).

The URP, first announced in 2004, has become Korea's evaluative framework designed to address the most pressing problems facing the higher education system—declining student enrollment brought on by demographic changes from low fertility rates and brain drain; isomorphism with lower-tier universities and colleges trying to emulate elite universities; high unemployment resulting from the mismatch of skill development with labor market needs (Kim, 2008); and low competitiveness vis-à-vis foreign higher education markets that continue to be more attractive to international students. The URP is a coercive process applying penalties to underperforming institutions with the aim of closing them while concentrating public resources in high-performing institutions (Kim, 2008). Penalties range from forcing enrollment cuts to the withdrawal of government student financial aid or even embargoes on private loans from commercial banks to students attending sanctioned institutions. The ultimate aim of the URP is matching higher education supply to a shrinking population of college-bound students. Korea's higher education system experienced a marked drop of 85,000 college applications in 2003 in comparison to 2002 (Kim, 2008). The declining number of applicants has worsened in recent years with no prospect of reversing.

2   FOMHEIS in Korea

In this intensifying regulatory environment and changing demographic landscape, most family-owned institutions may be facing significant challenges. As a result of their characteristics and circumstances (rural base of operations, financial instability, short history of operation, local community focus, and negative public perception) they are ill-adapted to compete on an unlevel playing field that favors "center" institutions (Riesman, 1958)—institutions with longer histories, a geopolitical advantage of operating in major cities, established social networks, and greater financial stability that are better positioned to manage environmental changes. These center institutions are national and public institutions that receive robust government financial support (Kim & Lee, 2006; Weidman & Park, 2002); private institutions founded by corporate conglomerates or religious groups; family institutions with longer histories located in major cities; or elite institutions that cut across all of these categorical types.

An in-depth discussion of the challenges facing most family-owned universities is presented later in this chapter following some context of the family enterprise in higher education. The next section offers a brief historical summary of the circumstances surrounding the appearance and proliferation of FOMHEIS, some information regarding governance and ownership patterns, and a statistical breakdown of their numbers across institutional categories

2.1   A Brief History

The first appearance of FOMHEIS on Korea's higher education landscape was in the late 1940s when the government created the Agricultural Land Act. This policy allowed the government to expropriate private lands for public agricultural use. This policy threatened the livelihood of many landowners, mostly farmers who lost their land to government appropriation. However, there were

a number of families who kept their land by satisfying one of three exceptions to the government seizures—the government could not take properties
used for scientific research, religious, or educational purposes (Park, 2000).
Together with the appearances of new churches, many farmers kept their land
by establishing higher education institutions on their properties. According to
Park (2000), 23 higher education institutions, presumably all family-owned,
were founded over a span of three years during this period.

Since then, the number of FOMHEIs has grown. In large part, their expansion
was borne out of necessity. FOMHEIs performed the crucial role of building
educational capacity during the 1980s and 1990s that led to the massification of
Korean higher education and knowledge-based economic expansion (Altbach,
2016; Yeom, 2016).

Several converging conditions led to the further proliferation of FOMHEIs—
rising income levels that brought a college education within the financial reach
of a larger part of the population, the elimination of government policies that
had limited upward educational mobility, and national economic strategies
emphasizing the need for a greater supply of more highly-skilled labor. These
factors shaped the political environment and drove support for greater higher
education capacity. However, the government was unable to accommodate
this need within the public sector for various reasons, namely scarce public
resources after investing heavily in primary and secondary education. The government's limitations became the perfect opportunity for more private actors
to participate in higher education delivery.

The government facilitated private entry by loosening requirements for
establishing new institutions. The shift in policy led to a marked growth in
institutional numbers from 168 institutions in 1970 to 419 by 2004 (Korean
Educational Statistics Service, 2017) and a spike in enrollment from 201,436
students to roughly 3.5 million students over the same period (Korean Educational Statistics Service, 2017). Many families launched higher education
enterprises around this time, either to make money or pursue a philanthropic
endeavor by operating a university or college.

While exact figures are difficult to confirm, it is estimated that roughly 200
or more family-owned or managed institutions operate in Korea today across
all institutional types. Family ventures account for around 65 of 189 four-
year institutions, a handful of the 19 cyber universities, and an overwhelming
majority of the 138 junior colleges. Indeed, their presence in Korea's higher
education landscape is significant. The figures suggest the valuable role this
type of institution has played in educating Korea's citizenry. Junior colleges
alone, that are mostly family-owned, account for 677,721 students of the total
college-attending population.

2.2   *Ownership Structure*

In Korea, all private institutions are established as a subsidiary of a foundation. Whoever controls the foundation (comparable to a holding company)—a
family, major corporation or religious group—is understood to control the
institution. In this way, "the government regard[s] private schools as the property of the founders that [is] used for educational purposes" (Park, 2000, p. 112).

In some cases, a family operates multiple institutions through a single foundation. It is thus not atypical to find an arrangement with several institutions
(a university, junior college, or even primary and secondary schools) under the
direction of a single family. These institutions operate as separate entities in
the sense that they are not necessarily connected to the same physical plant,
but decision-making is centralized because they share a single board within the
family foundation. While not always the case, this may result in the brothers
and sisters of the founder or members of the second or third generation sharing leadership positions and governance responsibilities across institutions. Of
course, there are some cases where non-family members are appointed presidents of FOMHEIS. However, the decision-making authority and other powers
of non-family presidents may be limited within a structure that situates the
family foundation and the family above the university

2.3   *Organization, Governance, and Leadership*

FOMHEIS in Korea follow a normative organizational structure required by the
Ministry of Education. Article 4 of the Enforcement Decree of the Higher Education Act and Article 14 of the Higher Education Act are particularly salient
to Korea's higher education organizational patterns. There are few, if any,
differences between FOMEHIS and their non-family-owned counterparts in
terms of governance. All institution types have boards of trustees, a president,
deans, professors, academic assistants, and administrative staff and operate
with an organizational hierarchy resembling those found in many parts of
the world.

However, some key differences may be discerned in institutional norms
around the hiring of top management personnel and the appointment of
board members. For example, the authority to select the leadership at public
institutions has at times come under the purview of the government. At other
times, public institutions have been self-governing, allowing faculty to vote
and promote other faculty members. Reforms resulted from faculty challenges
to government intervention. In contrast, neither the government or faculty at
private institutions have authority to choose management staff or board members. Rather, the board at FOMHEIS, and perhaps at other private types operated by corporations and religious groups, retains the right to select leadership

personnel, thereby allowing the university to control its institutional priorities and matters of fiduciary relevance, strategic planning, and human resources (Grubb, Sweet, Gallagher, & Tuomi, 2009, p. 77; Kim & Kim, 2015). For FOM-HEIs, the freedom to select their own leadership allows owners to preserve familial influence across generations through a "transgenerational succession process" (Otten-Pappas, 2013). The understanding is that families, in addition to choosing management staff from within kinship groups, choose non-family board members who agree to the idea of the "generational investment strategy" (Cennamo et al., 2012) that preserves the heritage, character, and vision of the founding family. Thus, anticipating and voting for a familial successor is a culturally accepted practice. In fact, the core administrative staff and faculty all have some familiarity with the idea of the generational investment strategy and accept it, whether they like it or not.

For the children and grandchildren of founders, planning their transition to leadership begins very early. Younger family members grow up at the institution their father or grandfather founded and they regularly interact with faculty and staff. To them, assuming a leadership role at the family venture is not so much a process of choosing a career but one of fulfilling a vocational purpose. This purpose was given to them at birth and cultivated from childhood. As they grow into adulthood expectations lead to considerable pressure and scrutiny as to whether or not they are fit for the role they are to assume. Familial successors are expected to receive a solid education at reputable domestic or international institutions. Further, they are expected to gain appropriate experience by first working as faculty or in administrative positions at their family's university or another institution. In this way, there is a huge commitment of personal time and resources on the part of the family and the successor that reflects the transgenerational investment strategy. Having the necessary qualifications is paramount to smooth transgenerational succession and presents the leadership transition to all university constituents as one earned on merit.

The transgenerational succession process typically begins with the president initiating a special board session for the purpose of presenting a familial successor of his or her choosing. In most cases this candidate will be the son, daughter, brother, or in some cases, a daughter or son-in-law of the incumbent. The board then votes to pass a special resolution related to leadership transition. At some FOMHEIs a minimum of 50 percent of the board's votes is required. At other institutions the number of votes needed for approval may be higher or lower. Once the familial candidate is voted in as president, the incumbent generally moves to the position of board chair. However, not all aspects of hiring and appointing leadership are locally determined and several government regulations may supersede institutional protocols. For example, family members may not occupy more than one-third of the board seats (Kim & Kim, 2015). FOMHEIS are also prohibited by law from appointing a single family member to multiple positions of power; the proprietor of an institution may not serve as both the chair of the foundation and the president of any subsidiary institution, nor may a single family member fill a leadership position at multiple institutions.

2.4   *Challenges Facing FOMHEIS*

Most FOMHEIS in Korea face myriad challenges. Some of these challenges may be common to many non-family universities and colleges worldwide. For example, funding issues are forever pervasive (Hauptman, 2006) and cut across all institution types. There are, however, a number of inherent challenges unique to the Korean context and the intersection of family and business systems. These challenges are important to consider, especially because they handicap the majority of FOMHEIS in their efforts to respond to increasingly strict government regulations under the URP and to compete with center institutions.

2.4.1   An Elite and Homogenous Education System

Most FOMHEIS in Korea are not widely known. This limited visibility extends to all universities in Korea that are eclipsed by Korea's elite universities. The best of these institutions forms the grouping that Koreans commonly refer to as SKY or Seoul National University (SNU), Korea University, and Yonsei University.

Korea's elite universities drive and shape higher education demand in the country. Demand is greatest for these institutions that attract students from all over the country. However, most of Korea's universities and colleges are best known within their local communities and surrounding region. This reality makes it very difficult for less-prestigious universities and junior colleges to distinguish themselves. Family-owned institutions, especially those located in the provinces, are no exception. For these, building reputational cache is a zero-sum game where capturing a share of the student market must be balanced against the reputational pull of center institutions. Center status is built on a combination of factors—urban location, financial stability, long history of operation, etc. Schools like SNU have all of these. These factors allow elite schools to recruit better qualified faculty, build better facilities, and secure substantial funding. The majority of family universities lack these characteristics making it very difficult for them to build both financial, capital, and reputational advantages.

2.4.2   Regional Disadvantages

Generally, urban institutions have a significant advantage in student recruitment compared with their rural counterparts. This advantage stems from the directional flow of college bound students in Korea, almost entirely towards major cities (mostly Seoul) where job and internship opportunities, entertainment possibilities, and options to supplement formal learning with private tutoring abound. Thus, it not surprising that city residents rarely consider relocating to small towns isolated from their family and friends, other environmental supports, or the vibrancy of city life (Grubb et al., 2009).

The pattern of student traffic from rural areas to major cities is historical and part of a wider trend of domestic migration. What are now Korea's metropoles were sites of intense urbanization that began in the 1960s and 1970s (Hashiya, 1996; Schwekendiek, 2016) with the government pouring significant resources into developing these areas as labor-intensive industrial complexes. As development continued and led to job creation, the distribution of Korea's population began to change (Rii & Ahn, 2002). Today more than 40 percent of Korea's total population lives in Seoul and the surrounding satellite cities as a result of these migration patterns.

Provincial FOMHEIS face the near impossible challenge of bucking a historical trend that favors major cities. For these institutions, attracting students from outside of their immediate surroundings is especially urgent because the local base of students is insufficient to meet the strict enrollment quotas of the URP. Many of these schools have been flagged for enrollment shortages and face the imminent reality of losing even more students as a result of government penalties. For these schools, closure or merger are perhaps the only options. However, a number of rural family universities have circumvented the recruitment challenge by locating a second campus or a small post, typically as an office or a building, near or in Seoul. For the time being, these institutions continue to meet enrollment targets with the benefit of their second location.

2.4.3   Public Opinion

In Korea, public discontent with FOMHEIS runs high. This is mainly a reflection of scandals involving families that have accumulated personal wealth and power at the expense of the academic mission (Kim & Kim, 2015; Kim & Lee, 2006). Instances of such activities are not hard to find in the media and are widely known. For example, Grubb et al. (2009) and Kim and Lee (2006) report cases where family-owned institutions have been guilty of embezzlement, fraud, and unethical hiring practices that concentrate power within the family by hiring relatives. Similarly, Bae, Kim, and Kim (2012) describe the exploitive practice of "tunneling" where family members appropriate institutional resources for the purpose of accumulating personal wealth. For example, a family may award a construction contract to a construction company that the family owns. Interestingly, all of this happens under the guise of their non-profit status. Those families who get caught become the center of criminal investigations for setting up profit-making shops connected to the university that divert institutional resources into personal bank accounts. These activities were so extensive that in the past FOMHEIS were called "ox-bone towers" instead of ivory towers referring to the popular joke that universities and colleges became rich off families who sold their ox as the only way to send their children to college (Park, 2000). Oxen were, and perhaps still are, invaluable assets to farmers and represent a significant cost.

It is not difficult to sympathize with public criticism directed at Korean FOMHEIS, especially when unscrupulous familial activities are at the center of institutional disputes. According to Kim and Kim (2015), there were 44 such demonstrations and disputes at FOMHEIS between 1994 and 2000.

2.4.4   Succession Problems

Leadership transitions at FOMHEIS in Korea are rarely uneventful and often breed political and competitive activity among family members and non-family personnel who vie for institutional control. Further, loyalty lines are often established between non-family constituents and incumbents that do not always carry over to successors. In fact, successors are critically evaluated and questioned during leadership transitions. As second or third generation family owners, they are subject to greater scrutiny than the first generation, regarding their qualifications, vision and experience that are often less developed relative to first generation leaders. Thus, the potential for FOMHEIS to experience greater organizational turmoil and conflict becomes higher with each passing leadership transition.

In rare cases, the government has been known to intervene when FOMHEIS in Korea become a site of extreme political unrest with tensions between constituents or when there is evidence of corruption as described earlier. Intervention typically means the appointment of ex-officio members to the board with the aim of increasing transparency and providing ongoing monitoring. At least a few universities in Korea have become subject of such heavy-handed intervention.

2.4.5   Funding Challenges

Many FOMHEIS have deep financial reserves due to individual family members who have acquired wealth from other business ventures. Others with longer histories have built wealth over time. However, many, if not a majority of FOMHEIS (especially newer ones) are not as well off as the public may believe. These institutions, like many around the world, find securing and generating revenue to be an enormous challenge. One reason is the disproportionate concentration of national research funding to a small group of elite universities. According to Kim (2008), top-tier institutions receive 46 percent of total disbursements. As a result, the remaining share of research monies become the focus of intense competition among the hundreds of lower-tier universities, including many FOMHEIS.

Another challenge lies in satisfying strict research funding criteria. Some government research funding is disbursed only when institutions can match funds or demonstrate linkages with local businesses. While fulfilling such criteria may be easy for wealthier universities in major cities where businesses abound, rural FOMHEIS find this difficult. Many rural FOMHEIS not only have fewer resources (making it difficult to match grants), but also operate in less developed communities devoid of businesses. They thus struggle to receive funding that requires partnerships with local businesses.

Demographic changes and the shrinking youth population pose an even greater risk to the financial footing of all institutions in the private sector. Private institutions depend on tuition revenue as their primary source of operating income. This overdependence is extremely risky in a context where low fertility rates and brain drain translate into rapidly declining student enrollment and large budgetary gaps. The imperatives are very clear—find ways to maintain enrollment or identify alternative funding strategies to offset shortages in tuition revenue. Unfortunately, for many FOMHEIS, pursuing either option offers little promise. The former is not easily addressed due to the shape of national demand in Korea and domestic migration patterns. The latter is equally challenging due to excessive government controls and URP penalty schemes that limit an institution's ability to recoup costs. While financial cost-recovery strategies such as raising tuition and transferring more financial responsibility to students and their families have been on the uptake in various parts of the world, the Korean government has taken a different approach. The government not only penalizes institutions for increasing tuition levels above socially determined limits, but also demands greater institutional student aid in line with URP goals. This has forced many underfunded FOMHEIS, or those anticipating funding challenges in the future, to rely on cost-cutting solutions to offset tuition losses and outlays for student aid. Cost-cutting solutions may range from academic retrenchment like discontinuing programs and courses to hiring more contingent (part-time) faculty. These solutions are temporary at best and may have an adverse effect on academic quality. Part-time faculty may not bring the same level of commitment to their work and research as their full-time peers.

A final funding challenge is unique to the financial structure of ownership. Historically, the financial structure was centralized, and the parent foundation and affiliated institutions shared a single accounting system. Such a structure allowed for the movement of funds among the different organizations controlled by the same family. This approach was useful for filling budgetary gaps at one institution by borrowing funds from another. Financial crises have been avoided with the ability to move funds around quickly and easily. Further, the centralized accounting system allowed for using surplus institutional funds as seed money to develop additional funding streams. For example, families would use university resources to establish business ventures that pumped profits into institutional accounts. Such a strategy, understood as a form of social entrepreneurship (Mair & Noboa, 2006), is allowed under Korea's Private School Act and may be vital to support financially floundering institutions that could use the extra financial boost in times of financial reversal. These financial strategies, however, can no longer be applied. The Korean government now mandates a decentralized accounting structure with controls in place to prevent the sharing of funds between institutions. While the "every tub stands on its own bottom" (Barr & McClellan, 2018) approach is well-meaning and perhaps necessary to keep owner families accountable and minimize "tunneling" activities, the new system seems to have created additional funding challenges for FOMHEIs.

2.4.6   Political Instability
Finally, FOMHEIs in Korea have a significant challenge in establishing a permanent identity and long-term strategic focus in a volatile political climate. Drastic and frequent policy swings are normal, even expected by society. The unstable political environment is connected to profound leadership changes (East-West Center, n.d.) that typically lead to drastically different directions under successive administrations. For example, President Rhee Syng-man's (1948–1960) view of low levels of regulation for private business was replaced by President Park Chung-hee's (1963–1979) preference for stricter oversight with the aim of ridding society including higher education of corruption (Kim & Lee, 2006; Yoon, 2014). Government controls reached into many facets of university affairs—governance, faculty appointments, expansion of programs, management practices, board structure, student admissions, and department enrollment quotas (Kim & Lee, 2006; Weidman & Park, 2000). This level of intervention in the private sector was made possible under broadly specified conditions largely determined by government authorities

(Kim, 2000) and with an amendment to the Private School Law in 1964. President Kim Young-sam (1993–1998) would reverse this policy through a comprehensive package of reforms emphasizing market forces and competition (Kim, 2008; Frank et al., 2013; Weidman & Park, 2000). President Kim is known for establishing the Presidential Commission on Education and revising the Education Law. These changes were directed at granting private institutions substantial procedural autonomy in many areas including program development and diversification, student quotas, tuition levels, distribution of students within the institution, and admissions standards (Kim & Lee, 2006; Shin, 2011; Weidman & Park, 2000). However, the level of institutional autonomy experienced under President Kim eventually came to an end with present-day Korea returning to stringent, rational planning, and close monitoring of the private sector.

The policy seesaw reflects the unstable political environment in Korea within which institutional identity seems to have less to do with the unique character and heritage of an institution than to conforming to the demands and expectations of the government currently in power. Korea's political landscape is disruptive to long-term strategic planning when strategies pursued under some presidents can be later reversed under others.

3   Conclusion

Historically, Korea's family-owned or managed higher education institutions have performed a critical role. They helped expand higher education capacity by absorbing excess demand as Korea reached universal access in the 1990s. Further, their involvement in higher education helped the transition of Korea from an agrarian society to a hyper-advanced economic and technological state. While this contribution has been significant, there has been an erosion of their purpose relative to the national direction of higher education as fashioned by Korea's government. This erosion is not just limited to FOMHEIs but affects all private institutions that fail to meet government-prescribed performance indicators for quality, enrollment, and institutional mission.

Lesser-known FOMHEIS are falling out of social favor. These institutions are the most sensitive to the challenges described in this chapter including demographic shortages, a domineering government, urbanization, brain drain, negative public perception, a volatile political environment, and funding issues. These environmental changes affect an institution's capacity to perform and survive under URP restrictions. In fact, the combination of environmental challenges and stricter regulations and intensifying controls have already forced the closure and mergers of a number of private universities and colleges, many being family-owned. FOMHEI closures include Daegoo Mirae University, Hanryuh University, Daegoo Waegookuh University, Gwangjoo Yaesool University, Gondong University, and Kyungbook Waegookuh University (News1Korea, 2016). There are also cases in which a family member acting as president has stepped down in response to public pressure after failing to move their institutions into compliance with URP goals. It is unclear how these resignations will affect the transgenerational succession at these institutions, but the reputation of these families as competent leaders in higher education is now in jeopardy. For these families, the prospect of maintaining long-term control over their institutions is quite low.

However, national, public, and elite private institutions are likely to survive the URP. Other privates backed by well-resourced corporations and religious groups are also likely to survive. FOMHEIs with the best future possibilities are those with a main or secondary campus located in a major city and those with longer histories. Institutions with geographic advantage, robust government support, and established social networks have already emerged as winners on an unlevel playing field.

If peripheral FOMHEIS are to survive the environmental shifts outlined here, they must reinvent themselves as innovative institutions. They must distinguish themselves from their better positioned peers. They need to articulate strategies that simultaneously and effectively address the challenges they face while remaining nimble enough to adapt to strict government directives. This may be difficult because of excessive government controls that constrain their capacity to respond to myriad environmental factors (e.g., penalties for tuition increases, the obligation to increase student aid, the inability to increase enrollment, or develop new programs). Notwithstanding, there are some general directions that seem prudent. Peripheral FOMHEIS might consider enhancing unique programs. These programs, if successful, could shape a new institutional identity that would not only target and attract niche students, but also improve the institution's visibility and reputation. Further, such a strategy aligns with government efforts to encourage specialized institutions and reduce isomorphism across the higher education landscape. Some FOMHEIS are already moving in this direction by branding themselves with marketable names. For example, one university is commonly known as the "government officer training school." This university promotes itself as the best pathway for students to receive policy and political training and enter government employment.

For provincial FOMHEIS, surviving enrollment shortfalls may mean developing degree and non-degree lifelong learning programs, online and face-to-face, that cater to non-traditional students who are either unwilling or unable to relocate from cities to smaller communities. Non-degree programs must be flexible in their scheduling with courses offered during evenings or weekends to accommodate working professionals. This may mean hiring new staff and faculty with the hope that these programs cover salaries and eventually produce a profit. Provincial FOMHEIS must consider whether demand for such programming exists. Non-degree professional programs, if not offered online, may not make sense in areas where businesses and working professionals are few in number.

Further, FOMHEIS in Korea may consider forging international partnerships with foreign institutions that may offer new sources of funding, research, and student recruitment. The establishment of international exchange programs and joint degree programs might attract students who desire an international education, but do not have the means to travel abroad. Having international programming, especially with reputable foreign institutions, may improve an institution's domestic reputation as well as offer international visibility.

While society may applaud the government for ridding the landscape of wasteful and, in some cases corrupt institutions, there has been a loss as well. This loss results from the government's blanket approach to evaluating performance with universal measures for the entire higher education system. URP performance measures are applied without consideration to unique local circumstances and neglects the local impact that universities and colleges have in their communities, not unlike provincial national institutions in the 1950s. According to Kim and Lee (2006), these institutions provided societal benefits in the form of educational and medical services as well as employment. In this way, many smaller towns depend on provincial FOMHEIS. These FOMHEIS provide career opportunities and services in collaboration with local non-profit agencies, businesses, and primary schools. They also provide an educational pathway for many citizens who otherwise cannot pursue education. These externalities are especially realized when family owners are motivated by educational objectives and a vision of social responsibility. For these families, owning a university is less about profiteering than transforming and growing the towns and cities they call home. In fact, businesses in many towns have opposed campus efforts to expand into other cities by those FOMHEIS held in high regard. The relocation of students, faculty and staff to alternate campuses implies a loss to the local economy. This is because provincial FOMHEIS often act as a magnet for urban development and economic activity in areas that otherwise host little. FOMHEIS often attract investors who establish restaurants and entertainment venues that generate economic growth.

In sum, penalizing these institutions may in fact have far-reaching implications not being considered. The government should perhaps consider devising alternative strategies to help these institutions improve their services and offerings—with the benefit of the community in mind—rather than subscribing to the current coercive URP framework.

References

Altbach, P. G. (2016). *Global perspectives on higher education*. Baltimore, MD: Johns Hopkins University Press.

Bae, K., Kim, S., & Kim, W. (2012). Family control and expropriation at not-for-profit organizations: Evidence from Korean private universities. *Corporate Governance: An International Review, 20*, 388–404.

Barr, M. J., & McClellan, G. S. (2018). *Budgets and financial management in higher education*. Hoboken, NJ: John Wiley & Sons.

Byun, K. (2008). New public management in Korean higher education: Is it reality or another fad? *Asia Pacific Education Review, 9*, 190–205.

Cennamo, C., Berrone, P., Cruz, C., & Gomez-Mejia, L. R. (2012). Socioemotional wealth and proactive stakeholder engagement: Why family-controlled firms care more about their stakeholders. *Entrepreneurship Theory and Practice, 36*, 1153–1173.

East-West Center. (n.d.). *Political challenges in Korea*. Retrieved from https://www.eastwestcenter.org/research/visiting-fellow-programs/posco-visiting-fellowship-program/political-aspects-of-korea-related-issues

Frank, R., Hoare, J, Köllner, P., & Pares, S. (2013). *Korea 2013: Politics, economy and society*. Boston, MA: Brill Publishers.

Grubb, W. N., Sweet, R., Gallagher, M., & Tuomi, O. (2009). *Korea: OECD review of tertiary education*. Organisation for Economic Co-operation and Development. Retrieved from http://www.oecd.org/education/skills-beyond-school/38092630.pdf

Hashiya, H. (1996). Urbanization in the Republic of Korea and Taiwan: A NIEs pattern. *The Developing Economies, 34*, 447–469.

Hauptman, A. M. (2007). Higher education finance: Trends and issues. In J. F. Forest & P. G. Altbach (Eds.), *International handbook of higher education* (pp. 83–106). Dordrecht: Springer.

Kim, J. (2000). Historical development. In J. C. Weidman & N. Park (Eds.), *Higher education in Korea: Tradition and adaptation* (pp. 7–53). New York, NY: Falmer Press.

Kim, S., & Kim, S. (2015). Private universities in South Korea. *International Higher Education, 37*, 20–22.

Kim, S, & Lee J. (2006). Changing facets of Korean higher education: Market competition and the role of the state. *Higher Education, 52*, 557–587.

Kim, T. (2008). Higher education reforms in South Korea: Public-private problems in internationalising and incorporating universities. *Policy Futures in Education, 6*, 558–568.

Korean Educational Statistics Service. (2017). *Educational statistics*. Korean Educational Development. Retrieved from Institute https://kess.kedi.re.kr/eng/stats/ school?menuCd=0102&cd=18508&survSeq=2017&itemCode=01&menuId= m_010202&uppCd1=010202&uppCd2=010202&flag=B

Ministry of Education. (n.d). *Higher education*. Retrieved from http://english.moe.go.kr/sub/info.do?m=020105&s=English

Otten-Pappas, D. (2013). The female perspective on family business successor commitment. *Journal of Family Business Management, 3*, 8–23.

Park, N. (2000). Continuing debates: Government financial aid to the private higher education sector and faculty tenure. In J. Weidman & N. Park (Eds.), *Higher education in Korea: Tradition and adaptation* (pp. 109–130). New York, NY: Falmer Press.

Riesman, D. (1958). The academic procession. In D. Riesman (Ed.), *Constraint and variety in American education* (pp. 25–65). Garden City, NY: Anchor Books.

Rii, H. U., & Ahn, J. (2002). Urbanization and its impact on Seoul, Korea. In *2001 Forum on Urbanizing World and UN Human Habitat II* (pp. 83–100). New York, NY: Columbia University.

Schwekendiek, D. J. (2016). *South Korea: A socioeconomic overview from the past to present*. Piscataway, NJ: Transaction Publishers.

Shin, J. C. (2011). Higher education development in Korea: Western university ideas, Confucian tradition, and economic development. *Higher Education, 64*, 59–72.

Shin, S, & Koh, M. S. (2005). Korean education in cultural context. *Essays in Education, 14*, 1–10.

Weidman, J., & Park, N. (2000). *Higher education in Korea*. New York, NY: Falmer Press.

Yeom, M. (2016). Critical reflection on the massification of higher education in Korea: consequences for graduate employment and policy issues. *Journal of Education and Work, 29*, 48–63.

Yoon, K. (2014). The change and structure of Korean education policy in history. *Italian Journal of Sociology of Education, 6*, 173–200.

CHAPTER 13

Mexico: The Complexities of FOMHEIS

Juan Carlos Silas Casillas

Research on private higher education has typically focused on corporate-owned or faith-based institutions. A study of family-owned or managed higher education institutions (FOMHEIS) has been lacking. Nevertheless, the role of families as owners or managers has begun to attract attention in an increasingly complex postsecondary environment (Altbach, 2005).

The higher education literature in Latin America has mostly ignored family ownership, possibly because of the difficulty in obtaining reliable data. In Mexico and other Latin-American countries, FOMHEIS tend to mask their ownership as family management is perceived generally as of lesser quality and primarily oriented towards generating revenue. As a result, identifying FOMHEIS is a challenging task.

This chapter contains three sections. The first presents the general context of higher education in Mexico focusing on the private sector and the trends of corporatization and fragmentation. The second discusses the general features of private ownership and presents some salient characteristics of FOMHEIS. The third presents an analysis of two cases that portray the unique operational issues and challenges of FOMHEIS in Mexico. The final section summarizes the findings.

The two cases, Universidad de la Vera-Cruz and Universidad Antropológica de Guadalajara, share several characteristics. The rectors are young and charismatic professionals; they are sons of the founder; both institutions operate under the legal status of *asociación civil* (non-profit); and historical events have shaped ownership. They also share the challenges of operating in a complex and competitive environment. On the other hand, the two cases have important differences. One is a niche institution, timidly venturing into mainstream program offerings and the other offers a range of programs while securing a position as a significant player in the city. One emerged from a legal dispute and the other evolved organically from a small startup to a mid-sized university.

1 The Context of the National Higher Education System in Mexico

The higher education milieu in Mexico reflects a mosaic of issues—years of national economic stagnation affecting business investment and family

© KONINKLIJKE BRILL NV, LEIDEN, 2020 | DOI: 10.1163/9789004423435_013

budgets, industrial transformations resulting from new technologies, and problems resulting from violence and migration. The public sector still dominates higher education with about 67 percent of national enrollment but faces significant budgetary restrictions that limit expansion, making private institutions (especially low-cost) attractive. As a result, the private sector continues to grow, although not at the accelerated pace of the late 1990s and early 2000s.

The private sector is experiencing a process of corporatization and fragmentation. On the one hand, large business groups are purchasing and taking over established universities, growing low-profile institutions targeting low-income students, while on the other hand there is a plethora of small narrowly focused institutions.

The largest private provider of higher education in Mexico according to 2016–2017 data is the US-based company, Laureate Education, Inc., with 126,219 students—65,566 at Universidad del Valle de México (UVM) and 60,653 at the Universidad Tecnológica de México (UNITEC).

The second largest private provider is the Instituto Tecnológico y de Estudios Superiores de Monterrey (ITESM or Tec de Monterrey) and its startup for working students and families from lower socioeconomic strata, TecMilenio. In total, these institutions enroll 68,015 students—52, 874 at ITESM and 15,141 at TecMilenio. ITESM is a long-standing, well-regarded institution in Mexico that reflects a multi-campus educational startup backed by corporate capital.

In third place are the universities that belong to Grupo Nacer, a Mexico City based business group with interests in different industries. In education, they control seven universities that enroll a total of 49,919 students. Additional corporate-owned institutions belong to companies as diverse as Anheuser-Busch, Fondo Topaz, (a diversified business group with interest in retail, oil extraction as well as education), London-based Pearson Education, Vanta Education (a subsidiary of the US-based Apollo Group), and London-based Galileo Global Education.

The total enrollment in corporate-owned-universities is 263,396 students, one fifth of the 1,291,954 undergraduate students in Mexican private higher education.

In addition to corporate-owned institutions, there is a fast-growing sector of independent universities focused on low-income families. Some started timidly in the 1970s and 1980s, then expanded rapidly during the late 1990s when these startups developed into multi-branch players. These institutions have grown steadily in a short period and generally appeal to first-generation students. These institutions are extremely dynamic and it is almost impossible to determine their size and impact as a group, but they probably account for

10 percent of private enrollment. Some of them launched as FOMHEIs but it is unclear whether they still are.

Religious affiliated institutions are also an important and growing sector. The total enrollment at universities affiliated with the Catholic church is 109,893 students or 8.5 percent of private enrollment. Other religious denominations operate higher education institutions but with less significant participation. The total of religiously affiliated enrollment is 112,456 students and although the group is quite heterogeneous, these institutions share features like the symbolic and financial support of their church and the funneling of students from the high schools they operate.

The second trend, fragmentation, is also very tangible. Data from the National Association of Universities and Higher Education Institutions from the 2016–2017 school year (ANUIES, 2017) show a plethora of small institutions—99 enroll ten or fewer students; 114 enroll between 11 and 20; 275 enroll between 21 and 50; 310 between 51 and 100; 285 with 101 to 200 students and 320 with more than 201 but fewer than 500. This reflects more than 1,400 institutions from minuscule to small providing degree programs in professions that range from chef to nurse to homeopathy as well as traditional programs like education, marketing, psychology, accountancy, or law.

1.1   Legal Framework for Private Institutions

In this complex environment FOMHEIs are hard to identify, especially in Mexico where legal and fiscal status are not linked to the authorization to operate schools or universities. There is no for-profit tax code for the education sector and although some FOMHEIs operate as for-profits they can be registered in different categories:

- Sociedad Anónima (SA) that allows an institution to operate as a business and retain profit.
- Sociedad Civil (SC) that can earn profit in exchange for professional services.
- Asociación Civil (AC) established for cultural purposes with limitations on the use of profit.

Individuals (*persona física*) and legal entities (*persona moral*) can obtain authorization to offer higher education as private providers but cannot indicate that their goal is to generate profit. They must prepare a case for every degree offered, showing academic and legal justification. FOMHEIs can be established under any of the categories above, but the third is the most common. The majority of higher education institutions in Mexico are property of *personas morales*, legal entities formed by five or more individuals as an *asociación civil*, when the main purpose of its operation is cultural or social development or as a *sociedad civil* when the purpose is business activity. FOMHEIS are usually established as *asociaciones civiles* because this does not imply a predefined agreement on the use of revenue. *Sociedades civiles* are established more frequently by groups of entrepreneurs.

Mexican law limits the use of the term "university" to institutions that offer at least five academic programs from at least three areas of knowledge. If the institution does not meet this requirement it must called "Instituto," "Centro de Estudios," "Centro Universitario," or "Colegio." In fact, there is a difference between the legal name and the commercial name. Therefore, it is not unusual for small institutions with registered names like "Instituto" or "Centro de Estudios" to have more appealing commercial names. One such case is addressed later in this chapter. For example, the legal entity, Centro de Estudios Universitarios Veracruz, operates commercially as UNIVER and Universidad UNIVER.

Regardless of the type of ownership, in order to have official authorization to operate any program, private higher education institutions in Mexico have four options for official recognition—*reconocimiento de validez oficial de estudios federal* from the Ministry of Education, valid in the whole country; *reconocimiento de validez oficial de estudios estatal* from the state board in which the institution would operate; *incorporación de estudios* implying operation under the auspices of a large federal or state university. The first two options protect independence from other institutions; the third and fourth require adherence to the academic criteria set by the sponsoring public university. Most FOMHEIS and other small or medium-sized private universities look for state recognition because it requires considerably less paperwork and because their primary constituency is local.

In brief, characteristics typical of FOMHEIS in Mexico are that they:
- are medium-sized institutions (between 1000 and 3000 students);
- have one large campus and perhaps two to four branch campuses in the same city or smaller cities located nearby;
- are authorized by state boards to operate specific program;
- have a commercial name related to the official name but is not always the same;
- are legally owned by a board and they are most often incorporated as an asociación civil;
- have diverse sources of income such as family businesses donating revenue to the university;
- operate primary and secondary schools whose students have preferential access.

2   Universidad de la Vera-Cruz

The Universidad de la Vera-Cruz is a FOMHEI that emerged from a complex
series of events and reflects how a university that responded to the rapid
growth of the 1990s and 2000s transformed from a joint venture between a
religious congregation and an entrepreneurial institution to a FOMHEI.

2.1   *History and Background*
This university was established officially in 2005; however, its history dates to
1948 when a congregation of nuns opened a school for women in Guadalajara
that offered primary and lower secondary education. After years of positive
relations with the community, a teacher persuaded the Mother Superior to
offer education at the next level and in 1955, Jorge Ramírez y Martínez Sotomayor developed the Escuela de Comercio y Decoración Veracruz (ECDV). The
ECDV enjoyed slow but steady growth targeting girls from affluent families in
the city.

Inspired by the creation of the Universidad Femenina de Guadalajara,
Mexico City, and Veracruz by philanthropists, Ramírez y Martínez Sotomayor
invited Carlos Gabriel López Aranda Muñoz to create a higher education
institution offering studies in interior design in Guadalajara. During the 1970s
and early 1980s the ECDV moved to a larger building. A period of growth and
diversification began in 1986 with the addition of two high schools, the Escuela
Normal para Educadoras Veracruz, and the Escuela Normal Primaria Veracruz,
providing teacher training. The schools were later authorized to offer undergraduate degrees in psychology, administration, and accountancy and opened
admission to male students.

With the registered name of Centro de Estudios Universitarios Veracruz
and the commercial brand of UNIVER, the institution experienced a period
of expansion during the late 1990s and early 2000s. At this point, there was
no board of trustees, only a written agreement between the Mother Superior
and the founders. The expansion funneled funds to the congregation and the
founders. With unprecedented demand the institution made the decision to
grow as much as possible. UNIVER rented and purchased large houses and
adapted them to university use. Enrollment skyrocketed from 1,200 in 1986 to
12,000 in 1998 as result of additional outposts in Tijuana, Morelia, La Paz, Los
Cabos, and other cities and the addition of the graduate studies division.

A combination of marketing, branches, and pricing allowed UNIVER to
profit handsomely during the economic crisis of the late 1990s. They adapted
to an environment that required access to inexpensive education for thousands of students while disregarding issues of quality and academic prestige.

Other universities increased their fees and became inaccessible to lower and middle-class families facing unemployment or salary reductions. At the same time, the public university, Universidad de Guadalajara (UdG), underwent significant changes. The UdG created regional campuses in smaller cities of the state in an effort to decentralize educational opportunities and at the same time dismantling corruption based on inflated enrollment figures to secure more public funding. The result was considerable resource reduction that limited the number of students that the university could absorb for several years. With limited access to established private universities and public institutions, families needed alternatives.

These conditions created perfect opportunities for educational entrepreneurs. UNIVER benefited from demand-driven growth, but economic success led to organizational, managerial, and academic problems. Former employees outside of Guadalajara lined up for the authorization to open a branch of the university that became a sort of franchising. Local managers received some training on how to run their branch campus and the rights to exploit institutional brand. UNIVER's central administration earned undisclosed compensation.

Central management lost control as decisions were made by branch directors without consultation about the use of logos, marketing strategies, admissions standards, hiring, or performance evaluations. The establishment of branches was done without planning, but more as a response to expanding demand that generated a lot of money.

This haphazard management triggered tensions between the founders and led the religious congregation to withdraw from the partnership. The founders pursued different objectives prioritizing a meaningful college education at all branches and emphasizing expansion to secure a larger market share while postponing attention to academic quality. Local educational entrepreneurs were more inclined towards the second strategy.

In early 2005, the mayor of the city of Zacatecas invited UNIVER to open a branch in the city. This is particularly important because it created the last branch officially under the name of UNIVER and because the person responsible for the initiative was Carlos Gabriel López Aranda Ramírez, the son of one of the original founders. Things went well. They began their first year with more than 300 first-year students. After a few years, this well-administrated campus suffered from the public's perception of poor quality of the brand and competition from several new institutions.

In 2008, after a series of negotiations UNIVER was sold to Grupo Nacer, triggering a number of legal problems. UNIVER went through difficulties that led to the reorganization of most of the branch campuses, the closing of some, personnel adjustments, and an aggressive marketing campaign to restore its reputation and recover enrollment.

After months of litigation, the transfer of ownership was finalized giving Grupo Nacer control of UNIVER and the family of Jorge Ramírez y Martínez Sotomayor leadership roles in the organization while the López Aranda Muñoz family retained legal rights to the brand and authority over the new branch campus in Zacatecas established with the name of Universidad de la Vera-Cruz or UVC.

2.2   Renaissance as a FOMHEI

The second stage of institutional history begins in 2009 after the sale to corporate owners. Under the new management, UNIVER continued to experience enrollment declines at most of the branch campuses. The UVC, on the other hand, expanded and established a new *asociación civil* as owner of the university with legal rights to the UVC brand and official recognition granted by the state board of education.

In 2009, the first cohort in Zacatecas completed their undergraduate studies. The rector and his staff turned their attention to local issues. They got a bank loan, purchased and adapted a six-story hotel building in a convenient part of the city. In 2012, the family launched a small branch campus in Puerto Vallarta with a cousin.

The sale of UNIVER in 2008 to Grupo Nacer was undoubtedly a pivotal experience for UVC, now fully under the leadership of López Aranda Muñoz. The UNIVER rector learned about the importance of immaculate legal and fiscal status the hard way.

2.3   The Higher Education System and the UVC

The state of Zacatecas and its capital city are consistently ranked low for economic development. The state's economy depends on agriculture, mining and the money sent by migrants working in the United States. There are a few factories in the state, generally small and located in or near the capital city. The city of Zacatecas is a colonial city, once home to wealthy mine owners and is becoming a popular tourist destination due to the grandeur of colonial buildings, cobblestone streets, and surrounding mountains. The result is a rapidly transforming economy in need of services in hospitality, gastronomy, and thematic tours. However, financial resources to build the sector are lacking.

The higher education system in Zacatecas is small as a result of its demographics, economy, history, and culture. Private investment in higher education is limited, which results in the lowest participation rate in Mexico at 12.4

percent, below the national average of 31.5 percent (ANUIES, 2017). In this sense, private institutions have to struggle to have "a larger slice of a small cake."

Relations among private institutions are cordial but competitive. The relationship with the public university is characterized by suspicion since the Universidad Autónoma de Zacatecas has launched undergraduate programs provided by private institutions but at a lower cost and has resources to support student transportation, books, and food. The environment for private universities is challenging and requires planning, careful use of resources, commercial intelligence, academic credibility, and good public relations.

2.4   Universidad de la Vera-Cruz in Context

The UVC combines aspects of a traditional university with an entrepreneurial spirit. Its legal ownership as an *asociación civil* means that it cannot pursue profit explicitly. The university offers traditional degrees without establishing academic departments or other traditional structures. Competitive advantages tend to be administrative innovations in student services, the promotion of opportunities for national and international mobility, and strategic partnerships with language schools.

The UVC mission is to cultivate entrepreneurs with leadership aspirations who generate change and prosperity. At UVC learning is directed towards personal happiness and self-fulfillment. It strives to become a prestigious institution in Mexico with an international network and graduates who are innovative entrepreneurs who will transform society in positive ways.

Tuition fees are in the middle range, oriented towards being a reasonably-priced university. The marketing strategy differentiates UVC from demand-absorbing universities (Levy, 2004) and low-profile institutions (Silas, 2005) and has positioned itself as a first option for middle-income families. UVC offers undergraduate and graduate degrees in many high-demand programs like communication studies and administration and some smaller programs in criminology and nutrition that are challenging as the public university can offer similar degrees at a lower price. UVC´s enrollment by program is shown in Table 13.1.

Official data from ANUIES show that UVC has experienced an enrollment decline of about 500 students in five years. This results from slow economic growth in Mexico and Zacatecas, higher investment from public institutions to increase their enrollment, and the creation of new low-cost private institutions in the city. Students who otherwise would enroll at UVC are now considering the public university, a cheaper private, or not enrolling in higher education at all.

TABLE 13.1   UVC 2016–2017 undergraduate enrollment

Faculty	Enrollment
Arts and Humanities	87
Graphic Design	55
Fashion Design	32
Social Sciences, Administration and Law	786
Business Administration	77
Administration of Tourism Business	45
International Commerce and Customs	110
Communication	107
Accountancy	19
Criminology	60
Law	78
Gastronomy	216
Marketing	26
Gastronomy and Hospitality	17
Psychology	31
Education	39
Pedagogy	39
Engineering, Manufacturing and Construction	53
Architecture	53
Health	56
Nutrition	56
Total	1,021

SOURCE: ANUARIO ESTADÍSTICO ANUIES 2016–2017

UVC hosted 6.8 percent of the city's higher education enrollment in 2012 and was the largest private institution with 1,514 students compared to 795 at the next largest institution. In 2017, it hosted 3.2 percent of the city's enrollment and occupied the second spot with 1,021 students, 89 fewer than the largest private institution. Nevertheless, the challenge for UVC is not from the private sector but the increased intake of students at public institutions. Examples are programs in psychology, law, and accountancy that suffered from increased opportunities at public institutions with a total enrollment double that of all private institutions in similar programs.

UVC is confronting these issues by opening new undergraduate programs also offered by other providers, starting new modes like flexible scheduling and evening classes; starting high-demand graduate programs like the MBA; adding value to existing programs with language certification or diploma courses that complement usual coursework; offering continuing education programs in gastronomy and other areas within the hospitality industry. The enrollment decline has stopped and from 2017 to 2019 grew by 400 students.

2.5   Governance, Management, and the Family

Five family-members formed the *asociación civil* established in 2009: the rector, his mother, his father, his sister, and his brother (who lives abroad). This is the governing board and they have periodic meetings in which the five members analyze all aspects of operation and make decisions about the coming year and semester. The rector, who knows the university best, is the primary decision-maker but is influenced by the other board members. The sister and brother are interested and emotionally linked, but mostly disconnected from daily operations.

The institution is organized to strengthen market position. The rector reports to the family board and has two positions reporting directly to him— director of public relations and an executive director who is in charge of the daily operation and assumes control when the rector is not present. The executive director is a key position and as an FOMHEI, it would be expected that this role would be assigned to a relative, but it is not. The person in this position has been working for UVC for years. Under the executive director, there is an administrative director, comptroller, marketing director, and academic director.

The family owns the university and manages it through the *asociación civil*. With the exception of the rector and a cousin who is the director of the branch campus in Puerto Vallarta, there are no relatives working at the institution. The rector is the critical link between the family and the university.

A key challenge at UVC will be the generational transition. After the sale of UNIVER, the reconstitution of the *asociación civil* and the transition to UVC from 2008 to 2009, the leadership was assigned to the rector. He is the heart of the university; his father, a UNIVER founder, provides moral leadership only. The challenge for the future is grooming someone to succeed him.

The head of the Puerto Vallarta branch campus is the cousin of the UVC general director although not in that position due to family ties but because he conducted the market studies that prepared the startup and initiated the venture. The family decided to establish the Puerto Vallarta campus as a "joint venture," a partnership of the rector, the branch director, and another person who is not involved directly in the university. This was a way to protect the interests of the family and to make it clear from the beginning that all commercial activity with the UVC was to be managed by contract to control the use of know-how and brand.

2.6   Challenges and Plans

As a FOMHEI, UVC has two primary challenges—how to survive as a university in a complex, competitive, cost-sensitive environment, circumstances that might affect its academic and business model, and how to consolidate the process of professionalization taking place at the institution. The rector has a key role to play in the maturity of UVC; he must refrain from making all decisions on his own and delegate greater institutional responsibility to UVC staff.

Enrollment seems to be recovering. Nevertheless, plans for the future focus on marketing, improving quality, and controlling costs, three strategies that do not necessarily align. If UVC succeeds, they can recover leadership in Zacatecas and grow in Puerto Vallarta.

The *asociación civil* will remain unchanged with the current configuration that keeps key decisions in the family in the short-term. Nevertheless, this exacerbates the risk that results from disproportionate dependence on the current rector.

Some of the challenges experienced by UVC seem to be common to other FOMHEIs with different origins and trajectories. The second case presented in this chapter shows how UNAG, a niche institution that grapples with competition in a large city.

3   Universidad Antropológica de Guadalajara (UNAG)

The history of the Universidad Antropológica de Guadalajara (UNAG) dates to 1985 when José Garza Mora, a psychology professor who taught courses on human resources, psychotherapy, and general psychology began teaching courses on non-mainstream psychology. Garza Mora started the Instituto de Especialidades de Guadalajara (IEG) while continuing to teach at two of the large private universities in Guadalajara. The IEG offered a few courses on homeopathy, human development, transpersonal, and humanist psychology. Students were interested in these topics but disinclined to pursue a degree in these areas. Early infrastructure consisted of a house near the "bohemian zone" of the city. Practicing psychologists and people involved in alternative health were the first students.

The IEG had slow but steady growth in enrollment and courses. In 1992 the IEG changed its name to Instituto Superior de Especialidades de Guadalajara (ISEG) and gained official authorization to offer graduate degrees in psychology and health from the state board of education, the Registro de Validez Oficial de Estudios (RVOE). In 2010 the institution changed its name to Universidad Antropológica de Guadalajara (UNAG) in order to have a stronger brand name.

The ISEG eventually received authorization to offer undergraduate studies in homeopathy, the first institution in the country legally authorized to award this degree. This was a major success and enrollment grew from a few dozen to hundreds of students. Although the expansion was slower compared to other private universities, the institution grew year to year with a focus on working adults instead of traditional-age students and secured a market niche. The average age of students during the 2017–2018 academic year was 36 years old, much higher than elite private or public universities. Additionally, focusing on alternative therapies like homeopathy, bioenergetics, and transpersonal psychology has strengthened its position further over the years.

3.1   The Higher Education System and the UNAG

Guadalajara is an extremely important city in Mexico. It is the capital of the state of Jalisco, the third largest contributor to national GDP, the second largest metropolitan area in terms population, and a major cultural center. It is home to all types of industries, financial services, commerce, and tourism requiring all sorts of qualified professionals.

The academic environment in Jalisco is complex and competitive. Guadalajara is host to 134 higher education providers and more than 186,000 students. This complex network includes 93 smaller institutions enrolling fewer than 500 students; about 40 have 100 students or fewer. There are also prestigious public and private universities enrolling several thousands of students. Academic options at the graduate and undergraduate level are plentiful and cover practically all disciplines. UNAG has found a niche and prospered in this complex environment.

UNAG has minor involvement with state government and public universities, limited mostly to formalities. The university maintains some professional linkages with other institutions, but these opportunities and relationships depend almost entirely on initiatives by the rector.

3.2   Universidad Antropológica de Guadalajara in Context

UNAG is a medium-sized non-profit institution characterized by slow and steady growth benefiting from the expansion of private higher education in Mexico and opportunities in its market niche. The organizational chart is nearly flat with a rector as the operational leader and below him, a director of quality management and development, an academic director, a research coordinator, and an educational technology coordinator. An administrative director, outreach director, and comptroller are also at the same organizational level. This configuration gives the rector a broad range of involvement in all areas and concentrates key decisions on his desk.

UNAG embraces institutional values such as liberty, respect, truth, harmony, happiness, responsibility, and the pursuit of common good. These elements are posted in every classroom, at two branch campuses and enunciated in the mission statement.

The UNAG's mission is to, "form professionals with scientific grounding, solid beliefs, who are effective, practical, and ethical in their profession, self-fulfilled promotors of social well-being, productive and motivated to continue their professional development, in constant search and transcendence."

The university emphasizes its relationship to the city and makes frequent mention of the importance of acting locally to help the community. Three years ago, the university created an alternative health clinic with the name of "Armonía de Vida" (Life's harmony) that serves the community offering inexpensive therapy to needy citizens.

UNAG developed the "PILARES model," an acronym for Proactividad (proactivity), Iniciativa (initiative), Logros (achievements), Aprendizaje dinámico (dynamic learning), Reflexión (reflection), Evaluación (evaluation) and Socialización (socialization). This model, developed by the coordinator of quality management and development, was made public in 2016 and defines the university's approach. All newly hired teaching staff are indoctrinated in the PILARES model.

The two branch campuses offer morning and evening courses on weekdays, intensive courses on Saturday mornings and online courses. Graduate courses are offered in additional cities.

UNAG could be described as a niche or boutique institution since it offers programs no other institution in the city offers. Its strongest program is perhaps the undergraduate program in homeopathy that has become the indisputable leader in Guadalajara in this field with 40 percent of the city's enrollment in this area. Other important programs like human development and social psychology contribute to a solid enrollment base that makes it possible to experiment and launch other programs without risk. In recent years, UNAG has started offering more mainstream programs like administration, accountancy, marketing, and law with decent results. A comparison of 2012 and 2016 enrollment pattern is shown in Table 13.2.

UNAG made decisions about starting new programs after careful consideration of the still growing market for private higher education in Guadalajara, reviewing strengths and weaknesses along with possible risks and costs. Although a latecomer to conventional undergraduate programs presents challenges, it reflects the UNAG's intention of becoming a larger comprehensive institution in the future. At least 20 universities in the city offer the same

TABLE 13.2   UNAG enrollment

Undergraduate program	2012	2016
Homeopathy	417	528
Social psychology	78	305
Human development	77	86
Family counseling	20	21
Business administration		61
Law		49
Accountancy		36
Marketing		25
International commerce		19
Total	592	1,130

SOURCE: ANUARIO ESTADÍSTICO ANUIES 2016–2017

programs that UNAG launched with law offered at 39 private and one public university.

Carefully developed graduate studies are also UNAG strengths. In 2012, they offered the only master's degrees in bioenergetics and family counseling and one of two master's in school management in Guadalajara. In 2016 UNAG offered the only master's degree in transpersonal psychology and one of two doctoral programs in human development.

UNAG's trajectory is one of slow and steady consolidation and growth. The owners monitor almost every development. Academic decisions about program offerings or delivery modes, as well as the development of the institution's image in the city, are always under scrutiny. The expansion of infrastructure is a good example. During the late 1990s and early 2000s, the owners rented an old, large attractive house and used it as the campus. The charming building became an icon of the institution. Nevertheless, the opportunity to buy an old hotel on a central avenue of Guadalajara helped to create room for growth.

The year 2010 was particularly significant in UNAG's development. The founder had to step aside for health reasons and invited his oldest son, Alejandro Garza Preciado, already working at the university, to assume institutional leadership. This shift forced the family to restructure the *asociación civil* and ownership of the university (from Instituto de Especialidades de Guadalajara Asociación Civil to Instituto Superior de Especialidades de Guadalajara

Asociación Civil). During 2010, the institution also obtained a bank loan to purchase the old hotel in order to expand infrastructure and changed the commercial name to Universidad Antropológica de Guadalajara.

3.3   Generational Transition

Rector Alejandro Garza Preciado started working for the university during the early 2000s. He holds a degree in industrial engineering and could have pursued a career in any institution or industry but had to assume responsibility in the family business. In 2010 when the father stepped down, he was the obvious choice to assume the role of rector. The founder's daughter has a degree in education and works as the coordinator of quality management and development. Both of the founder's children play key roles at the university as owners and members of senior management.

UNAG's history is defined by two distinct stages—when the founder created, staffed, stabilized, and led the institution from 1985 to 2010 and the period of expansion starting in 2010 when UNAG expanded infrastructure and academic offerings. The second stage has taken place under the leadership of the second generation.

The inclusion of the children in management was expected. The founder's son had participated in many institutional activities, had deep knowledge of most processes and knew (and was known by) university personnel. His experience and knowledge made him a strong candidate when the founder stepped down. His sister, coordinator of quality management, was also an obvious choice for a managerial position as she held a degree in education and like her brother, had intimate knowledge of the university as a member of the *asociación civil.*

There are cases of other relatives employed as teachers, but their participation has not led to any special consideration and their contracts have been based on merit.

3.4   Governance Structure

Universidad Antropológica de Guadalajara or UNAG is property of an *asociación civil* (ISEG AC) comprised of six members—the founder, his wife, son, daughter, an expert in education, and an expert in tax and finances. Before 2010 the *asociación civil* included additional relatives of the founder but with symbolic roles. Once the founder's children reached adulthood and were clearly committed to the institution, it was clear that they would become owners and managers of the university. They were included in the *asociación* and the other relatives were asked to leave. The transition was handled smoothly since the departing relatives did not have an active role in university management.

A critical decision was the inclusion of experts who were not part of the family with the aim of minimizing family biases in university decisions. The current rector presented the idea to the family in the interest of a stronger institution. The two experts play an active role in analyzing opportunities and advising the family, but their involvement does not dilute family control as two-thirds of the association are family members; the experts help to fine tune decisions.

The *asociación civil* summons the rector, quality assurance coordinator, and founder frequently to present a detailed report and plan for the next year. Although retired, the founder remains an almost daily presence at the university.

The *asociación civil* has been satisfied with the institution's performance and is not likely to pursue major change. The participation of the second generation as owners and managers seems to be producing good results. The main challenge ahead is expansion without losing its essence as an institution with a humanist orientation and values and without impact on quality. The family hopes to grow to 2,000 students. In order to accomplish this, they will need a well-designed financial strategy and the capacity to attract accomplished scholars that likely implies hiring faculty on an hourly basis from other prestigious local universities. The objective is to become the least expensive among the established universities in the city and to expand into the traditional-age student market successfully.

4 Conclusion

Higher education institutions in Mexico can be classified in several ways although distinctions among institution types are not entirely clear (Muñoz, 2004). The analysis of the two cases in this chapter sheds some light on FOMHEIs.

FOMHEIs are separate from corporate-owned or faith-based private institutions. They typically receive their authorization from state boards and operate under commercial names that often differ from the name used for their legal incorporation. They are generally small, enrolling on average 1,000 to 3,000 students, and often operate across multiple campuses.

These institutions are owned by families that dominate the membership of an *asociación civil* that operates as the board of trustees. FOMHEIs have diverse sources of income that may include revenue from other family-owned businesses. They generally own and operate primary and secondary schools and students who attend these schools have preferential access to the family's university.

In addition, FOMHEIs in Mexico seem to grow from similar patterns—a visionary establishes an institution that evolves into a family-controlled enterprise where family members play an active role in oversight and management. Children of the founder become second generation management and endeavor to protect the original vision of the founder while adapting to changing conditions and opportunities in the environment.

Motivations for creating the university vary. Frequently they involve the desire for intellectual and financial independence. FOMHEI's cannot be successful without knowledge of educational management and academic culture. Most FOMHEI founders have been university faculty or teachers or have had experience in government with public education.

Management frequently reflects centralized administrative control; senior managers tend to make most of the decisions without deference to the traditions of academic life or shared governance. Collegiality is not a priority; trust and loyalty are key elements of the organization. Charismatic leadership is a critical feature of successful FOMHEs.

FOMHEIs face many challenges. How they develop and grow in the future will determine whether they can survive in a complex and competitive environment.

References

Altbach, P. G. (2005). Universities: Family style. *International Higher Education, 39,* 10–12.

ANUIES. (2017). *Anuario estadístico de la educación superior 2016–2017.* Retrieved from http://www.anuies.mx/informacion-y-servicios/informacion-estadistica-de-educacion-superior/anuario-estadistico-de-educacion-superior

Levy, D. (1986). *Higher education and the state in Latin America.* Chicago, IL: Chicago University Press.

Muñoz, C. (2004). *Desarrollo y heterogeneidad de las instituciones mexicanas de educación superior de sostenimiento privado.* Mexico: Universidad Iberoamericana.

Quintero, L. (2011). The impact of demand-absorbing universities in Mexico's higher education system. *Reflecting Education, 7*(1), 55–66.

Silas, J. C. (2005), Recognizing the subsectors in Mexican private higher education. In P. Altbach & D. Levy (Eds.), *Private higher education: A global revolution* (pp. 241–243). Rotterdam, The Netherlands: Sense Publishers.

CHAPTER 14

The Philippines, Part 1: The University of Cordilleras and Its Place in Philippines Higher Education

Rene Joshua M. Verdote

The Philippine postsecondary education landscape was greatly disrupted in 2016. The implementation of the senior high school program replaced an obsolete ten-year combined basic and secondary education program. This new program posed various threats to higher education institutions (HEIs) such as possible faculty retrenchment resulting from projected low enrollment figures, particularly during the initial five-year transition period.

In addition, the populations of faculty and students in private HEIs were at risk of declining with the national rollout of a government scholarship program that granted free tuition to all qualified students at state-owned universities and colleges (SUCs). University coalitions decried the program citing a significant decrease in their population during the pilot implementation year.

In broader perspective, the advance of "Industry 4.0," the age of the Internet of Things, and artificial intelligence, also affects how universities and colleges approach and deliver education. The rapid emergence of new trends in technology has implications for the future workforce and the skills demanded of its workers. Hence, universities are pressed to update curricula to be responsive and remain relevant to the needs of the industry with special attention to technical skills.

All these factors, local and beyond, press HEIs in the Philippines to catch up with this drastically shifting landscape. This chapter looks at how the University of the Cordilleras (UC), a 73-year old family-controlled higher education institution in Baguio City in the Philippines, confronts these disruptive trends in Philippine higher education.

1 An Overview of the Philippines Postsecondary Education Landscape

In August 2017, the British Council reported 1,943 HEIs in the Philippines—1,710 private universities and colleges (88 percent) and 233 state universities and colleges (12 percent). Approximately 54 percent of students are enrolled in private higher education and 46 percent in public. UC is among 59 schools granted autonomous status by the Philippines' Commission on Higher Education (CHED).

Autonomous HEIs are the top HEIs in the country that "demonstrate exceptional institutional quality and enhancement through internal quality assessment systems and demonstrate excellent program outcomes through a high proportion of accredited programs, the presence of Centers of Excellence and/or Developments ... In particular, they show evidence of outstanding performance consistent with their horizontal type" (Commission on Higher Education, 2012, p. 9).

With this distinction, UC and other autonomous HEIs may function with limited supervision from the commission. These schools are a priority for research and scholarship grants and are allowed to offer three new programs a year by simply submitting all necessary documents to the commission.

Universities and colleges face three key issues in Philippine postsecondary education—massification, privatization, and internationalization. Massification results from higher education being more readily accessible to the general population with a total of 2,981,803 students enrolled in higher education according to a report of the Commission on Higher Education for academic year 2017–2018 (Higher Education Enrollment by Region and Institution, 2018). Due to the availability of scholarships and grants, students will be able to enroll in either private or public universities. This may cause an increase in class sizes and affect the absorption abilities of a university.

Privatization is a result of massification. Due to the high demand for education, commercialization (as corporations open their own schools or take over established HEIs) is becoming more common. In the Philippines, major business conglomerates have now entered the education industry and are becoming key players by establishing or acquiring their own educational systems all over the country.

Finally, due to the increased mobility of students and teachers in the world, internationalization may deprive local students of spots in universities, especially for schools that have met maximum absorption capacity. The Philippines, a member of the Association of Southeast Asian Nations, is gearing for the ASEAN integration that will allow freer exchange of services including education.

2   More Funding, Free Tuition in State-Run HEIs

The implementation of the government scholarship program through the Universal Access to Quality Tertiary Education (UAQTE) Act provides free tertiary education in state and local universities and colleges (SUC/LUC) and free technical-vocational education and training in state-run technical-vocational institutions. It operates in conjunction with the Unified Student Financial Assistance System for Tertiary Education (UniFAST) Act that consolidates all government-funded scholarships, loans, and grants and is projected to significantly impact private university faculty and students. A total of P8.3 billion pesos (US $157M) has been allotted to the program.

Section 4 of the UAQTE provides for free higher education in SUCs and LUCs for students who have met the school's admission and retention policies. This provision is limited to first-year students. Learners who have previously earned their degree in a state or private university and plan to pursue a second or graduate degree are ineligible for the scholarship. CHED Commissioner J. Prosero De Vera III (2018) said the tertiary education subsidy (TES), a grants-in-aid program, is for the "poorest of the poor" and potential beneficiaries must be included in the Department of Social Welfare and Development's "Listahan 2.0" or the National Household Targeting System for Poverty Reduction, a database of impoverished families and potential beneficiaries of social development programs.

Salvador B. Belaro Jr. (2017), a representative in the Philippine Congress, argued that the enactment of these laws will pose a threat to enrollment at private universities. He added that faculty members may also "flock to SUCs because the now better funded SUCs will be able to provide them with better job security." Low participation in postsecondary education was often attributed to the poverty rate of the country. A large number of UC's students and other family-owned or managed universities come from low to middle-income families and the opportunity to study for free will definitely appeal to these students and impact UC's enrollment.

Established institutions, including UC, have not felt the impact of the free tuition program. In the national capital region, Visayas and Mindanao regions, institutions are beginning to feel the impact of this program; smaller schools are facing possible closure or are beginning to shift to offering only senior high school due to declining enrollment.

In August 2018, the Catholic Educational Association of the Philippines (CEAP) reported that private universities in Metro Manila "have experienced lower student enrollees." They added that schools in the Visayas regions noted a "migration of their students to the nearest state universities."

The effect may be attributed to the following major factors.

- Parallel programs. The academic programs offered by a private university may be similar, if not the same, to the academic program offerings of a state university or college. A student who may have difficulty in supporting their studies may opt to transfer to an SUC and receive the same degree for a fraction of the cost.

– Proximity. Records show that universities cater to students coming from various parts of the country. With scholarships available in sucs in their hometowns, students have the option to study locally and save on lodging and transportation costs.
– Job Security. Positions in government offices or universities are sought after due to their compensation and benefits package that include allowances, research incentives and the like.

As a response to the government scholarship program, private universities have begun offering a variety of scholarships to students that include grants for members of varsity teams and performing arts groups. In addition, special scholarship grants are available to honor students and persons with disabilities. One major scholarship is the student assistantship program that requires students to work for six hours in a university office. In turn, they receive 100 percent tuition remission, miscellaneous fee discounts, and a monthly allowance.

3   Access to Postsecondary Education

Commissioner J. Prospero E. De Vera III (2018) believes that lack of resources is the main determinant for whether individuals continue their education. De Vera presented figures that show that 32.1 percent of high school graduates are not in college because of the high cost of education.

The Philippines has only about 28–30 percent of the age cohort enrolled in postsecondary education (Yee, 2017). This can be linked to data in a Philippine Statistics Authority report (2018) that show that 5 of 10 Filipino families lack even basic education.

Yee (2017) asserts that 61–80 percent of families who earn a monthly income between P5,106 (US$99) to P12,987(US$253) are not able to attend college. Among the poorest families with an estimated monthly income of P5,106 (US$99) and below did not or cannot attend college. This is in comparison with high-income families earning at least P115,428 (US$2,250) monthly where only 19 percent are not enrolled in college.

Business administration and related programs account for the greatest concentration of enrollment with 775,805 (26 percent) of postsecondary students during 2017–2018. Business fields are followed by education and teacher training (21.43 percent), engineering and technology (12.43 percent), information technology (10.59 percent), and medical and allied health fields (5.92 percent) (Higher Education Enrollment by Discipline Group, 2018).

Program choice is likely influenced by economic need and potential. These programs are aligned with a specific career path and good opportunities for employment upon graduation. Many students consider education as a key path out of poverty and that a degree will allow them to better provide for their families soon after graduating.

Further, Yee (2017) says that most disciplines offered most frequently "are largely the easiest to offer and inexpensive ... that do not require as much investment."

The Cordillera Administrative Region (CAR), where the University of the Cordilleras is located, recorded a higher education participation rate of 45.93 percent. This is the second highest participation percentage after the national capital region that enrolls 51.47 percent. The Autonomous Region in Muslim Mindanao posted the lowest participation rate in the country at only 17.97.

4 First Higher Education Institution in the Cordillera Administrative Region

Baguio Colleges, as the University of the Cordilleras was originally known, pioneered tertiary education in the mountain highlands of the Cordillera region amidst devastation in and around Baguio City after the Second World War.

Despite a pessimistic outlook and bleak prospects permeating the climate of any undertaking at the time, Attorney Benjamin Romero Salvosa (BRS) envisioned Baguio City as an educational center in northern Luzon, beyond the city's status as a hill station for the Americans and the country's 1903 summer capital. This vision stemmed from the fact that there were no colleges in the city. This was brought up during the founder's discussion with prominent Baguio personalities such as Sinai Hamada who was BRS's fellow alumnus at the University of the Philippines.

Establishing a university was not BRS's main objective for moving to Baguio City from his hometown in Unisan, Quezon Province. He was diagnosed with tuberculosis and moved to Baguio City because his doctor believed that the air and climate of the city would improve his health. Terminally ill, he was known as "the young man who came to Baguio to die."

In spite of his affliction, BRS lived his life without concern for the lingering possibility of death. He went to Manila and recruited unemployed schoolteachers, sold all his assets in Manila and in his hometown, and pursued his vision by founding the first college in the Cordillera region, earning him the title "Father of Higher Education" from the city government of Baguio 60 years later.

On June 19, 1946, Baguio Colleges (BC) officially opened. The founding date was deliberate to coincide with the anniversary of the birth of Dr. Jose P. Rizal, the Philippines national hero whom BRS greatly admired. As the only college at the time, 156 students enrolled in BC in the teacher training and liberal arts courses offered.

In 1966 Baguio Colleges was converted into an educational foundation and was renamed Baguio Colleges Foundation (BCF). The founders signed a deed of donation transferring all their corporate and personal assets to the school, shifting the beneficiaries from stockholders to "learners and knowledge workers." This meant that all earnings would be reinvested in the school and the students. BRS was the chairman of the board of trustees and president until his death in 1994.

As BCF, the campus relocated to its current location on Governor Pack Road. BCF began offering more degree programs and its population grew with learners now coming from various areas of northern Luzon.

In 2003, BCF was granted university status by the Philippines' Commission on Higher Education (CHED) and was renamed University of the Cordilleras (UC). Despite dropping the word "foundation" in its name, UC remains a foundation. From Baguio Colleges to Baguio Colleges Foundation and then University of the Cordilleras, the school increased offerings to include early childhood to postgraduate studies to over 18,000 students.

4.1   UC's Vision, Mission, and Philosophy

UC envisions itself as a community of scholars aggressively involved in the pursuit of knowledge to help preserve Filipino culture and values to act positively by training them to think critically and creatively. UC's mission is to provide functional knowledge and skills, dynamic interaction, and leadership in various disciplines for a better quality of life (UC Student Handbook, 2016).

UC is committed to education as the foundation of a progressive nation, training the youth for civic responsibility and the development of moral character. The institution maintains the belief that the benefits of higher education should be made accessible to everyone who deserves it.

4.2   UC on the Postsecondary Education Landscape

The University of the Cordilleras is one of the most prominent HEIs in northern Luzon based on its official recognitions, accreditations, and the qualifications conferred by the Commission on Higher Education (CHED) and other reputable accrediting institutions.

UC is recognized nationally for being the top performing criminology school in the Philippines for 43 consecutive exams. UC is likewise the only law school north of Metro Manila to produce two top scorers on the bar (the professional) examination. Notably in March 2019, Atty. Janet Abuel, UC's top scorer on the

1998 bar examinations, was named officer in charge of the Department of Budget and Management by Philippine President, Rodrigo Duterte.

CHED has conferred Center of Excellence status to UC's criminology, information technology, and teacher education programs. This is the highest recognition awarded to any academic program.

The Commission has also identified UC as a "delivering higher education institution" for graduate program scholarships in the K to 12 transition program which includes the off-campus delivery of a master's in information technology and a doctorate in information technology in the provinces of Bicol, Abra, and Tuguegarao. As an off-campus program, UC-IT faculty travel from Baguio City to the three provinces on weekends to deliver the MIT/DIT programs to fellow IT educators who are under a CHED scholarship grant. The degrees may be completed in two years.

UC is also part of the Commission's "Train the Trainers Program." UC faculty train senior high school teachers from various parts of the country on the new syllabus and methodologies in the delivery of various general education courses.

UC offers a total of 33 bachelor's programs across nine disciplines, 15 postgraduate programs (master's and doctorate), law, and basic education from early childhood to senior high school.

In total, UC has three campuses that house different programs. Early childhood to basic education is housed at the Campo Libertad Campus in Hamada Road Subdivision. The college of criminal justice education occupies the Legarda Campus. The main campus on Governor Pack Road houses the rest of the undergraduate and graduate programs as well as the senior high school. All key offices are found in the main campus. Students and staff converge in the main campus during institutional activities.

UC, as of the first trimester of 2018–2019 hosted the following number of students:
- Postsecondary (including postgraduate and law students), 11,102.
- Senior high school, 6,945.
- Junior high school, 526.
- Primary school, 882.

UC has the largest number of international students among HEIs in Baguio City with 461 students representing 47 different nationalities.

4.3   Governance and the Family Coalition

The university's chain of command is divided into the board of trustees, the executive council, academic council, administrative council and finance committee, and information technology systems and services (ITSS).

The board of trustees is composed of six members from the six branches of the founder's descendants. The board is headed by an ex-officio chairman, elected by a majority vote of the members. Membership of the board is a combination of executive and non-executive trustees. Executive trustees report to the university on a regular basis and they are directly involved in the school's operations.

According to UC's code of corporate governance, members must be direct descendants of Benjamin and Evangelina Salvosa, have at least a bachelor's degree and at least three years of work experience. According to executive trustee, Nene Salvosa-Bowman, the board ensures that the philosophy of the founder will be preserved. As of 2019, the Board is composed of second and third generation Salvosas with the eldest son of the founder as chairman.

Since its founding, the university has seen the leadership transition from first generation Salvosas (starting with the founder) to the second generation Salvosas, the children of the founder, who are currently holding top management positions as university president and chairman of the board of trustees. Other second generation Salvosas are members of the board.

In 2018, third generation Salvosas assumed key internal management positions as assistant vice-president for finance, assistant vice-president for human resource and development, and director of quality assurance.

The board assumes responsibility for decision-making on matters that greatly affect the organization at large. It exercises all corporate powers of the university, conducts all business, controls and holds all its properties, and has such powers and authority as provided by the UC by-laws and the laws of the Republic of the Philippines.

The board of trustees appoints members of the executive council led by a president and/or executive vice president who shall act as their chief executive officer and implement necessary policies to sustain the university. It is also the board's responsibility to periodically evaluate and monitor the implementation of policies and strategies such as business plans and management performance.

The executive council is composed of the president, executive vice-president, vice-president for academic affairs, vice-president for administration, assistant vice-presidents for finance, and a legal counsel. The executive council oversees day-to-day operations of the university and is largely responsible for formulating strategic policies from academics to student services, subject to the approval of the board.

Decisions are usually reached between the board and the executive council during a board meeting. Decisions that would greatly impact the organization at large are made by the board of trustees. For example, if there is a proposal for the construction of a new building, final approval must come from the board.

Decisions that are purely operational can be decided upon by the executive council, specifically the president and the executive vice-president or their respective vice-presidents. Matters such as the school calendar, curricula, and university programs can be acted upon by top management. In cases that involve smaller units of the university, middle management may step in. It should be noted that the executive council must still present their proposals on matters beyond day-to-day operations for the board's review and approval.

The councils and committees, on the other hand, headed by their respective vice-presidents, report directly to the president of the university. The academic council is composed of the VP concerned, dean of student affairs and services, the college deans, the basic education's principal, and senior high school academic director. They are in charge of the university's academic programs, functions, and services. Coordinating closely with the Commission on Higher Education, Department of Education, Legal Education Board, and other agencies, they ensure that all academic-related functions of the university are in compliance with the standards imposed by the commission.

The academic council, in coordination with the office of quality assurance (also under the office of the president) handles the accreditation requirements of the university to ensure and maintain the quality of education provided by the UC.

The administrative council handles various student services with a special focus on alumni concerns, health, and infrastructure issues such as buildings and facilities management. The finance committee is tasked to manage and secure the university's financial matters while the ITSS manages the university's ICT needs that include network and software infrastructure, online services, and social media.

The faculty, often referred to by UC's founder as "knowledge workers," is expected to deliver courses as prescribed in the curriculum. They are trained to deliver "outcomes-based education." Moreover, faculty are largely engaged in research with some research initiatives funded by Philippine government agencies. Faculty publications, specifically on information technology and computer science, have been indexed by international databases such as SCOPUS and ISI.

4.4   *Decrease in Market Share*
Aside from the national scholarship programs, with Baguio City being tagged as the Educational Hub of Northern Luzon, competition is inevitable.

In Baguio City, UC is one of three major private universities dominating market share; data show UC alternating between the second and third spot in terms of enrollment.

UC posted the largest high school enrollment in the entire region with 6,419 students in grades 11 and 12. This number could be attributed to the fact that public schools offered a limited number of sections during the implementation of the K to 12 program that resulted in students from public schools enrolling in private schools. Public schools have begun constructing new buildings to accommodate a larger number of students in their senior high school program. However, with the rise of more SUCS/LUCS and private institutions in other provinces in the Cordillera region, students from UC's major feeder areas no longer need to travel to Baguio City and may opt to enroll in HEIS opening closer to home.

Surprisingly, despite a projected decrease in population due to the K to 12 transition period, UC recorded an increase in student enrollment during 2017–2018. This increase may be attributed to UC's uniquely designed senior high school program. In 2018–2019, UC recorded almost 7,000 students in grades 11 and 12. The UC senior high school program was designed so that senior high students are treated like college students. The high school occupies the science building of the main campus complex. There they are integrated with college students and able to use the same facilities.

In addition, senior high school students are included in university activities such as sports, literary, and musical competitions. Moreover, senior high students are able to socialize with college students and join college organizations thus giving them early exposure to university life. UC was able to enroll a significant percentage of its 3,500 grade 12 students in its university programs.

Still, UC has designed a multi-level marketing campaign targeted at recruiting potential students. Other strategies include UC participating in quality assurance programs, discussed in the next section.

4.5   UC's Continuous Quality Assurance Efforts
In the context of growing competition and threats to private HEIS, UC has pursued quality assurance and accreditations to distinguish itself and ensure quality education.

Joshi Zarah (n.d.) observes limited success in the Philippines private sector commenting "private, non-sectarian institutions show the poorest results in the professional board examinations." UC challenges this by recording satisfactory performances in most of its professional board examinations. This has been achieved by subjecting its academic offerings to stringent quality assurance accreditations from various accrediting institutions.

It should be noted that the quality of education between private and public universities cannot be easily compared as certain SUC/LUCs fulfill a specific mandate that is reflected in its program offerings and services. However, private universities are applying to various quality assurance programs to demonstrate that they are delivering quality education and providing adequate and appropriate student services.

Specifically, UC is subjecting its academic programs to quality assurance assessments and accreditations from private accrediting bodies. It should be noted that 60 percent of UC's programs have received Levels I to III accredited and re-accredited status from two separate accrediting institutions.

In 2019, UC was given its ISO 9001:2015 certification from TUV Rheinland after a stringent review of its operations, processes, and client satisfaction. UC was found to be compliant with international standards in relation to its delivery of academic and student support services.

In the same year, UC subjected itself to the Commission's Institutional Sustainability Assessment (ISA) which assesses an HEI's institutional sustainability in five key result areas namely governance and management; quality of teaching and learning; quality of professional exposure and research; creative work and innovation; support for students; and relations with the community. The ISA measures an HEI's ability to translate its vision, mission, and goals into programs that effectively deliver expected outcomes.

Aside from its QA efforts, the offering of new programs also reinforces UC's stance. In 2018–2019, UC has offered four new bachelor's degree programs—behavioral science, forensic science, data analytics, and a business administration major in digital marketing. These new programs are aligned with the demands of the international workplace, especially in the entry to "Industry 4.0." This era requires a totally different skill set from workers and a different approach on the delivery of education and the programs offered. This has led academic managers to coin the phrase, "Education 4.0."

UC's data analytics program, a specialization under the broader data science field, is among emerging professions in information technology. The employment-oriented website, LinkedIn, in its 2017 emerging jobs report, indicated a 650 percent increase in opportunities in data science. The United States alone needs more than 200,000 data scientists by 2018, according to a report by Burning Glass Technologies. This is one of UC's first steps towards updating its offerings to fit the current industry trends.

Further, UC continues to update and revise its curricula alongside its industry advisory board, a group composed of industry representatives, to review proposed curricula. This ensures that the skills and knowledge expected from UC graduates are in sync with what is expected and required in practice.

It is notable that UC did not lay off faculty during the K to 12 transition period. This is a credit to UC's faculty development program where faculty members are required to pursue graduate programs aligned with their respective disciplines through the Commission's scholarship program.

5   Conclusion

For the 73 years since Atty. Benjamin Romero Salvosa founded Baguio Colleges, UC continues to be managed by the founders' family to ensure the preservation of the original philosophy and core values. UC is a testament of an organization that has evolved and developed while remaining true to the enduring legacy of its founder—to be a higher education institution that recognizes education as a birthright and a citadel for learning for those who seek it.

As a FOMHEI in the Philippines, UC relies greatly on tuition fees to sustain its operations, yet it continues to provide quality and affordable education to thousands of students. As a FOMHEI, UC is able to implement policies that will benefit the students and the institution. As such, UC continues to improve its educational facilities and record satisfactory performances in various state licensure examinations amidst all the changes on the educational landscape. It is vital for UC's survival to undertake quality assurance efforts to ensure relevant and responsive education to Filipino youth. Following the implementation of a national scholarship program, UC recalibrated its academic offerings to keep up with the growing competition amongst public and private higher education institutions.

Moving forward, UC is planning on undergoing ASEAN University Network Quality Assurance to harmonize its educational offerings with universities in Southeast Asia and bolster UC's research culture and teaching practices.

References

Belaro Jr., S. (2017, August 9). *Disadvantages of free college education law.* Sun Star Davao. Retrieved from https://www.pressreader.com/philippines/sunstar-davao/20170809/281741269514801

Commission on Higher Education. (2012). *Policy-standard to enhance Quality Assurance (QA) in Philippine higher education through an outcomes-based and typology-based QA* (Commission Memorandum Order No. 46, s. 2012). Retrieved from https://ched.gov.ph/wp-content/uploads/2017/10/CMO-No.46-s2012.pdf

Commission on Higher Education. (2018). *Higher education enrollment by discipline group: AY 2007-08 to AY 2017–2018.* Retrieved from https://ched.gov.ph/higher-education-enrollment-by-region-and-institution-type-ay-2017-18/

Commission on Higher Education. (2018) *Higher education enrollment by region and institution type: AY 2017–2018.* Retrieved from https://ched.gov.ph/higher-education-enrollment-by-region-and-institution-type-ay-2017-18/

De Vera III, P. (2018). *Expanding access to tertiary quality education* [PowerPoint slides]. Retrieved from https://www.slideshare.net/christiantabilin2/slides-forcommdeverafinal

De Vera III., P. (2018). *Tertiary education subsidy in full swing.* Retrieved from https://ched.gov.ph/blog/2018/09/18/tertiary-education-subsidy-in-full-swing/

Hernando-Malipot, M. (2018, August 20). Free higher education 'killing' private schools slowly – CEAP. *Manila Bulletin.* Retrieved from https://news.mb.com.ph/2018/08/20/free-higher-education-killing-private-schools-slowly-ceap/

Philippine Statistics Authority. (2018). *Filipino families are most deprived in education* [Press release]. Retrieved from https://psa.gov.ph/sites/default/files/attachments/ird/pressrelease/mpi percent20press percent20release.pdf

Yee, K. (2017). *Re-imagining Philippine Higher Education* [PowerPoint slides]. Retrieved from https://pdfhost.io/v/q7mRnQsCX_05_Mr_Karol_Mark_R_Yee_Re_Imagining_Philippine_Higher_Educationpdf.pdf

Zarah, L. (n.d.). *Work conditions and management issues in a family-owned college in the Philippines.* Retrieved from https://researchedworks.com/work-management-family-college-philippines

CHAPTER 15

The Philippines, Part 2: Holy Angel University—A Catholic Family University

Alma Santiago-Espartinez and Leopoldo N. Valdes

Holy Angel University (HAU) is a non-profit Catholic Higher Education institution in Central Luzon committed to providing access to high quality education from primary school to graduate study. HAU has a seven-hectare campus located in Angeles City and a 10-hectare property in Ayala Alviera in Porac, Pampanga in anticipation of growing enrollment in the coming years.

Holy Angel University is part of a narrative of the Nepomuceno family and their family enterprises that dates back to 1933. The Nepomuceno descendants continue to run several for-profit businesses in Angeles City and institutions that offer quality education in Angeles City with the notable successes and setbacks normally associated with family-run firms. Having begun on a one-hectare lot, Holy Angel University's idyllic campus now sits on a prime property in the heart of Angeles City. Its story is one of a family-owned operation emerging from a painful past to a promising present and a hopeful future; from a struggling unknown to an internationally recognized institution. After close to a century, the Nepomucenos still manage the business, cognizant of the challenges of a changing and more competitive world.

1 History

In 1933, Juan D. Nepomuceno started Holy Angel Academy (HAA) as a family-owned enterprise with the purpose of establishing an affordable quality Catholic coeducational high school in the Philippines founded by the laity. Juan D. Nepomuceno established the school with the help of Fr. Pedro Santos, regarded as the school's co-founder (Mendoza, 2004). One of the motivations was that his eldest son wanted to attend high school in their hometown.

After engaging Ricardo Flores as the principal, Fr. Santos and Nepomuceno spent a frantic summer and several thousand pesos of Nepomuceno family money to start the school. They were passionate about providing affordable and quality Catholic education; the origins of this venture have been chronicled in Ricardo Flores's memoirs (1992). Its growth over the years from high

© KONINKLIJKE BRILL NV, LEIDEN, 2020 | DOI: 10.1163/9789004423435_015

school to college and later to university in 1970 was marked by obstacles and challenges. Today, Holy Angel University (HAU) has become an indispensable contributor to the quality of life and prosperity in Angeles City.

2   From Academy to University

Holy Angel Academy (HAA) began as a four-year high school in an empty parish residence in June 1933 with a total enrollment of 78 students. During the following two years, enrollment rose to 89 and then to 150.

Hours after the attack on Pearl Harbor on December 8, 1941, Japanese forces invaded the Philippines. HAA along with all schools in the Philippines ceased operations. At the end of WW II, the founders regrouped and HAA reopened. The challenges to restore normalcy included reacquiring the main building from the American military forces, finding, and re-hiring teachers and managing a large intake of students who had not attended school for several years.

Until 1945, all administrators had been male and all instructors, female. With the hiring of male instructors, the problem of gender-pay equity emerged. At the same time, movements towards unionization and leftist politics were growing with consequences for HAA.

In 1947, HAA acquired a license from the Bureau of Private Schools to start a two-year junior normal college and offer a non-degree elementary teacher's certificate in response to an increasing demand for qualified teachers following the war. At the same time, HAA started an evening high school to serve the workers of the nearby Clark airforce base.

In 1948, HAA opened the College of Commerce, the first college established at HAA. Javier Nepomuceno was named the first dean of the College of Commerce and launched a three-year bachelor's of science in commerce diploma patterned after the Dela Salle College curriculum. With their first graduates in 1951, Holy Angel Academy became Holy Angel College (HAC) with Juan Nepomuceno as its first president. Due to its growing population and increasing curricular offerings, the Colleges of Arts and Sciences and College of Education were established. In the 1960s, other colleges were opened offering secretarial education and engineering. The graduate school opened in 1966 with a master's of the arts in education.

On December 4, 1981, Holy Angel College became Holy Angel University (HAU) with Mamerto Nepomuceno, a younger sibling of Javier, as the first university president.

HAU started out on one hectare surrounded by sugar cane fields owned by Juan Nepomuceno. HAU expanded into a prime seven-hectare property that the Nepomuceno family continues to lease to HAU for lower than market rates as part of the legacy of Juan D. Nepomuceno.

3   Challenges Faced by the HAU Founders and Leaders

The efforts that have been made by the founders to address serious challenges at different stages of development, supported by Monsignor Pedro Santos who provided spiritual guidance, have largely made the university what it is today. Juan D. Nepomuceno with his wife Nena Gomez Nepomuceno provided direction and resources. Ricardo Flores worked tirelessly to implement what needed be done to operate the school. Its changing leadership would lead to diverse opinions about its sustainability.

The initial challenges of starting and sustaining a quality provincial high school, restoring services after World War II, and dealing with leftist elements earned these founders the town's respect and admiration. Until HAU became a college in 1951, the founders assumed leadership of the school. Juan D. Nepomuceno was then installed as its first president until his passing in 1973. His son, Geromin Nepomuceno, took over after having overseen the construction of new buildings resulting from the school's unprecedented growth in the 1960s.

The 1960s and early 70s were challenging times for Angeles City. A militant communist group, the New People's Army (NPA), threatened businesses and the school to extort funds. Some of its leaders were HAU graduates and they would influence growing unrest among teachers and students. Geromin had to respond to NPA threats, including threats to the security of his family. In 1972, Philippine President Ferdinand E. Marcos declared martial law that eased tensions in Angeles City throughout the Marcos dictatorship.

In 1975 Geromin passed away in his office from heart failure. In an effort to provide continuity, Ricardo Flores became the first non-family member to serve as president of HAU. He served a single five-year term. Another son of Juan Nepomuceno, Mamerto, became president in 1980.

When HAU became a university in 1981, HAU leadership returned to the Nepomuceno family. Despite its new status as a university, the board favored appointing family members over non-familiar academic leaders. It was during Mamerto Nepomuceno's presidency that student enrollment soared to 28,000, beyond the university's capacity. Access to quality education was no longer the driving force and average class size expanded to 65 students. Different leadership was badly needed for HAU to regain its lost stature.

In 1985, Sr. Josefina Nepomuceno, the youngest daughter of Juan Nepomuceno, assumed the presidency and initiated much needed reform towards

academic excellence with a strong Catholic orientation. She had strong credentials for institutional leadership having served as president of St. Scholastica's
College in Manila for ten years.

During the term of "Sister Jonep," as she was called, she weathered two major
challenges. Nearby Mount Pinatubo erupted in 1991, destroying some infrastructure. Later, a student boycott disrupted classes for several weeks. In both
situations, Sister Jonep successfully engaged teachers and staff to return HAU
to normal operations quickly. She pushed for the accreditation of programs
and the expansion of programs at all levels. She was the last Nepomuceno
descendent to lead the university, but when she left in 1995, her legacy was the
university's first accreditations from the Philippine Accrediting Association of
Schools, Colleges, and Universities (PAASCU).

In 1995, Bernadette "Bernie" Nepomuceno, daughter-in-law of Mamerto, was
installed as president. She continued to balance accreditation, maintenance,
and campus expansion. She empowered staff and instituted many educational
reforms.

Arlyn Sycangco-Villanueva, the second non-Nepomuceno family member to
lead, took over in 2006 and developed "a more professional and business-like
university" (Tantingco, 2009). However, Villanueva was a maverick who grew
tired of changing accreditation standards. She wanted to prove that HAU's priorities lay not in its compliance with accrediting bodies but in its reputation
with its community. She oversaw the largest renovation of the HAU campus
to make it into one of the most beautiful campuses in the Philippines. These
actions led to undesired long-term consequences as PAASCU downgraded
HAU's accreditation, undermining its position in comparison to major universities in Metro Manila. Additionally, capital expenditures without significant
improvements to compensation led to yet another union strike in 2012.

4   Swings between Accessibility and Quality

One of the founding values of HAU is to provide access to quality education.
HAU has struggled to find a balance between accessibility and quality. HAU's
past leadership emphasized one or the other, with some trying to achieve
both. These shifting priorities have resulted in both positive and negative
outcomes.

Overcrowded classrooms resulted from the need to finance capital expenditures. Enrollment hit a peak of 27,000 students in 1983. As a low-cost university
with overcrowded classrooms many compromises were made that led to faculty burnout, lower student engagement, union strikes, and infighting within
the administration.

After recovering from the Mount Pinatubo eruption and growing student unrest, Sister Jonep had pushed staff and faculty by embarking on PAASCU accreditation, a process of several years. To have a competitive edge, higher educational institutions (HEIS) apply for accreditation as an indicator of continuing improvement of quality. Unaccustomed to the effort required for accreditation, HAU staff and faculty were tested and this led to widespread pushback.

Arlyn Villanueva set out to create an environment within the university that heightened the student's intellectual experience and pride in the institution by creating a campus seen as a desirable destination. She focused on the improvement of facilities and construction of new buildings more than decreasing class size and improving student-to-faculty ratios. The Villanueva presidency also saw the downgrading of PAASCU accreditation from Level 3 to Level 2, two years before the end of her term although HAU managed to maintain its autonomous status from the Commission on Higher Education (CHED).

5   A New Vision for Leadership and Governance

The perception that the professional leadership was not in line with the tradition of HAU was augmented by a 2014 independent survey of the state of the university. The survey results indicated a desire to return the presidency to a descendant of Juan D. Nepomuceno. Indeed, during the transition following Villanueva's term, Geromin T. Nepomuceno, Jr., the eldest son of president Geromin Nepomuceno, acted as officer-in-charge of HAU. In an effort to ease labor tensions that had led to a 53-day strike, Geromin T. Nepomuceno appealed to staff to work together by calling everyone a "member of the family." This message from a grandson of the founder was well-received.

In 2015, after an exhaustive search, HAU hired Luis Maria R. Calingo, the first professional with prior experience as a university president and international exposure. This was a promising decision towards professionalizing the stewardship of Juan Nepomuceno's educational legacy.

5.1   *Reclaiming Quality*
Luis Maria Calingo introduced comprehensive internationalization to Holy Angel University. At the time it was difficult to predict the changes that Calingo would usher in or whether power would ultimately remain with the Nepomuceno family. While the university was still under the full control of the Nepomuceno family, the institution had already begun to move towards professional, rather than family, practices.

Calingo was given a free hand to lead the university to higher levels of excellence. He was a career academician and higher education leader from the United States, a staunch Catholic with family roots in the Pampanga region of the Philippines. He was perceived as a highly qualified leader who shared the values and vision of the founders. His reputation as a quality assurance guru in the Philippines and in the ASEAN region attracted attention from CHED and other leading institutions.

Calingo's challenge was to transform the university from its insulated state in 2015 into a higher education institution worthy of national and international recognition. Moreover, in the new millennium HAU was a far more complex organization than the Holy Angel of its founders. There would be many issues to tackle simultaneously and priorities to balance while staying true to original founding values.

Starting with a downgraded PAASCU rating meant that the accreditation journey would take several years. With the mantra "We're all about students," Calingo sought to change the tendency of measuring schools based on the board examination performance of their graduates and institutional compliance to the requirements of Philippine accreditors. This meant looking for other measures of institutional effectiveness, including those used in other countries.

Calingo believed that a university is not only about its buildings and grounds, but also about its product—graduates with highly-valued degrees—and its people—the students, the faculty, non-teaching staff, and administrators—who work together to transform students into persons of conscience, competence, and compassion.

By 2018 Calingo had achieved the following:
– Received the Philippine Quality Award in 2016 based on Malcolm Baldrige Quality Award as a result of sound organizational processes and excellent results in student retention and learning, student and stakeholder satisfaction, and budgetary and financial performance;
– Recipient of the 2018 Global Performance Excellence Award from the Asia Pacific Quality Organization;
– Renewal of accreditation from the International Accreditation Commission for Business Education (IACBE);
– International accreditation from the Accreditation Commission for Programs of Hospitality Administration (ACPHA);
– Achieved improvement in *Chronicle of Higher Education's* "Great Colleges to Work For" survey from very good to excellent in 2016, to 86 percent in 2018 exceeding the 63 percent average for US Catholic university peers and 77 percent for the US Honor Roll;

- First in the nation to be designated "National School of Character" by the Character Education Partnership;
- Listed in the *Newman Guide to Choosing a Catholic College of the Cardinal Newman Society* as a role model of faithful Catholic education.

Further, strategic planning in 2015 and 2017 articulated the direction of the organization for the next decades. Part of the plan was a decade-long road map for the continuing recognition of HAU's programs and operations. During the first three years of his leadership, Calingo achieved additional accomplishments. He resolved the four-year impasse with the union by concluding a collective bargaining agreement on the first day of negotiation. He launched pioneering academic programs including the country's first professional master's degree program in cybersecurity with support from USAID; Southeast Asia's first MBA program in sustainable enterprise; the country's first "College First Year Experience" program based on the study of "Big History," an innovative program adapted from the US and Australia; and raised 104,000,000 Philippine pesos (US$5.7 million) in government grants for research and development.

Calingo's legacy, as demonstrated by the achievements of his presidency, has brought Juan Nepomuceno's vision to a higher level as a world-class Catholic university, making it more attractive to potential faculty, employers, and students and contributing to the reduction of rural-to-urban migration by helping develop the countryside.

5.2   *Governance*

HAU has a nine-member board of trustees. The trustees include at least five descendants of Juan D. Nepomuceno, one member of the Catholic clergy, and three independent trustees. A non-family member usually serves as chair of the board. The board of trustees (BOT) appoints the president. The president reports to the board and serves a term of three years that can be extended up to 10 years.

Three out of the five Nepomuceno members of the board of trustees are surviving children of Juan D. Nepomuceno; the other two are from the third generation. Although Juan D. Nepomuceno's third and fourth generation descendants are numerous, planning for membership on the board mirrors succession challenges among the Nepomuceno family enterprises—finding engagement, qualifications, and interest from the family pool.

University leadership is also a challenge. Calingo's term ends in 2020. Considering the decade long scope of the road map and the absence of an obvious successor among the descendants of Juan D. Nepomuceno, it makes sense that Calingo's term be extended. However, if Nepomuceno family involvement is viewed as critical to the reputation of the institution, the board of trustees must consider alternative leadership structures for a growing, internationally recognized university as well as prepare a new generation of board members. One possibility considered is that the president would continue to operate as the chief executive officer with a provost or chancellor who is a Nepomuceno descendant.

6   Past and Future Challenges

Two historical external events challenged HAU's development. The first was World War II, the Japanese occupation, and the use of the campus by the Japanese forces as a base and a place of execution. HAU did not operate from 1941–1945. With the resumption of classes many students had to enroll in the first year of high school leading to the largest graduating class in 1949. The second event was the eruption of Mount Pinatubo that suspended classes for almost two months in 1991 while power and classrooms were restored (Tantingco, 2009).

According to President Josefina Nepomuceno (2017), the greatest challenges were the student boycotts and teacher strikes in 2012–2014. She noted that while natural disasters brought out the best in people, the student or teacher-led disruptions brought out the worst.

There have been many challenges due to the shifting emphasis on quality versus affordability and presidents have emphasized one of these over the other in the past.

In a country where the density of private higher education institutions is relatively high, there is a perception that higher education is a profitable venture. At least one investment group has offered to take over HAU, but the offer was refused by the Nepomuceno family. After close to a century, the Nepomucenos still manage the institution.

Working with members of the third and fourth generation, the Nepomucenos have decided to form a family council to draft a constitution that will guide the governance of their family-owned enterprises, including non-profit foundations. It will also serve as a forum for family members to discuss issues such as engagement and succession.

Holy Angel University is working towards a vision of becoming a role model for rural development and one of the best-managed Catholic institutions in the Asia-Pacific region. HAU is expanding its high school facilities and building a 10-hectare campus in Porac, Pampanga. New and expanded academic offerings will accompany those changes.

7   Conclusion

What is unique about Holy Angel University as a family-run organization is that the shared values and vision of its administrators remain aligned with the vision of the founders. In recent years, Holy Angel University has transformed into an innovative higher education institution of significance.

During HAU's history, there has been a steady stream of pioneering efforts making it "a first" in many areas. To face the challenges of the future, HAU strives for excellence and explores innovations that reflect the founders' vision that all efforts are for the greater good of the city and the region.

HAU has had ten presidents with different leadership styles. Despite the difference in their initiatives and approaches, HAU's values and mission have remained the same—providing accessible quality Catholic education. The resolution of crises involved compassion, altruism, and transparency from HAU's leadership. To become a great university to work for, HAU leadership must continue to emphasize those values.

HAU will continue to encounter challenges. The institution is profoundly important to the Nepomucenos; it is in their best interest to lead with purpose to guarantee future success. The fourth generation must continue the legacy of attracting the most promising students and talent in coming years. How the campus operates, how it appears, how it runs, how it binds people and spaces, and how it presents itself to others will determine the extent to which HAU remains an institution of significance.

References

Flores, R. V. (1992). *A memoir of Holy Angel University.* Angeles City: Holy Angel University Alumni Association.

Mendoza, E. P. (2004). *A cofradia of two: Oral history on the family life and lay religiousity of Juan D. Nepomuceno and Teresa G. Nepomuceno of Angeles, Pampanga.* Angeles City: The Juan D. Nepomuceno Center for Kapampangan Studies.

Nepomuceno, J. G. (2017, June 2). Speech of PAX Awardee Sister Josefina Nepomuceno at Saint Scholastica's College.

Tantingco, R. P. (Ed.), (2009). *Destiny and destination: The extraordinary story and history of Holy Angel University 1933–2008.* Angeles City: The Juan D. Nepomuceno Center for Kapampangan Studies.

CHAPTER 16

United Arab Emirates: The Al Ghurair University Case

Chester D. Haskell

This chapter examines Al Ghurair University of Dubai and its broader context. Al Ghurair University is in some ways a prototypical family-owned or managed institution. However, its national environment, the United Arab Emirates, is uncommon as an extremely wealthy, dynamic and competitive federation with regional and global aspirations. This context is essential to appreciating Al Ghurair's history and future opportunities. Furthermore, Al Ghurair University's strategy for success within this environment may provide useful lessons for academic institutions with similar ambitions elsewhere.

1   Historical Background

The United Arab Emirates (UAE) is a young nation celebrating its 50th anniversary in 2021. A federation of seven separate emirates spreads along the Arabian Gulf. Prior to 1971, these entities operated independently under British protection while being left to manage their internal affairs independently.

The UAE has become a vibrant and successful nation state. Abu Dhabi and Dubai are the largest of the emirates. Abu Dhabi is by far the wealthiest of the emirates as it has the vast bulk of the federation's estimated oil and gas reserves, 94 percent and 90 percent respectively (Gonzalez, 2008). The ruler of Abu Dhabi heads the nation and the ruler of Dubai is the vice president and prime minister. While Abu Dhabi is the seat of national authority, each of the autonomous emirates is still governed by a ruling family, thus allowing for diverse policies, norms, and attitudes within the broader context.

1.1   *Dubai within the UAE*

Autonomy has allowed the second largest emirate, Dubai, to evolve differently from its neighbors. While this chapter will discuss the larger UAE context, it will concentrate on Dubai, the location of the family-owned institution studied in this chapter.

The ruling families of the various emirates were never absolute in their power (Al Sayegh, 1998). This was especially true in Dubai where powerful tribal and merchant families shared governance. Lacking fossil fuel resources, Dubai built on its lengthy history of trade by members of its merchant class. Dubai today is an outward-looking, free trading, entrepreneurial business and financial community that has become a global crossroads, an entrepot with aspirations to become the Singapore of the Middle East.

In many ways this vision has already been realized considering Dubai's success as a financial, commercial, and travel center. Its principal airline, Emirates, is the world's largest in terms of international passengers (International Air Transport Association, 2017). Its container port is the busiest between Rotterdam and Singapore (LaGuardia, 2018). A range of visitors and expatriates come to Dubai, not only from the region, but from around the globe. Dubai has become the sixth most popular tourist destination in the world after Paris (CNN Travel Dubai, 2018). Its relative openness, tolerance, and security have made it a destination for business, investment, and relaxation for the entire region. At the same time, Dubai is an integral part of the UAE working closely with its partner emirates to build the nation as a whole.

1.2 *Key Demographics*

Understanding the UAE as a whole requires appreciating its unusual demographics as these are important drivers of national policies. Similar to other wealthy Gulf states, the UAE population is skewed heavily towards expatriates. The total UAE population in 2018 was 9.54 million with 8.44 million (88.5 percent) expatriates. Nationals (referred to as Emiratis) make up only 11.48 percent of the total. This situation is even more pronounced in Dubai where the Emirati population is only 245,000, 8.4 percent of the total 2.9 million (Dubai Statistics Center, 2018).

This demographic reality has important implications. Contrary to the experience of other nations with large expatriate communities, expatriates in the UAE are not just low-level manual laborers, construction workers, chambermaids, or taxi drivers, they also fill a wide range of professional, management, and executive positions. The UAE economy is fully dependent on expatriate labor and expertise in almost all sectors including higher education.

At the same time, expatriates are constrained in various ways. Legal residence for most workers is dependent on the issuance and renewal of work permits that can be revoked at any time, a factor that creates an uncertain future for many residents (Gulf News, 2018).

Gonzalez (2008) offers a detailed discussion of the human capital and labor market challenges facing the UAE. The fact is that the Emirati population is too small and growing too slowly to meet the labor market demands of a successful economy. At the same time, the UAE government has embarked on a policy of "Emiratization" creating preferences and incentives for Emiratis to replace expatriates in governmental and private settings. One outcome of this situation has been to emphasize education for both Emiratis and non-citizens.

The role of women is another central challenge for human capital and labor markets in the UAE. Unlike more conservative Arab states, the UAE and Dubai have acknowledged the importance of the participation of women in the labor market. Indeed, it is recognized that Emiratization cannot succeed without significant numbers of Emirati women entering the workforce. Emirati and expatriate women play important and growing roles in the public and private sectors. Forty-two percent of Emirati and expatriate women work but make up only 11.56 percent of the total workforce because the expatriate population is heavily male (Butteroff et al., 2018). Emirati women have ample opportunities, not only in the private and service sectors, but also in government including sensitive areas restricted to Emiratis such as the military and security services, even serving in combat positions such as fighter pilots.

2   Higher Education in the United Arab Emirates

The combination of a small Emirati population and the demands of both public and private sectors for educated workers drives many of the higher education policies at the national and emirate levels. There are strong incentives for women as well as men to participate in higher education and the UAE government has invested heavily in providing appropriate educational opportunities.

This investment has taken two forms. First, the national government has created educational institutions to serve Emiratis. Since 1976, three public, government-funded universities have been established—United Arab Emirates University (UAEU), Zayed University, and the Higher Colleges of Technology (HCT). There are limited opportunities for non-citizens at these public institutions. Until 2009, Zayed was open only to Emirati women. Tuition and other costs of attendance are free at all three institutions. Perhaps the most striking aspect of the public institutions is the participation of young women—82 percent of the students at UAEU are female despite it being a coeducational institution (Pennington, 2017).

However, these public institutions were never expected to fully meet the demand for higher education. Thus, the establishment of private institutions (for-profit, non-profit, and international) has been allowed and encouraged from the early days of the nation. These private institutions serve expatriates, Emiratis, and international students.

The Ministry of Education and Higher Education Affairs is the government body responsible for promoting and regulating higher education. Public institutions are directly under ministry oversight. Private institutions—local and international branch campuses—operate within carefully designed regulatory structures. The Commission on Academic Accreditation (CAA), a unit of the Ministry, is responsible for licensing most of the non-government operated institutions and for assuring minimum quality standards through the accreditation of individual programs. The CAA does not award institutional accreditation; quality assurance is managed mostly at the program level.

The mission statement of the CAA expresses the general view of the value of higher education and orientation to program evaluation.

> The colleges and universities of the United Arab Emirates, government-supported and private alike, play an essential role as we here in the UAE seek to realize the tremendous potential of a knowledge-based future. It is therefore of the utmost importance that institutions in the UAE. offer the highest quality academic programs, programs that are recognized both within the country and internationally for their excellence. (Commission on Academic Accreditation, 2018)

Despite policy and structure at the national level, considerable leeway exists for individual emirates in the promotion and oversight of higher education. Dubai is the leader in this respect, having established free zones for international universities under the auspices of its Knowledge and Human Development Agency (KHDA). The largest of these zones, known as Academic City, is located in the south of the emirate. Within the zones, KHDA oversees the licensing and quality assurance of branch campuses of international academic institutions as well as several local private universities. Institutions in the free zone can be 100 percent foreign-owned, are tax exempt, can repatriate 100 percent of profits, and are exempt from licensing and accreditation by the CAA (Knowledge and Human Development Agency, 2018). KHDA operates a parallel regulatory and quality assurance regime within the free zones on behalf of the government of Dubai and in collaboration with the national government. Together, the CAA and KHDA license and oversee more than 120 institutions across the UAE, a large number for such a small nation.

In addition to the public institutions and local private institutions, the UAE is host to a third model that expands the higher education space—the international branch campus. A variety of institutions from outside the UAE have established operations in the country. Some initiatives were highly publicized such as those established by New York University, Paris Sorbonne, and the Ecole Polytechnic Federal de Lausanne. Other less well-known institutions including the Universities of Birmingham, Middlesex, and Heriot-Watt (UK); Rochester Institute of Technology (US); Wollongong University (Australia); Birla and Amity Universities (India); and Azad University (Iran) have also established branches.

NYU Abu Dhabi is licensed by the CAA but is accredited in New York. Others, especially those in the academic free zones of Dubai under the auspices of KHDA, range from tiny rental ventures to major investments, all regulated by their home campus while also meeting KHDA standards. In 2018 there were 36 international branch campuses within the UAE with the majority in Dubai.

The combination of strong government support and encouragement for higher education has been wildly successful. Not only are there multiple educational opportunities for Emirati students, but also for the larger expatriate community. In keeping with its entrepot vision, Dubai has attracted students from nations and communities across the region and beyond. A supportive governmental regime, an encouraging academic climate, pressures from labor markets, and growing student demand have led to an increasingly diverse and competitive higher education environment throughout the UAE.

2.1   *Higher Education Competition in the UAE*
Since every UAE institution has to be licensed in line with standards set by the CAA or KHDA, certain basic threshold standards have been met by all. Therefore, since the early 2000s, several public and private institutions have sought ways to distinguish themselves in different ways. One way of doing this is through rankings. As is the case globally, in the UAE tremendous attention is paid to the various commercial rankings despite the broad skepticism and criticism of their value within the academic world (Hazelkorn, 2015). Rankings are influential in the UAE even though local institutions rarely appear in them. Additionally, Noori and Anderson cite Lindblad and Lindblad's 2009 research that shows the undue influence of ranking algorithms on the strategic management decisions of many academic institutions (Noori & Anderson, 2013). Many UAE institutions see recognition through rankings as a primary objective and tout these successes on institutional websites when they occur.

International accreditation has provided another visible path to differentiation. Al Ghurair University, like many UAE institutions, has sought to have their best academic programs recognized by international accreditors such as the Accreditation Board for Engineering and Technology (ABET) or the Association to Advance Collegiate Schools of Business (AACSB). International program accreditation is quite common today among UAE universities in addition to the program accreditation required by CAA and KHDA.

Some of the stronger institutions see international accreditation as a way to demonstrate their quality. The American University of Sharjah (AUS) was established in 1997 by Dr. Sultan bin Muhammad Al Qasimi, the ruler of Sharjah and a distinguished academic. As a private, non-profit entity, AUS was the first UAE institution to obtain institutional accreditation from the Middle States Commission on Higher Education in the US in 2004. AU Sharjah also has the distinction of having one of the most international student bodies in the world with 84 percent of the students coming from outside the UAE (Kamal & Trines, 2018). Other institutions have followed with institutional accreditation of the American University of Dubai and American University of Ras Al Khaimah by the Southern Association of Colleges and Schools (SACSCOC) and to Abu Dhabi University by WASC Senior College and University Commission, both in the US. Amity University of India operates a branch campus in Dubai in an impressive facility within the KHDA area and has also been accredited by WASC Senior College and University Commission.

The public institutions have also pursued international quality recognition. Zayed University was the first public institution to seek American institutional accreditation, succeeding with the Middle States Commission on Higher Education in 2008. UAEU expanded its programs and achieved programmatic accreditation from ABET and AACSB and institutional accreditation from the WASC Senior Colleges and University Commission in 2016. HCT also moved aggressively to develop programs more directly related to employer demand, influenced by the community college and vocational education models in Canada and elsewhere.

The quest for international accreditation among local institutions reflected the desire to promote academic quality and to be recognized for achieving international standards in a crowded marketplace. While international accreditation protocol is not well understood by the general student population or their parents, US institutional accreditation has been presented by the institutions to reflect a global seal of approval and acknowledgement of their superior academic quality. These achievements have fueled the increasingly competitive higher education environment to the detriment of smaller, less well-resourced institutions such as Al Ghurair University.

However, the US system, like the CAA and KHDA, confirms only minimal thresholds of quality. This is the only way US institutional accreditors can accommodate the wide diversity of institutions seeking accreditation. Quality beyond the threshold varies among institutions. UAE-based institutions accredited in the US make much of the fact that they have the same type of accreditation as Stanford or Princeton. While this is technically true, institutional propaganda implies that this has significant implications for comparable quality.

International accreditation presents the risk of isomorphism as described by DiMaggio and Powell (1991). Examples of the tendencies they identify include coercive isomorphism, mimetic processes, and normative pressures. This raises the question of whether it is desirable for all academic institutions to hold similar values and norms and whether the broader objectives of higher education are furthered by homogeneity.

Wilkins and Huisman (2012) also explore this question in their examination of international branch campuses. These institutions may be seen as providing access to somewhat different models of higher education, although others question their influence towards greater isomorphic tendencies. Altbach (2010) criticizes the trend towards international branch campuses questioning the motives of the institutions involved. Altbach also argues that "foreign institutions do not enter an overseas market to provide a guide to best practices or to stimulate reform. Rather, they come for pecuniary purposes or to promote international student mobility" (p. 13).

Noori and Anderson go further, looking at the proliferation of American-style institutions as an "unexamined dimension of both globalization and America's influence in the region" (2013, pp. 160–161). They cite Mazawi who argues that current research efforts "have neglected the social, cultural, and geopolitical forces that shape the modes of [institutional] governance prevalent in developing countries." One of their points is that US accreditation agencies, lacking the experience and background in the UAE, may reach determinations that are actually detrimental. Another concern is that accreditation agencies working in places like the UAE provide less emphasis on values and practices critical to the success of US institutions such as academic freedom, shared governance, and community engagement (pp. 159–172). Indeed, experience shows that American accreditors are somewhat uncritical in the application of US standards to the UAE context.

3 Family-Owned or Managed Higher Education Institutions (FOMHEIS)

In addition to Al Ghurair University, there are at least two other FOMHEIS in the UAE—the College of Islamic and Arabic Studies, founded by Jumal Al Majid, and the Gulf Medical University, founded by Thumbay Mohideen. Gulf Medical University is located in Ajman, one of the smallest UAE emirates. It is not clear to what degree the founders, both prominent businessmen, maintain control over the institution. Both institutions have governing boards with a majority of non-family members. Instead, the boards are composed of important representatives from the government and private sector. Nevertheless, in

UAE culture, influence and control can be informal and managed through networks. The fact that both institutions are highly specialized speaks to the vision of the founders. Gulf Medical University has developed into a leading local medical institution.

There are other types of private institutions established by a philanthropic founder like the American University of Sharjah (AUS), but that now operate under a diverse and representative board of trustees. There are institutions founded by groups like the Chamber of Commerce or a network of private investors. Some institutions are explicitly for-profit while others are non-profit. Indeed, the most obvious FOMHEI, other than Al Ghurair, may be Amity University Dubai, an international branch campus.

While it is clear that powerful, wealthy, and politically connected individuals have played central roles in developing many UAE institutions, these actions have taken place through networks that are not necessarily based on family relationships. This is not to say that family connections are irrelevant. Emirati family connections are extremely important in almost every context but seem to be less significant in higher education.

4   The Case of Al Ghurair University

One of the most important merchant families in Dubai is the Al Ghurair family. Their involvement in education includes the establishment of Al Ghurair University, an example of a small family-owned institution striving for success in the competitive UAE environment. Abdulla bin Ahmad Al Ghurair, the family patriarch, is a self-made billionaire businessman. Together with his brother Saif and other family members, he built a diversified business empire from a holding company established in 1960. Over the years, they established the Mashreqbank bank, now the largest in the UAE, as well as companies in varied industries such as cement, milling, water, food imports, and construction. They also made a large number of real estate investments in Dubai. These various business investments benefited greatly from the UAE oil boom that began in 1969. One was the Al Ghurair Centre, the first major shopping mall in Dubai. The Al Ghurair construction group was central to major projects such as the Dubai Metro and the Burj Khalifa (Wendel, 2018). The brothers decided to divide the holdings in the early 1990s with Abdulla retaining the construction and food businesses along with a major share of the bank and real estate company.

Today, Al Ghurair Investments (AGI) is a family conglomerate. Abdulla's son, Abdul Aziz, is the chief executive officer (CEO) of the bank and has played an important political role in the UAE. His brothers run the other principal components of AGI, while a non-family member is the CEO of the conglomerate. Abdulla bin Ahmad Al Ghurair is today the wealthiest individual in the UAE and the family is considered the wealthiest family with a net worth estimated at US$4.6 billion (Billionaires, 2019).

Education has always been an interest of Al Ghurair family, beginning with an elementary school that they established in the 1960s. Al Ghurair has said, "To me, education is the true enabler of Arab youth and the backbone of their social and economic development" (Wendel, 2018). He sent his three oldest sons to the United States for undergraduate degrees at California Polytechnic San Luis Obispo, University of San Diego, and Boston University. In 2015, he pledged a major portion of his assets (US$1.1 billion over ten years) to fund the Abdulla Al Ghurair Foundation for Education. The purpose of the foundation is to provide scholarships and education programs for students from the UAE and other Arab nations, including those in conflict zones, to study outside the Middle East, principally in the United States, Canada, and Western Europe.

In 1999, prior to the establishment of the foundation, the Al Ghurair family founded Al Ghurair University, a private higher education institution owned and controlled by the family. Established in Dubai on land owned by the AGI group and with family funds, the university's objective was to provide educational opportunities for diverse students so as to prepare them to participate in the local community and the larger world. A modern academic and administrative building was constructed on the site. An expatriate was hired as president along with a largely expatriate faculty. The language of instruction was set as English with the exception of Arabic in the law program. The university was licensed by the CAA in 2001.

The University's initial programs were in electrical engineering, computer science, and business administration and were accredited by the CAA at the undergraduate level. Interior design, law, education, public relations, architecture, and mechanical engineering were added between 2004 and 2016. Master's programs in engineering management with public and private law were initiated in 2011 and are under CAA review. In addition, a master's program in business administration was accredited by CAA in 2016. Particular emphasis was placed on engineering and the bachelor's of science (BS) degree in electrical and electronics engineering was accredited internationally by ABET in 2014.

According to Al Ghurair University data, undergraduate enrollments grew steadily reaching a high of 1,370 in 2010 but declined to 1,100 by 2017. There were several reasons for this decline, the most important being increased competition from other institutions. Master's programs enrolled only 107 students by 2017. Approximately 57 percent of undergraduate students were men in 2017, an enrollment pattern that continues in the graduate programs. Women outnumber men in several programs, including business administration, computer science, engineering, interior design, architecture, and education. Approximately 28 percent of all students are Emirati, while two-thirds are expatriate with the remaining 5 percent coming mainly from the Middle East region.

In 2018 the university operated on an annual budget of approximately 41 million AED (US$11.1 million) with most of the revenue coming from tuition. The university owns a modern 275,000 square foot academic and administrative building on a large property adjacent to the Academic City Free Zone of KHDA.

In 2018, the university had 42 full-time faculty members, all with terminal degrees in their fields and with considerable academic experience elsewhere. As is the case in most UAE institutions, 98 percent of all UAE faculty members are expatriates, another consequence of the small Emirati population (Kamal & Trines, 2018). Almost 40 percent of Al Ghurair faculty come from the Middle East or North Africa region, a third from South Asia, and the remainder from Western Europe and North America (Office of the President, private communication, July 2018).

The university has struggled to maintain and grow enrollment since 2010 because of the intense competition among institutions. Basic questions have been raised about its strategic plan and implementation. As is the case with most institutions dependent on tuition, the budget is closely tied to enrollments and tuition revenues. Unlike some other local institutions, Al Ghurair receives no direct support from its owners, although the AGI has provided bridge financing and other forms of indirect assistance, treating the university as an affiliated enterprise.

The initial university governing board was composed of five members, including three members of the Al Ghurair family, a business partner involved with the Al Ghurair construction group, and the board-appointed president of the university. In this way, the owners put the institution into the hands of a professional administrator. This governance structure is common to family-owned institutions in other settings and allocates considerable authority to the president and CEO for advice and expertise on matters of higher education policy and practice (Altbach, 2005). This binds institutional success in large part to the skill and competence of a single person.

4.1   *Crisis and Change*

In 2013, representatives of the Al Ghurair family decided to examine ways to strengthen the university. There were conversations with knowledgeable higher education leaders in the UAE and elsewhere, some of which led to the engagement of consultants. The clear intention was to align the university with international standards in order to improve quality and increase enrollments. Indeed, Abdul Aziz Al Ghurair, the AGI chairman, noted that he and his brothers had been educated in the US and that they wanted Al Ghurair University to be successful and eventually to become a "new Harvard" (private interview, 2015).

The university had several academic advantages at that time. As noted earlier, the undergraduate electrical engineering program was accredited by ABET, the leading international accreditor in engineering and technology and the business program had begun taking steps to gain AACSB accreditation. The interior design program was also positioned to pursue accreditation in that field. All programs had successfully been accredited and reaccredited by the CAA. While most of the faculty members were expatriates, they were well-qualified and generally well-regarded.

However, the institution also faced several important challenges. First, it operated in a competitive environment but without the advantages of the high visibility, recognition, reputation, or the external accreditation of some of its competitors. Indeed, its reputation was viewed as eroding because of efforts to maintain enrollments at the expense of selectivity and quality. Second, it did not have a history of best practice in internal academic administration, enrollment management, student services, financial aid, budget management, or marketing. Its organizational structure was centralized in the office of the president and it lacked experienced professionals in several key positions. The net result was that the university was losing money because of falling enrollment.

From the beginning, the Al Ghurair family expected that the university would eventually be fully self-supporting. In the early years, healthy enrollments masked potential problems. As the higher education environment became more crowded and more competitive, AGU did not make the investments and adjustments necessary to stem enrollment declines, nor did it have adequate surplus resources to do so. It also lacked the required professional expertise and leadership needed. It sought to maintain enrollments by discounting tuition, focusing like many small institutions on headcount instead of net tuition revenue. Yet the relationship to the Al Ghurair family and AGI and assumptions about available resources hid cashflow limitations and other financial problems. It is likely that internal and external actors assumed that the Al Ghurair family was backing the institution, thus obscuring growing budgetary pressure. The institution found itself in a sort of stasis without a strategy to resolve its difficulties.

In the face of these problems, the university and the family might have simply sought a new president in the hope that different leadership would lead to improvement. Yet the family decided to take a more comprehensive look at the institution's governance and other practices. Instead of seeking to ensure continued direct family control as is common to FOMHEIs, they sought a different path, one they hoped would lead to the quality outcome to which they aspired.

This decision led to the establishment of a new governing board designed to be more in line with good practice in higher education elsewhere. New by-laws were drafted using models recommended by the US-based Association of Governing Boards (AGB). These stressed board independence with a majority of board members not connected to the Al Ghurair family or the institution. The board would assume clear fiduciary responsibilities, avoid real or perceived conflicts of interest, and incorporate other traits of a governance structure common among US private, non-profit institutions.

It was agreed that the new board would start small and gradually be augmented over time. The board is chaired by Ibrahim Al Ghurair, one of the brothers active in the oversight of the AGI. It also includes an experienced UAE academic and former senior administrator at UAEU, two international scholars with lengthy experience—one the former rector of a Spanish university who is deeply involved in Spanish and European accreditation affairs and an American academic administrator with more than 40 years of experience in several US universities—and the CEO of the AGI conglomerate. The plan is to make the changes and investments necessary for an institutional turnaround and longer-term success. Once this is fully underway, it is expected that the board will be expanded to engage representatives of the UAE business community and government, including women board members.

With this decision in place in 2016, a review was undertaken of the university's status and numerous recommendations were made for its improvement. During the following two and one-half years an enrollment management leader was appointed, administrative systems overhauled and reorganized, and a worldwide search was conducted for a new president with the assistance of an executive search firm. This search led to the appointment in 2017 of someone with a distinguished academic and teaching record in the US, who speaks Arabic and English fluently, and has a Syrian background. Under the new president's leadership, highly qualified deans have been hired for the engineering and business programs. In addition, an experienced enrollment management team has been recruited and installed. Financial aid policies have been reviewed and revised. Student support activities, large and small, have been instituted or upgraded.

The financial side of governance is perhaps the most interesting aspect of these changes. Like many private institutions in the UAE and elsewhere, AGU was established under a corporate legal model. In some cases, UAE-based institutions were explicitly set up as for-profit companies with profit as a prime objective. Two of the first UAE institutions to seek and gain international institutional accreditation (AUD and ADU) were structured this way. In this model the basic assumption seems to have been that in order to attract investment capital to start a university there had to be a return on investment. Some investments were made as loans to be repaid. In other cases, there was an expectation that portions of operating surpluses would be returned to investors. Indeed, in one case the bylaws of an UAE university stipulated that the chairman of the board received 10 percent of any institutional budget surplus.

Given a general lack of transparency, it is difficult to document the internal financial workings of many institutions. However, it is possible to observe how other private institutions in the UAE have addressed this question. The American University of Sharjah is a non-profit with its benefactor and founder explicitly rejecting financial returns. Al Ghurair University is a similar case. While the original bylaws were similar to other family-owned or established institutions, the principal motivation was always to promote education, not make money. In its renewed structure, the family has made this more explicit, promising that any surpluses will be reinvested into the university. In other words, Al Ghurair University is operating in line with the traditional financial model of an American non-profit institution.

The Al Ghurair family can and does support the university in other, less direct ways. For example, with the consent of the new board, the AGI professional staff has begun a review of the potential utilization of 55 acres of property owned by the university. AGI's real estate professionals are exploring the development of that property for ancillary educational use like housing for students, athletic facilities, or the establishment of a secondary school. AGI financial and human resources professionals have provided advice to university leaders. Plans are evolving to better link AGU with AGI units for internships or employment opportunities. However, it is important to note that AGI is not expected to make donations or offer other direct financial support. Rather, the plan is to connect the university with the AGI in ways that will be more important in the long-term.

The challenges facing Al Ghurair University are similar to those faced by many smaller, tuition-dependent institutions in the UAE and elsewhere. Similarly, the prescriptions for addressing these challenges are well-documented in higher education. Enrollments need to grow so that net tuition revenues rise. Expenses need to be controlled and available resources utilized effectively. Academic and program quality must improve so that graduates are successful. Marketing and recruiting operations need to be modern and cost-effective. Financial aid policies must be targeted for maximum leverage. Institutional reputation must improve and connections must be expanded.

4.2   *Good Governance*

The components needed to build enrollment are widely understood and include effective leadership, good faculty, high-value degree programs, competent administrative professionals, and a culture supportive of student success. Many institutions hope to use this model to create a virtuous cycle of growing enrollments and revenues. Effective institutional governance and leadership must be at the core of such strategies.

Bloom and Rosovsky (2011) argue that there are certain characteristics of the best research universities that are central to the quality of these institutions and that understanding these characteristics provides useful guidance for other types of academic institutions seeking to promote quality. They did not argue that most academic institutions should imitate the most prominent universities. Indeed, the capacity to do so is rare. But there are hundreds or thousands of other academic institutions that seek to improve their quality and reputation that might draw useful lessons from elite institutions.

Bloom and Rosovsky note that characteristics of the top universities relevant to other institutions seeking improvement in quality might include the following.

- Institutional autonomy and self-governance. Whether public or private, the best universities have a governance structure that is independent and under a governing board that can act as a bridge or buffer between the institution and external governments or societies.
- Organizational leadership appointed by a governing board. Appointing (and when necessary firing) appropriate, qualified leadership is essential to ensure accountability and appropriate strategic decisions. Institutions with traditions of elected leadership lack this key ingredient.

In addition, Bloom and Rosovsky noted the importance of commitment to academic freedom, shared governance between faculty and administration, meritocratic selection of faculty and students, a clear understanding of rights and responsibilities, financial stability, and a culture of quality.

In this sense, institutional governance is the key means to improving institutional performance in teaching, research, and service. The authors also call for governance that appropriately recognizes institutional and cultural heterogeneity. The principles are not absolutes, but they argue that it is difficult to pursue excellence in their absence. These are the basic building blocks of highly effective academic institutions.

Appropriate institutional governance, the interaction between an independent governing board with fiduciary responsibilities and strong institutional executive leadership may be the essential element in an institution that seeks quality for the benefit of its students and community. Al Ghurair University would seem to be in a position to model many of these characteristics to its longer-term benefit. Inadequate governance structures and processes can easily result in insufficient accountability or decisions that are not in the interests of students.

Governance is a central issue for every academic institution and no less so for family-owned universities. The reality is that higher education institutions operate in highly complex environments, the UAE being a good example. Effective institutions recognize the need for governing boards that are more than a rubber stamp for the chairman or institution's president. Operating in such a context demands more than the good judgement of a single individual. Rather, as William Bowen notes, a board provides a form of checks and balances, protecting the institution from "abuses of power, self-dealing, favoritism and just plain foolishness" (2011, p. 20). Bok agrees, observing that board members who seek to influence internal decisions or actions can "cause a lot of mischief" (2013, p. 46).

But these are dangers that may arise from a family-controlled board. Without proper independent governance, a family-controlled institution faces many potential risks, all of which may affect the quality and integrity of the institution and the programs it offers. Families or individual founders often create institutions in pursuit of an honorable vision of serving students and society. But founders or families may have different visions that may or may not be consistent with higher education values and practices. One example is the establishment of an institution for purposes of self-aggrandizement. Another might be to promote a specific worldview at odds with principles of scholarship, truth, and knowledge.

A properly structured and functioning governing board protects against these and many other risks. Such a board can provide the checks and balances Bowen suggests. It can offer perspective, expertise, and experience to complement the vision of the family. Ties to the broader external world can be richer and more diverse. The institution's responsibilities to society, particularly important if a non-profit is offered certain tax advantages, can be assured. An independent board, commonly required by some institutional accreditors, assures the institution of the diverse perspectives that lead to the best sort of planning and strategy. And, finally, the fiduciary duties of a board can be spread across multiple shoulders instead of resting only with the founder or the family.

One other consideration raised by Bloom and Rosovsky (2011) involves the importance of the meritocratic selection of faculty and students. When a board is dominated by family, it may be influenced by familial ties over other selection criteria. A board prone to meddling may seek to make some selection of deans or other administrators, faculty members, or even students dependent on family approval.

These are but some of the reasons Al Ghurair University offers a different model for a family-supported institution. By crafting a governance structure and composition that will gradually protect a truly independent board, the Al Ghurair family has recognized that providing excellence in education requires excellence in governance and leadership beyond what the family can provide. While the family will no doubt continue to be closely engaged with the university, their willingness to cede some control demonstrates their commitment to their vision. Other family institutions could learn from this.

5   Conclusion

Examination of the phenomena of family-owned or managed higher education institutions reveals various structural models and motivations. Success in the competitive higher education environments usually requires capacity, experience, and expertise that may be beyond the capabilities of the family owners. A common response in this case is to hire a skilled executive to lead the institution on behalf of the family. In this way, family control is assured. However, when such a strategy does not lead to the desired outcomes, the limitations of the family model may become evident.

Amity University of India appears to reflect an evolution similar to Al Ghurair University. With several internationally-accredited campuses, including the one in Dubai, Amity's history is instructive. Founded by a successful Indian businessman with a deep interest in education, Amity has evolved from governance largely controlled by the founder and his sons to a board structure of sufficient breadth and diversity to remain independent.

The realities of informal institutional control cannot be underestimated. Universities like Amity may have broadened their governing boards sufficiently to meet institutional accreditor standards for independent boards. However, as noted earlier, the way that these boards are constituted is not necessarily divorced from family influence. Some of this is due to deference, some to the fact that some board members are not truly independent. Instead, many boards are populated by individuals who may meet the accreditor's test of no direct financial or legal ties, but who are, in fact, friends, or associates of the family.

By taking a different path, the Al Ghurair family has implemented a plan that should ensure the university's independence from the family. One might argue that by taking this path, Al Ghurair University might become simply another "American-style" institution. However, this coincides with the Al Ghurair family's aspirations and its views of quality, in part influenced by their personal experiences in the US. Whatever the case, the university is set to evolve from a family-managed organization to one more in line with international standards of quality and effectiveness. It is doing so in an extremely competitive academic environment that exhibits demographic and social characteristics far different from any US-based institution. The governance model that has been chosen will be an essential element on a path to achieving success. Other family-owned institutions of higher education might do well to observe and learn from Al Ghurair University's example.

References

Al-Sayegh, F. (1998). Merchants' role in a changing society: The case of Dubai. *Middle Eastern Studies, 34*(1), 87–102.

Al-Serkal, M. (2018, May 9). Top 3 reasons for revoking UAE work permits. *Gulf News.* Retrieved from https://gulfnews.com/how-to/employment/top-3-reasons-for-revoking-uae-work-permits-1.2218601

Altbach, P. G. (2005). Universities: Family style. *International Higher Education, 39,* 10–12.

Altbach, P. G. (2010). Open door in higher education: Unsustainable and probably ill-advised. *Economic and Political Weekly, 45,* 13–15.

Billionaires: The richest people in the world. (2019, March 5). *Forbes.* Retrieved from https://www.forbes.com/billionaires/#70195b5f251c

Bloom, D., & Rosovsky, H. (2011). Unlocking the benefits of higher education through appropriate governance. In P. G. Altbach (Ed.), *Leadership for world-class universities: Challenges for developing countries* (pp. 71–89). New York, NY: Routledge.

Bok, D. (2013). *Higher education in America.* Princeton, NJ: Princeton University Press.

Bowen, W. (2008). *The board book; An insider's guide for directors and trustees.* New York, NY: W.W. Norton & Company.

Butteroff, G., Welborne, B., & Al-Lawati, N. (2018). *Measuring female labor force participation in the GCC 2018* (Issue Brief No. 01.18.18). Houston, TX: Rice University Baker Institute for Public Policy.

CNN Travel, Dubai. (n.d.). Retrieved from https://www.cnn.com/travel/destinations/dubai

DiMaggio, P., & Powell, W. (1991). The iron cage revisited: Institutional isomorphism and collective rationality in organizational fields. In W. Powell & P. DiMaggio (Eds.), *The new institutionalism in organizational analysis* (pp. 63–82). Chicago, IL: University of Chicago Press.

Dubai Statistics Center. (2018). Retrieved from https://www.dsc.gov.ae/en-us

Gonzalez, G., Karoly, L., Constant, L., Salem, H., & Goldman, C. (2008,) *Facing human capital challenges of the 21st century, Education and labor market initiatives in Lebanon, Oman, Qatar and the United Arab Emirates.* Los Angeles, CA: Rand Corporation.

Hazelkorn, E. (2015). *Rankings and the reshaping of higher education.* London: Palgrave Macmillan.

International Air Transportation Association. (2017). *World Air Transport Statistics.* Retrieved from https://airlines.iata.org/data/2017-world-air-transport-statistics

Kamal, K., & Trines, S. (2018). *Education in the United Arab Emirates.* Retrieved from https://wenr.wes.org/2018/08/education-in-the-united-arab-emirates

LaGuardia, A. (2018, June 21). The Gulf: The new Arab revolution. *The Economist,* 3–12.

Noori, N., & Anderson, P. K. (2013). Globalization, governance and the diffusion of the American model of education: Accreditation agencies and American-style universities in the Middle East. *International Journal of Politics, Culture, and Society, 26*(2), 159–172.

Pennington, R. (2017, August 26). Women continue to dominate UAE federal colleges and universities. *The National.* Retrieved from https://www.thenational.ae/uae/women-continue-to-dominate-uae-federal-colleges-and-universities

Wendel, S. (2018). The wealth of wisdom. *Forbes Middle East, 70,* 44–47.

Wilkins, S., & Huisman, J. (2012). The international branch campus as transnational strategy in higher education. *Higher Education, 64*(5), 627–645.

PART 3

Conclusion

∵

A Model of Family-Based Higher Education Management—Challenges and Opportunities

Edward Choi, Mathew R. Allen, Hans de Wit and Philip G. Altbach

Family-owned or managed institutions (FOMHEIS) are a worldwide phenomenon in higher education that has been almost entirely ignored. They are without question established parts of the private higher education environment. As stated in the introduction by Philip G. Altbach, it is hard to generalize about this special type of academic institution. The case studies in this publication illustrate the variety of FOMHEIS within the private higher education sector. In this concluding chapter, we analyze this phenomenon as a basis for further study and for understanding this understudied but substantive dimension of private higher education.

On the surface, FOMHEIS resemble their non-family counterparts in private sector higher education. Commonalities may be evident along several lines including academic offerings, challenges related to funding and compliance, and institutional capacity. Some FOMHEIS are small—Corporación Universitaria del Meta (UNIMETA) in Colombia has 2,600 students. Others are much larger, such as Symbiosis International University in India, with around 18,500 students.

From an organizational perspective, FOMHEIS share similar characteristics with both non-family private institutions as well as public institutions. In fact, government classification systems worldwide do not differentiate FOMHEIS as a separate category of private institutions. In this way, their identity is blurred. However, we offer a different perspective. Our primary argument is that the obvious parallels between FOMHEIS and non-family institutions mask family-based organizational peculiarities that, upon closer inspection, set FOMHEIS apart from the prototypical higher education institution. FOMHEIS are unique because they possess a duality of organizational properties. On the surface, they most resemble non-family private higher education institutions in key characteristics. However, they also bear many of the trappings of the prototypical family-owned business. The similarities between FOMHEIS and family businesses highlight a "family" dimension in FOMHEIS that has never been researched. As a significant and important part of the postsecondary environment in many countries, the family dimension of FOMHEIS along with other distinctions deserve further attention and analysis. Our goal in this chapter and this volume is to examine this entirely unexplored phenomenon for the first time, taking into account different national and institutional contexts and histories.

The chapter is organized as follows. In the first part, FOMHEIS are discussed as part of the private higher education sector, demonstrating, as Levy notes in his chapter, organizational and operational qualities that typify all private higher education institutions. Next, FOMHEIS are compared to family-owned businesses to highlight the "family" character of their operations. The commonalities drawn between these two groups differentiate FOMHEIS from non-family organizations in higher education. We conclude with discussion of the key distinctions between FOMHEIS and the broader higher education landscape. Specifically, because of family involvement in management, FOMHEIS exhibit differences both organizationally and operationally. Each founder and family has a special story underlying their involvement in higher education. These stories demonstrate how family values and beliefs drive and shape the vision as well as influence the organizational culture of FOMHEIS in unique ways.

1   FOMHEIS and Non-Family Higher Education Institutions

In many ways, FOMHEIS appear no different than their non-family private higher education counterparts. Both groups reflect similar organizational and operational properties driven mostly by conforming to contextual forces and pressures common to all other private institutions. These similarities are consistent across the case example chapters. A discussion of typical higher education traits found in both non-family private higher education as well as FOMHEIS is provided below.

1.1   *Origin and Role*
The dramatic expansion of private higher education globally, as Levy notes in his chapter, stems in large part from the phenomenon of massification of postsecondary education and the inability of governments to respond to the demand for access through the expansion of public postsecondary institutions.

Thus, many private institutions, including FOMHEIS, were established during the past half-century, although some, including many religiously affiliated institutions, have a much longer history. Several of the institutions discussed in this book, such as those in Korea and Japan as well as parts of Latin

America, are examples of the early development of private higher education, and the early appearance of FOMHEIS.

Industrialization and higher education massification have resulted in the significant presence of FOMHEIS in several of the countries discussed in this book. In India, for example, where the number of private institutions are outpacing their public counterparts, FOMHEIS makeup a significant segment of the higher education system. The same is true in South Korea, Ethiopia, and Japan. A number of FOMHEIS may also be found in Brazil, Colombia, Bangladesh, China, and Armenia.

Some of these countries are still in the process of industrialization and massification. Thus, the need for private actors in higher education delivery is ongoing and FOMHEIS play an important societal role. In this way, the emerging economies of India, Ethiopia, and Bangladesh demonstrate an increasing FOMHEI presence. In other countries, however, the growth of FOMHEIS and other private institutions has stabilized somewhat and even reversed in some cases. A number of factors contribute to this reality—slow economic growth as in the case of Mexico; stringent market entry regulations as in the case of China and Korea; or new policy directions as in the case of the Philippines where free public education now threatens student enrollment in the private sector. Market, demographic, and government forces may drive institutional mergers, acquisitions, and in some countries, closures as in the cases of Brazil, Japan, Korea, and Armenia. Additional factors determining the health and survival of FOMHEIS are related to funding, competition, and student recruitment. In Armenia's case, more than 50 FOMHEIS have exited the market over the last two decades as a result of such pressures.

As we will discuss later, many families created their institutions based on wealth generated in other businesses. But there are also examples of founders that have a background in politics (the Colombian cases) or as teachers in other universities (Symbiosis for instance).

1.2   *For-Profit or Non-Profit*

Like private non-family institutions, FOMHEIS operate as both non-profit organizations and for-profit businesses. In some countries, where education is largely considered a public service, all private institutions, including FOMHEIS, operate as non-profit organizations by law. This non-profit requirement exists in several of the countries discussed in this book including Colombia, South Korea, Japan, India, and Bangladesh. In these countries, distributing profits to family members, or shareholders in the case of publicly-listed FOMHEIS, is not a goal and is indeed unlawful. This does not exclude the fact that in some cases families generate income from their involvement in the institution through real estate and services.

However, in other countries families own and operate for-profit institutions where such commercial activity in higher education is allowed. Examples from the case chapters include the Philippines, China, Ethiopia, Armenia, and Brazil. Families in these countries can take advantage of looser regulations determining tuition levels as well as other market-related factors in order to produce profit. According to Reis and Capelato, authors of the Brazil chapter, this flexibility allows the founding families of the 647 family-owned or managed higher education institutions in Brazil to profit from elementary, middle, and high schools as well as the higher education institutions they operate. While profit-making may not be the only goal, it is a key goal of these for-profit institutions. As the literature reviewed in Chapter 3 suggests, founding for-profit higher education institutions may be less about maximizing social impact through education than about the bottom line. For-profit status, of course, does not preclude taking education seriously or offering quality programs.

Several for-profit institutions are discussed in the case chapters. Most notable is the China Education Group, which is not only for-profit, but also publicly-listed on the Hong Kong Stock Exchange. The two individuals owning the group hold a majority stake in the company and, as Yu states in the China chapter, are "ultimately accountable to shareholders." Other for-profit examples come from Armenia and Ethiopia. In the latter, FOMHEIs, constitute a significant portion of the 113 private institutions in the country (91 percent) and operate as private limited companies (PLC). A PLC is essentially a business with private shareholders who cannot trade shares publicly.

1.3   *Academic Focus and Research*

Like most private institutions around the world, FOMHEIs generally focus on offering programs with market relevance. These are often applied programs in popular fields such as engineering, business, medicine, law, IT, and computer science. Private higher education is generally more attuned to shifting and expanding employer demand and programs consistent with consumer interests. A different dynamic is found in public higher education where institutions are typically bound to offering traditional academic programs. Interestingly, traditional public academic institutions in some countries are also embracing market relevancy in the programs they develop. China is no exception. Shifting markets in China "increasingly demand graduates with professional skills," as Yu explains.

FOMHEIs do not generally focus on research. This is evident in several of the case chapters including Ethiopia, Bangladesh, Brazil, Colombia, and Armenia.

The low research output is common not only to FOMHEIs, but also most private higher education institutions around the world. While a lack of involvement in research on the part of FOMHEIs is typical, there are exceptions to this in a handful of countries such as the United States, Japan and Korea. In this volume, Tamagawa University in Japan, Symbiosis International University in India and to a lesser extent, the American International University-Bangladesh, are institutions recognized for their research orientation.

1.4   *Accreditation and Educational Quality*

Most institutions around the world must meet some minimum level of quality. Typically, the government or an independent, non-governmental accreditation or quality assurance agency enforces this standard. For example, Armenia has the National Centre of Professional Education Quality Assurance Foundation (ANQA); Japan has the Japan University Accreditation Association; Dubai has the Commission on Academic Accreditation (CAA).

All of the case studies presented in this book operate as fully-accredited universities at the institutional or programmatic level(s). Some are even reviewed by international accreditation or quality assurance agencies against international standards of educational quality. Al Ghurair University in Dubai, received accredited status at the programmatic-level from the Accreditation Board for Engineering and Technology (ABET) headquartered in the US. Another example is Holy Angel University in the Philippines, whose accreditation comes from multiple international sources including the Accreditation Commission for Programs of Hospitality Administration (ACPHA) and the International Accreditation Commission for Business Education (IACBE). The international level of accreditation provides these institutions with a reputational advantage in their countries.

However, our understanding is that many FOMHEIs around the world, specifically those operating in developing countries, are not accredited and of lower quality as Levy states in his chapter. For example, Burgos Mantilla notes in the Colombia chapter that only six percent of nationally-certified academic programs (approximately 1,444) are offered by FOMHEIs. Ethiopia is another country where FOMHEIs typically do not have accredited status. According to Tamrat, this is a result of weak accreditation assurance processes.

1.5   *International Activity*

No corner of the globe or institutional type is immune to the call to internationalize in some fashion (Rumbley, Altbach, & Reisberg, 2012, p. 3). Globalization has motivated all institution types, including FOMHEIs, to internationalize. As the world becomes increasingly interconnected, FOMHEIs are not exempt from the sweeping effect of globalization and the need to remain internationally relevant in an increasingly competitive market.

This observation is consistent with this book's case studies. Several of the cases, notably Eurasia International University (EIU) in Armenia, Symbiosis International University (SIU) in India, and the American International University-Bangladesh (AIUB) were established with internationalization as integral to their mission. These institutions provide services and programs consistent with their international branding. They have overseas institutional partnerships, international research projects, and university-wide policies, activities, and services promoting an international dimension at home.

In SIU's case, promoting intercultural reciprocity and learning in the programs and services the faculty and staff provide is crucial to making the sizable and increasing international student population feel welcome. For this institution, internationalization has been a key element of the university since its founding in 2002. Currently, there are 2,200 international students at SIU from over 20 countries or about 12 percent of the student body. Also notable are EIU and AIUB, both of which incorporate an international dimension measured by international research projects or foreign language skills as key criteria in the hiring and promotion of faculty. At EIU, internationalization at home is taken seriously as indicated in their strategic plans. EIU is part of the Bologna Process, a regional initiative aimed at increasing student and staff mobility, not to mention the exchange of knowledge, skills, and ideas within the European Union.

Other examples of internationalization and international engagement are found in Universidad de la Vera-Cruz in Mexico, Tamagawa University in Japan, the China Education Group in China, Toledo University Center (UNITOLEDO) in Brazil, Holy Angel University in the Philippines, and the University of Cordilleras, also in the Philippines. At all of these FOMHEIS, various international activities expand their sphere of operations to a global level. But with the exception of the first three, their international engagement and reputation remains relatively marginal.

1.6   *Funding*

Most FOMHEIS around the world have been established by individuals or groups of individuals using a combination of personal and external resources. External resources include bank loans, capital investments, and donations. Donations are both financial as well as in-kind, such as land grants from local and federal governments. Toledo University Center in Brazil, for example, was founded with the personal funds of the founder, land donations, and bank loans. Based on the cases, it is typical for founders to commit significant personal resources to the establishment of their institutions. FOMHEIS are often bankrolled by wealthy families or individuals. Often, founding an institution of higher education is not their first venture. These families and individuals already operate successful businesses outside of higher education that have generated significant wealth. This wealth is used toward establishing institutions of higher education. Such is the story of Al Ghurair University in Dubai, founded by the Al Ghurair family, one of the wealthiest families in the United Arab Emirates (UAE). They built their wealth through various business ventures and investments including running one of the largest banks in the UAE.

Whether FOMHEIs result from mergers between smaller FOMHEIs, private investment from wealthy families, or by borrowing money from banks, all FOMHEIs rely heavily on tuition revenue to sustain operations. This funding structure mirrors that of the broader category of the private higher education sector. Tuition revenue at most private institutions is significant relative to other revenue sources such as research grants, donations (virtually nonexistent in most countries outside of the US and UK), and direct government assistance. In most of the case studies, the government does not provide direct assistance at all. The exceptions are Korea, Brazil, and Colombia where public resources—though insubstantial in the case of Korea and irregularly disbursed in the case of Colombia—flow to the private sector.

Some FOMHEIs supplement tuition revenue with other forms of income. Publicly-listed FOMHEIs generate additional cash flow by attracting investors seeking some stake in company equity (e.g., China Education Group). Others benefit financially or from in-kind charitable donations from their wealthy founders. Still some FOMHEIs complement main revenue streams with income generated through social entrepreneurship. In this arrangement, families draw funds from other non-education businesses they establish to support the academic mission of their institution. And finally, some institutions are part of a family-owned educational conglomerate that may include primary and secondary schools. Such arrangements may be found in Japan, the Philippines, India, Brazil, Armenia, and other countries in Asia and Latin America. The lower-level schools may generate additional revenue through fees that may be allocated to the postsecondary institution and vice versa. Revenue is shared among different organizations within the family conglomerate.

1.7   *Government Oversight*

FOMHEIs worldwide are generally subject to government controls and guidelines targeting the higher education sector that can be quite stringent. Thus, FOMHEIs are no different from their non-family counterparts in terms of their relationship with the government and the degree of institutional autonomy they possess.

As some of the institutional cases suggest, external controls reach deeply into many facets of institutional operations including governance structures, curricular development, how land and buildings are owned, and financial regulations of various kinds. Strong government regulations may be found in some of the countries discussed in this book, notably China, Armenia, Korea, Japan, and the Philippines.

However, centralized external regulation is not found in all countries. This is especially true in developing country contexts and where for-profit higher education and FOMHEIS dominate such as in Brazil, Mexico, and Ethiopia. While the case studies do not address the reasoning for different levels of regulation, the level of government oversight seems indirectly related to the need for higher education capacity in that country. Where needs are mostly being met, the government will focus more on regulation, but where needs are unmet the government might turn a blind eye in favor of increasing the capacity to meet demand for higher education.

2   The "Familiness" of FOMHEIS

FOMHEIS also possess special organizational characteristics that set them apart from the non-family mainstream in higher education, including other private institutions. These characteristics mostly relate to the way that families approach the management of their institutions. Family involvement is understood to bring a unique family dimension to the organizational and governance culture.

The family dimension suggests that FOMHEIS are not only higher education institutions but also a family-managed enterprise. The family dimension further suggests that families bring their own stories, values, and beliefs to bear on organizational objectives. In this section, the lens of family-owned business research is applied to more fully understand when and why these organizations are more or less successful.

According to family business research, families who own and manage commercial businesses pursue what Berrone, Cruz, and Gomez-Mejia (2012) refer to as socioemotional wealth (SEW), described as non-financial benefits of business ownership. These non-financial benefits may refer to five distinct components—family influence, identity, binding social ties or social capital, emotional attachment, and renewal through the preservation of organizational influence accomplished by transgenerational succession.

The scholarship of family-owned businesses explains that preserving these benefits is important above and beyond financial motivation. A focus on community status related to ownership or leadership, or related political capital derived from ownership, are examples of this type of wealth. While difficult to measure directly (Berrone et al., 2012), a focus on socioemotional wealth preservation can often be seen in family efforts to maintain control of the company through family succession even if that is not in the best interest of the organization.

The cases discussed in this book provide some evidence that families involved in higher education ownership and management also pursue non-financial benefits derived from ownership including those related to control in organizational affairs. In the following section, this evidence is discussed through the framework of sew theory, which has been fully described in Chapter 3.

2.1 *Influence*

A common theme in family business research is the influence that the family has on the business and business decisions (Chrisman, Chua, Pearson, & Barnett, 2012). Families in family-owned businesses have long been recognized as influencing decisions within the business based on their beliefs, ideals, and values (Hubler, 2009). The case chapters suggest that family-owned or managed institutions are no different and that family beliefs and values are central to how FOMHEIs are founded and operate. For example, in the Bangladesh case study, American International University-Bangladesh, the family passion for education was a driving force behind the decision to get involved in higher education. Similarly, the founding and management of Symbiosis International University (SIU) may be traced to the values and vision of its founder, Dr. S. B. Mujumdar. His early experiences, working as a warden of a boy's hostel learning about the adjustment challenges that foreign students faced, shaped his vision and deep resolve to provide them with a "home away from home." Dr. Mujumdar's story became central to the vision of SIU that is to promote international understanding through quality education.

The case chapters are consistent with the family business literature in another regard. Across most FOMHEIS presented in this volume, family influence is exercised and also maintained over time through governance arrangements, rules, and processes that favor family involvement. One of the primary ways that families influence decision-making is through family members occupying key leadership positions. This control can be maintained over time by implementing hiring and promotion practices favoring family over non-family candidates.

In most cases, family influence is concentrated and exercised at the board level. As the highest governing body of any organization, the board has a strong influence on organizational decision-making. It oversees matters affecting larger organization-level objectives and strategic decision-making.

Representation of family members on the governing board varies by institutional case. At some FOMHEIs, family members have majority representation on the board such as at the American International University Bangladesh, Corporación Universidad Piloto de Colombia, Universidad Antropológica de Guadalajara (UNAG) in Mexico, and University of Cordilleras (UC) in the Philippines. UC is notable for having their entire board controlled by family related to the founder. Family members come from second and third generations with the eldest son of the founder occupying the position of chair.

In many FOMHEIs family influence is further strengthened at the management level through family members occupying leadership positions that report directly to the board (e.g., president, rector, or vice chancellor). According to the family firm literature, the occupation of both board and management positions by the family means less agency conflict around organizational decision-making. This is because the board and management (also referred to as principles and agents, respectively) are controlled by members of the same kinship group who are likely to share the same values, goals, and interests.

In this book, a notable example where such a dynamic may exist is at Corporación Universitaria Rafael Núñez in Colombia. As noted by Burgos Mantilla in the Colombia chapter, "The second generation maintains control, not only of the general board, but of relevant management positions in the institution, such as the rector's and registrar's offices."

Many FOMHEIs further concentrate influence by having the same family member occupying multiple leadership positions within a single organization or across several institutions controlled by the family. For example, a single family member may act as a board member and hold a senior position at the management level. Another scenario is where a family member occupies the position of president in one institution and at the same time, another leadership position at a different family-affiliated institution. Such is the case in Tamagawa University in Japan. The chairperson of the parent group, Tamagawa Gakuen, also holds the positions of university president and principal of the K-12 school.

Finally, family influence is strengthened through family-centric hiring practices. Many of the cases indicate that other family members, including relatives and those connected through marriage, become actively involved at the family institution. In the China chapter Yu notes that it is not uncommon for the founder or family to extend employment opportunities to relatives.

It is important to note that many reasons abound for family-centric hiring and that there is not always a self-serving agenda. In many institutions, the family involved in management possesses a deep sense of empathy for struggling family members seeking employment and extends invitations to join the university staff. In other cases, the managing family is pressured into hiring extended family because of entitlement expectations. Relatives feel entitled to leadership positions and a stake in the university. Finally, there are cases where family members, both immediate and extended, become professionally involved based on relevant experience and merit. In these cases, the appointment of new family members is less about strengthening familial influence than about hiring a strong candidate for the job. As discussed in the family firm literature, family members are more committed to seeing their organizations succeed than non-family members of the organization. In this way family involvement represents a benefit to the entire organization, not just the family unit.

Centralized governance structures and hiring practices that favor family in management positions typify FOMHEIs worldwide. However, there are exceptions. In some FOMHEIs, organizational structures and practices promote shared governance in decision-making across family and non-family groups within the institution. In this book, exemplary cases with such a dynamic include Symbiosis International University in India, Al Ghurair University in Dubai, and Holy Angel University in the Philippines. In all of these cases, governing boards have significant, if not a majority, representation of non-family members. Some of these institutions also have non-family members in key management positions.

A special case is Holy Angel University. Both the board chair and president positions are filled by non-family members. Holy Angel University is distinguished further because the president has a fixed term. This is not common at most FOMHEIs. In most cases, family members occupy the presidency for the span of their professional career. It is not uncommon for a family member to occupy the presidency for upwards of 20 or even 30 years. In the case of Korea, successors to the position of chairman of the board are appointed only after the incumbent retires or moves on. Ohanyan, author of the Armenia chapter, states that the average number of years of service for rectors of FOMHEIs in Armenia is 24 years.

Another special case is Al Ghurair University. The family proactively took steps to minimize continued direct institutional control by the family. These steps included drafting new bylaws modeled on best practices developed by the US-based Association of Governing Boards (AGB). Notably, the bylaws stressed board independence with a majority of board members not connected to the Al Ghurair family or the institution, clear fiduciary responsibilities, the avoidance of real or perceived conflicts of interest, and other facets of a governance structure common to US private, non-profit institutions. Additionally, non-family candidates were appointed to leadership positions through a competitive recruiting process.

In some countries, family influence is limited by government regulations. In Korea, government policy dictates the appointment of board members. Family members may not occupy more than one-third of board seats (Kim & Kim, 2015). It is unlawful in Korea for a single family member to occupy more than one leadership position in the same educational organization. In Japan government mandates supersede institutional protocols that determine the formation of the board. Relatives of the founder may not be appointed board members. There are even countries where FOMHEI boards include government representatives to insure accountability. In Bangladesh's case, this is enforced by the University Grants Commission whose aim is to align institutional priorities with socially determined purposes.

2.2   *Succession*

Another common theme in the family-business literature is that of succession (Breton-Miller, Miller, & Steier, 2004; Dyck, Mauws, Starke, & Mischke, 2002; Tagiuri & Davis, 1996). For the family, passing the business to the next generation is very important as this preserves the vision and goals of the founder. Further, family-based succession is the most important defining characteristic of the family-owned business. As the literature review in Chapter 3 explains, this dimension of socioemotional wealth (SEW) is frequently referenced. Our understanding is that a family-owned business may be defined by a family-based succession process, even when other SEW dimensions are absent.

Like in other family-owned businesses, the families involved in higher education management tend to recruit board members and management staff from within kinship groups. Successors are typically the son or daughter of incumbent leaders. In some cases, FOMHEIs are passed on to brothers and sisters or other relatives. In Corporación Universidad Piloto (UNIPILOTO) in Colombia, first generation members have appointed several second-generation members to the board.

Other examples where leadership has transitioned or involved second or third generations of the founding family in management are Corporación Universitaria Rafael Nuñez in Colombia, Corporación Universitaria del Meta also in Colombia, Dom Bosco University Center (UNDB) in Brazil, and University of Cordilleras and Holy Angel University, both in the Philippines. In the case of Corporación Universitaria del Meta, the institution has been passed to the founder's brother and two nieces. One of the nieces became president of the institution.

In some cases, family-based succession is institutionalized by university bylaws, as in the case of American International University-Bangladesh. Whether bylaws exist or not, family-based succession is shaped and driven by cultural values, pressures, and expectations coming from family incumbents and other university constituents within the family-based organizational environment. Family and non-family constituent expectations and pressures drive leadership transitions in all FOMHEIs around the world. At Universidad Antropológica de Guadalajara (UNAG) in Mexico, for example, the current rector accepted university positions based on a career trajectory planned by his parents.

Further, such expectations begin early in childhood as evidenced in the Korea, Ethiopia, and Brazil chapters. For next generation successors, commitment to take over the institution is cultivated as children grow up. The children of family incumbents are integrated into the culture of succession. For example, the current rector at Toledo University Center (UNITOLEDO) in Brazil assumed his position having grown up within his family's institution. The Ethiopia chapter also explains that many leaders of FOMHEIs focus on preparing their children for succession. Not only do they provide them with academic training, but also have them attend institutional meetings, in some cases before being designated officially as university personnel.

As part of the grooming process, familial successors are expected (and even pressured in many cases) to pursue appropriate credentials and experience for leadership. This expectation is also found in family-owned businesses in other sectors. Having the right credentials and experience is an important component of a successful organization, especially when leadership is chosen from within the family (Chang & Shim, 2015). At the most basic level, successors in higher education should have a doctoral degree. In many cases, a PhD is required by the institution to satisfy job requirements. This approach is not significantly different from leadership requirements in non-family institutions. The difference, however, is the grooming process driving next generation family members to earn appropriate credentials.

A final note regarding family-based succession relates to cultural forces beyond the expectations and pressures arising from within the institution. In countries such as Korea, Japan and India, family-based succession is a product of national ideological and sociocultural norms. The cultures of Japan, India, and Korea favor the unity of the family even after children become adults. It is not uncommon for children to live with and even receive financial assistance from their parents after marriage and building successful careers. Transferring the wealth of parents, including the family business, to children is a common cultural practice. Thus, in nations with a strong inclination towards intergenerational unity and wealth transfer, family-based succession is deeply rooted in culture.

3   Identity, Binding Social Ties, and Emotional Attachment

Like family-owned businesses, the case chapters suggest that other socioemotional wealth (SEW) besides family influence and renewal shape the organizational culture at FOMHEIs. The Armenia and Ethiopia chapters suggest that family members make a significant emotional investment in the success of their institution compared to non-family personnel. According to Deephouse and Jaskiewicz (2013) this is because their identity is deeply tied to the organization. Organizational success sustains a positive identity for the family and other benefits including a good reputation, social prestige, and financial security. Organizational success also means that the community (inside and outside of the business) continues to accept the family's control over the organization in perpetuity. Organizational success legitimizes the socioemotional wealth dimension of renewal. In contrast, institutional failure reflects poorly on the family name and may portend personal financial risk in the long-term, not to mention loss of control of the family organization.

Families involved in business management are also understood to cultivate the SEW dimension of binding social ties or positive relationships within their firms, not just between family members, but among all personnel. Families often create an organizational culture based on relationships rooted in loyalty, reciprocation, and trust (Cennamo, Berrone, Cruz, & Gomez-Mejia, 2012). The literature of family-owned businesses suggests that the desire for such a culture is stronger at family-based than non-family businesses.

The case chapters suggest that families involved in higher education management are also interested in cultivating social capital. In the Mexico chapter the author discusses decision-making at Universidad Antropológica de Guadalajara in the context of relationships rooted in trust and loyalty. Likewise, similar language is used by the Bangladesh author in his discussion of employee turnover, noting that strong relationships between employees and the leadership result in employee retention within FOMHEIs. Additional examples of binding social ties come from the India and Mexico chapters. According to the authors, senior leadership at both Symbiosis International University (SIU) (India) and Universidad Antropológica de Guadalajara (UNAG) (Mexico) has tacit knowledge of the organizational culture and maintain positive relationships with other family members and non-family personnel. With such evidence, however, these examples do not provide sufficient proof to conclude that FOMHEIs have more social capital than non-family institutions or that family-based leadership is more interested in cultivating this SEW dimension. More research is needed in this area.

Finally, family members within their business develop strong emotional attachments to one another (Berrone et al., 2012). These emotional attachments may be projections of pride or love or they may manifest as disappointment, frustration, or anger. Further, the emotional state of the family can spill over into the business and blur the distinction between family and business ecosystems. In other words, the intra-family emotions tend to affect interactions within the business for good or bad, depending on the emotional state of the family. Negative emotions that lead to family disagreements (Benedict, 1968; Breton-Miller, Miller, & Steier, 2004; Lansberg, 1983; Tagiuri & Davis, 1996) adversely impact performance. On the other hand, positive intra-family emotions may lead to a friendly environment where employees feel welcome and supported.

Our understanding is that the emotional state of families involved in higher education management affect business practices. The chapter on Bangladesh provides the most direct evidence of this. In an observation of the general landscape of FOMHEIs in Bangladesh, the authors state that family-based conflict often jeopardizes the ability of leadership to ensure smooth university operations and the proper handling of finances.

4   Challenges and Opportunities

FOMHEIs face myriad challenges. Some, such as demographic factors, funding challenges, increasing regulatory oversight and competition, relate to circumstances common to all private higher education institutions. There are also special challenges and opportunities relating to the family dimension of FOMHEIs. These challenges and opportunities are the focus of this section.

4.1   *Family-based Management Challenges*
4.1.1   Challenges Related to Centralized Governance
A key problem cited in most of the chapters relates to FOMHEIs operating with centralized governance and hiring from within family kinship groups. For example, the authors of the Bangladesh chapter discuss the leadership of FOMHEIs in light of their reluctance to share decision-making authority with non-family members. Family influence prioritizes the family's interests and perspectives over concerns raised by professors and even government officials who may sit on the board at Bangladeshi universities. Similarly, the authors of

the Mexico and Ethiopia chapters indicate that leadership in FOMHEIS gives little priority to shared governance. This is echoed by Reis and Capelato in the Brazil chapter. They explain that families involved in higher education management concern themselves primarily with the interests and opinions held by family-run boards of trustees although Dom Bosco University Center (UNDB) has moved forward towards professionalizing governance. A similar situation evolved at Al Ghurair University in Dubai. The Al Ghurair family, recognizing the dangers associated with excessive family control (e.g., poor organizational performance), has taken measures to reform the institution's governance model.

Human capital issues result from the family's desire to maintain control over institutional affairs and the leadership competency of family members is not clear (Schulze, Lubatkin, Dino, & Buchholtz, 2001). When the primary desire is to maintain family control through management, family leaders can be chosen who lack the necessary skills to effectively run the organization (Schulze, Lubatkin, & Dino, 2003). For example, hiring family members, including relatives and those affiliated through marriage, is quite common worldwide and evident in several of the case chapters. Hiring within kinship groups and honoring blood ties may compromise efforts to recruit more qualified professionals as Tamrat suggests in his chapter on Ethiopia. He notes that university positions are often given to family members and relatives with limited qualification and experience.

This reduced pool of human capital resulting from a focus on family dominance can be detrimental to the overall performance of the organization. While not prevalent in all of the cases, examples of an effort to control decisions through family management can be seen in Armenia, Colombia, and Ethiopia. While this issue has been demonstrated in many types of family businesses, it is possible that the problem is even more severe in the context of family-owned universities because of the high levels of education and experience required to manage a university.

The essential compromise between maintaining family control, or at least significant influence, on the one hand and the need for competent leadership on the other is a central issue for FOMHEIS worldwide. How institutions handle this question may determine their success or failure.

4.1.2   Challenges Related to Succession

The family-owned business literature states that passing leadership and ownership to the next generation while maintaining business effectiveness can be difficult (Handler, 1990). Families struggle to motivate, prepare, and transition to the next generation (Davis & Harveston, 1998). Furthermore, the probability of failure increases as leadership progresses down generational lines.

Similar themes regarding generational transition can be seen in the case examples. As a stark example, the Japanese case points out the increasingly negative public perception of heredity, making the process of family succession even more difficult. In Japan, family succession, understood as a form of wealth transfer, has become the subject of societal criticism and perceived as perpetuating class divisions. The same sentiment has taken root in Korean society.

Similar challenges related to family succession in higher education exist elsewhere. As Yeravadekar states in the India chapter, successors are constantly compared to the founder on their ability to function as intellectual equals to the staff and faculty below them and on their qualifications and experience. The comparisons and judgments become tougher for subsequent generations. Third and fourth generation successors may be held to higher standards and subjected to greater scrutiny. Based on the family-owned business literature, successors often diverge from the founder on personal ideals, vision, and values. As the case chapters suggest, this may be because of a loss of interest regarding the family business down generational lines. Later generations often embrace different aspirations that conflict with those of earlier family leadership or have little interest in academic leadership. Furthermore, later generations may not possess appropriate qualifications. Lack of academic qualifications provide additional basis for public skepticism when family successors clearly do not meet expected standards for leadership.

In some cases, the challenges of succession at FOMHEIs have led incumbents to consider selling their institutions, merging with other institutions, or assigning leadership to non-family successors. The options of selling or merging are more realistic in countries where major educational groups monopolize the higher education market such as in Brazil, China, or Mexico. Larger, for-profit institutions or companies are actively on the lookout for opportunities to acquire smaller FOMHEIs. However, these options are seldomly pursued. Generally, families prefer to keep their institutions within the family.

In sum, smooth family-based leadership transitions are rare. In fact, they are a source of significant conflict involving myriad constituents who may resist the leadership change. Succession at most if not all FOMHEIs is a disruptive process.

4.1.3   Challenges Related to Public Perception
There are many reputable FOMHEIs worldwide, including those examined in this volume. However, FOMHEIs in general suffer reputationally because of

corruption tied to some family-based management practices. In some countries, the poor reputation of FOMHEIS may stem from systemic corruption within the FOMHEI landscape. In other countries all FOMHEIS suffer reputationally as a result of a handful of corrupt FOMHEIS. Regardless, corrupt FOMHEIS make it difficult for those that pursue a serious academic mission to build reputational wealth.

Public perception of FOMHEIS as corrupt institutions is discussed in many of the chapters. Ohanyan states that many FOMHEIS in Armenia focus on profit-making and are often described as diploma mills. She explains that these FOMHEIS harm the broader status of FOMHEIS in society, creating an environment of public mistrust towards the sector as a whole.

In observing the general landscape of FOMHEIS in Ethiopia, Tamrat draws attention to institutional activities and characteristics that hurt the broader reputation of FOMHEIS. These include poor organization, opaque business practices, excessive commercialization, embezzlement, and blatant abuses of power.

Another example is presented in the Korea chapter. Choi notes that some families profit by creating businesses that funnel institutional resources into personal bank accounts. A family may award a construction contract from the family's university to a construction company also owned by the family. Sometimes this is done without a competitive bidding process. While such a scenario is unlawful in Korea, it nevertheless takes place. Profits made from the services rendered are pocketed by the family.

And while not evidence of corruption, the authors of the Bangladesh chapter allude to other perceptions that shape public opinion. They discuss a general landscape of family-run universities that deemphasize areas such as the professionalization of staff or curriculum development while favoring activities that preserve or enhance social status and power. The authors explain that FOMHEIS often become mired in family conflict to an extent that jeopardizes university operations. They note that "the interlacing of family and university matters ... becomes a frequent challenge for the family run unit ... [that] sometimes results in mismanagement and even mishandling of university funds."

In sum, the notoriety of FOMHEIS results from families that abuse their leadership in the organization for personal gain or become victims of family infighting. Our understanding is that family-based governance, when favoring excessive family involvement, provides opportunities for the family to engage in corruption more than in non-family institutions. This is because governance structures and modalities under family leadership may preclude the implementation of controls that ensure accountability and prevent the accumulation of decision-making power in any single stakeholder group.

It is important to note here that the poor reputation of FOMHEIs is not always based in reality. Sometimes, the public may inaccurately interpret certain family decisions that were made in the best interest of the institution, as in the Korean example. Unlike families motivated by profit, some families create side businesses that are used to provide services at a low cost to the institution, thereby freeing up resources for academic purposes. In these cases, the proceeds from the rendered services may be funneled back into the institution and used, for example, to train staff and faculty, or provide scholarships. There may always be a disconnect between the intent of the certain decisions and how society perceives them.

4.2   Family-Based Management Opportunities

Research has shown the businesses run by families in non-academic sectors demonstrate certain strengths that make them more competitive than their non-family-run counterparts (Anderson & Reeb, 2003). The various cases in this book provide evidence that family-run institutions experience similar strategic benefits. In Japan, universities where the founder or family leader is both the CEO and president of the university the institution, appear to be nimbler and quicker in making decisions and change. Centralized governance, while having its own set of problems, may in fact be a strength when circumstances call for efficient decision-making. As mentioned earlier, there is often a reduction in conflict because key decision-makers are family members who converge around similar beliefs, values, and interests.

Another strength of FOMHEIs is the focus on preserving the values, beliefs, and practices of the organizational culture. These dimensions are preserved primarily through family-based succession. Successors, having been groomed by the family, sustain the culture and may ensure the preservation of these qualities through their management strategy. However, the same cannot be said of successors in non-family-based institutions where successors and incumbents share fewer connections. A change in leadership, therefore, may bring about a new vision for the institution rooted in values and beliefs that may diverge from those of past presidents, rectors, or chancellors.

The organizational culture is further preserved because leadership does not change often. As mentioned earlier, it is not uncommon to find a single family member filling a leadership position for the duration of his or her career, often lasting 20 to 30 years or longer. Continuous, uninterrupted leadership offers some advantages. Whereas projects initiated by past presidents are re-evaluated or may even be terminated under new presidents, continuity may sustain projects and initiatives in the longer term. In other words, the family-based leadership model minimizes the disruptions that frequent leadership changes may have on long-term strategies.

A final strength of FOMHEIs, according to the family-owned business literature, is that families invest heavily in their institution's success to enjoy the personal rewards of remaining in control. These rewards have already been discussed (e.g., financial security, social status, etc.) and are linked to socioemotional wealth. However, a deeper reflection explains the indirect impact that these personal rewards may have on the institution as a whole.

The prospect of personal financial stability and social prestige drives the family's continued commitment to organizational success. While financial stability and social prestige are personally motivated rewards, the family is not the only stakeholder group that benefits from organizational success. Faculty, staff, students, and the local community stand to benefit from the high engagement of the family when the institution climbs rankings, attracts top talent, or attracts resources. As Choi notes in the Korea chapter, the community benefits from the institution in the form of employment, an educated citizenry, and economic activity as businesses crop up around the institution.

5   Can FOMHEIs Be World-Class Research Universities?

The question is sometimes raised as to whether private higher education institutions in general, and FOMHEIs in particular, can rise to the stature of elite, research-intensive universities. As is clear from the case studies in this volume and from the research on private higher education generally, the vast majority of private universities worldwide generally focus on teaching courses in high demand by the job market. However, a small but growing proportion of private institutions have aspired to the ranks of elite or semi-elite universities, providing top-quality teaching and in a few cases focusing on building research capacity to become recognized in global rankings and achieve national esteem. Financial, staffing, and other limitations mean that only a few private universities can achieve top status within their country.

For many reasons, it is extraordinarily difficult for FOMHEIs to develop a research focus and join the top ranks of universities in nationally or globally. However, it is not impossible. Two of the cases analyzed in this volume, Symbiosis International University in India and Tamagawa University in Japan have achieved significant success in research. It will be extraordinarily difficult, and probably impossible, for most FOMHEIs to join the ranks of elite, world-class universities for many reasons although it is possible for them to build research capacity and encourage quality teaching with careful planning, appropriate investment, and a commitment to social and academic mission. Institutions with a for-profit orientation are much less likely to achieve this level of excellence.

6   Conclusion

FOMHEIs are special institutions. They are a hybrid combining organizational properties found in both higher education institutions and family-owned businesses. The convergence shapes a unique organizational culture. As a private institution, FOMHEIs conform to economic, political, and sociocultural realities inherent in the higher education systems in which they operate. They reflect characteristics that typify all private institutions. And as a family-owned organization, they exhibit many of the characteristics common to family-based management.

The case chapters in this book were analyzed in order to summarize the similarities and unique qualities of FOMHEIs as well as their role in society and on the higher education landscape. A key conclusion is that FOMHEIs are complicated institutions whose unique organizational and operational characteristics can be both opportunistic as well as detrimental to effective organizational operation.

This concluding chapter focused on the challenges and opportunities related to family influence and family-controlled, centralized governance. Indeed, many of the case chapters highlight the dangers of centralized governance that may jeopardize organizational and academic performance and allow for corruption. However, centralized governance can also result in efficient decision-making that can be crucially important in moments requiring immediate action. Further, where families demonstrate social values, a strong family role in decision-making may be beneficial and conducive to driving performance towards standards of excellence.

Our conclusion is that family involvement in higher education institutions has, and continues to have, a significant and positive impact on global higher education. That said, like other family businesses, if not properly managed, the involvement of the family can also create tensions that can produce a negative impact on the institution and its overall mission. Whether or not the involvement of the family is positive or negative depends on balancing the needs of the family with the core purposes of the institution they own. Where families can apply their experience, convictions, and values to enhancing academic excellence, family involvement will promote success. When families are focused inwardly, when they are more concerned with their own status, position, power or profit than with their students, faculty, or contribution to society, their involvement can impede the success of the organization.

Governance structures such as requiring non-family board members, establishing stringent qualifications for hiring of family members, and stipulating family values that align with the purpose of the organization mitigate the potential negative impact of family involvement. However, as is evident in cases with this volume, many FOMHEIS operate successful institutions without such mechanisms to limit family control or involvement.

Based on this set of cases, one conclusion is clear. FOMHEIS, represent a unique and interesting subset of the higher education environment and warrant additional study and exploration. Still, there are also key differences among FOMHEIS. We can infer from the chapters included here that FOMHEIS have differences because of the differences among the families involved in their management. Each founding family has a unique story driving their involvement in higher education. These stories shape the vision, values, and beliefs of the families and influence the organizational culture of their institutions differently.

Differences are evident in the leadership styles employed by different founders and their successors. Families with a strong commitment to educational excellence may approach management thoughtfully and with more sensitivity to the needs of faculty, staff, and other constituents. These families may shape organizational cultures that reflect shared governance, similar to many of the world's most renowned universities. These families may respect the autonomy of faculty as essential to educational progress and may fashion their institutions to resemble a prototypical higher education institution more than a business.

In countries where for-profit education is allowed, many founders have a commercial interest in establishing ventures where profit-making is blended with a social mission. There are also publicly-listed FOMHEIS where, as Yu notes in the China chapter, the family is ultimately accountable to the shareholders of the company. However, some founders and families may believe in education as a public charity. In these cases, FOMHEIS may be established with the single purpose of maximizing social impact in the communities where they operate. FOMHEIS and the families operating them are ultimately accountable to society.

In sum, FOMHEIS are not a monolithic group. While circumstantial and contextual factors account for some of the differences, most of the differences result from the unique vision and beliefs of the families operating them. It is clear from the case studies included in this book that FOMHEIS are a significant presence worldwide and a special higher education phenomenon in an increasingly complex global environment.

References

Anderson, R. C., & Reeb, D. M. (2003). Founding-family ownership and firm performance: Evidence from the S&P 500. *The Journal of Finance, 58*(3), 1301–1328.

Benedict, B. (1968). Family firms and economic development. *Southwestern Journal of Anthropology, 24*(1), 1–19.

Berrone, P., Cruz, C., & Gomez-Mejia, L. R. (2012). Socioemotional wealth in family firms: Theoretical dimensions, assessment approaches, and agenda for future research. *Family Business Review, 25*(3), 258–279.

Breton-Miller, I. L., Miller, D., & Steier, L. P. (2004). Toward an integrative model of effective FOB succession. *Entrepreneurship Theory and Practice, 28*(4), 305–328.

Cennamo, C., Berrone, P., Cruz, C., & Gomez-Mejia, L. R. (2012). Socioemotional wealth and proactive stakeholder engagement: Why family-controlled firms care more about their stakeholders. *Entrepreneurship Theory and Practice, 36*(6), 1153–1173.

Chang, S. J., & Shim, J. (2015). When does transitioning from family to professional management improve firm performance? *Strategic Management Journal, 36*(9), 1297–1316.

Chrisman, J. J., Chua, J. H., Pearson, A. W., & Barnett, T. (2012). Family involvement, family influence, and family-centered non-economic goals in small firms. *Entrepreneurship Theory and Practice, 36*(2), 267–293.

Davis, P. S., & Harveston, P. D. (1998). The influence of family on the family business succession process: A multi-generational perspective. *Entrepreneurship Theory and Practice, 22*(3), 31–53.

Deephouse, D. L., & Jaskiewicz, P. (2013). Do family firms have better reputations than non-family firms? An integration of socioemotional wealth and social identity theories. *Journal of Management Studies, 50*(3), 337–360.

Dyck, B., Mauws, M., Starke, F. A., & Mischke, G. A. (2002). Passing the baton: The importance of sequence, timing, technique and communication in executive succession. *Journal of Business Venturing, 17*(2), 143–162.

Handler, W. C. (1990). Succession in family firms: A mutual role adjustment between entrepreneur and next-generation family members. *Entrepreneurship Theory and Practice, 15*(1), 37–52.

Hubler, T. M. (2009). The soul of family business. *Family Business Review, 22*(3), 254–258.

Kim, S., & Kim, S. (2015). Private Universities in South Korea. *International Higher Education, 37*, 20–22.

Lansberg, I. S. (1983). Managing human resources in family firms: The problem of institutional overlap. *Organizational Dynamics, 12*(1), 39–46.

Rumbley, L. E., Altbach, P. G., & Reisberg, L. (2012). Internationalization within the higher education context. In D. K. Deardorff, H. de Wit, J. Heyl, & T. Adams (Eds.),

The Sage handbook of international higher education (pp. 3–26). Thousand Oaks, CA: Sage.

Schulze, W. S., Lubatkin, M. H., & Dino, R. N. (2003). Toward a theory of agency and altruism in family firms. *Journal of Business Venturing, 18*(4), 473–490.

Schulze, W. S., Lubatkin, M. H., Dino, R. N., & Buchholtz, A. K. (2001). Agency relationships in family firms: Theory and evidence. *Organization Science, 12*(2), 99–116.

Tagiuri, R., & Davis, J. (1996). Bivalent attributes of the family firm. *Family Business Review, 9*(2), 199–208.